SLEEPING
WITH
LIONS

LEE ANNE McILROY

SLEEPING
WITH
LIONS

A Year in Tanzania

atmosphere press

© 2022 Lee Anne McIlroy

Published by Atmosphere Press

Library of Congress Control Number: 2022915923

Cover design by Matthew Fielder

atmospherepress.com

CONTENTS

For my Bukoba family

PART 1
Nests

Kila ndege huruka na mbawa zake.

"Every bird flies on its own wings."

— Tanzanian *kanga*

GOING APE OVER AN
EMPTY NEST

I saw the mother's reflection first. Then, the blinking eyes of the baby clutched onto her back. In the hilltop pool surrounded by gardens and woodlands above the western shores of Lake Victoria, I came up for air and observed the intangible gray and black furry visage shimmering like a family ghost through a crystal ball. At the water's edge sat her flesh-and-blood twin. The Vervet monkey and her baby had appeared within arm's reach, just as Beatrice had once foretold. Equally intrigued by her own reflection and my presence, the mother exchanged glances with her own untouchable image and then with me. Our identical eyes met for a moment that was simultaneously mysterious and familiar, both miraculous and mundane. The casting of a spell, a silent incantation, an opening of a portal. Suddenly, the spell was broken. The portal closed, and she looked away while drawing her baby close in one arm. She leapt into the trees and gradually disappeared, swinging through the vines of double helix tendrils that were draped like garland through the fertile, ancestral forest.

One year earlier, I had seen another mother with a baby monkey under much less natural and wondrous conditions. I was wasting the sunshine and the nearby Pacific Ocean on a perfect Southern California day laid out like a corpse on the sofa and crying as I watched television. The tears streamed down my face as I watched a middle-aged woman on an afternoon talk show who had a chimpanzee dressed as a baby sitting in her lap. Next to the woman sat her husband with a glazed, deer-in-the-headlights expression across his face. The woman explained that her psychotherapist had recommended the chimpanzee as a surrogate child to help her through her crippling Empty Nest Syndrome. When asked why she didn't just get a dog or a cat, the woman said that the life span of those animals was simply too short to get her through: Only the monkey, with its extended dependency on her for the entirety of its thirty-plus years of life, was able to soothe her sense of loss.

I cried, not out of pity but out of terror. I identified too strongly with that chimpanzee mother. Just a few months away from my youngest daughter going half-way across the country for college, I was actually crying a lot in those days at the idea of both daughters leaving home. I was trying to think of better coping strategies when I saw that woman on television, and for just the briefest of moments, I thought: "What a *great* idea!" Actually, I had even more frightening potential because of my particular fondness for turtles with their limited ability to run away and life spans of up to 150 years. I wondered where one could find baby clothes to fit over the shell of a 100-pound amphibian.

I had already started to venture into crazy-cat-lady territory by offering a veritable open doggie door for rescued felines. After my divorce, I had started to let the cats sleep with me. Those tiny nocturnal lions comforted me with reassuring cuddles as I awoke startled and fearful at random hours of the night. As my daughters prepared to leave home, I became addicted to the opiate, leonine purrs. My veterinarian started to greet me with expressions like, "Couldn't you at least get a *healthy* one?" or "Of course it's another cat."

Although they offered comfort, all those perfectly baby-sized felines with their finely-honed snuggling skills neither lived nor stayed forever.

I expanded my horizons when I took a course at the local animal wildlife sanctuary to learn how to care for injured birds. I started nursing them back to health in an aviary-sized birdcage in my front yard. I helped rehabilitate one crow who, upon his release, waddled slowly down the street like Charlie Chaplin until he awkwardly took flight while a neighbor remarked, "That is the ugliest looking bird I have ever seen."

I thought he was magnificent.

As I reveled in that bird's flight, I realized that I would never find what I was looking for by holding anyone or anything else back from moving on.

Luckily, I had a job to distract me from the Maternal Sword of Damocles looming over me. Before I had become a mom, I had been an ambitious young linguist, but once my first daughter was born, virtually all that ambition disappeared and was replaced by an obsessive motherly devotion of religious proportions. I nursed both daughters on demand and long enough for them to speak in full sentences and say things like, "Hey, Mom, this is getting a little awkward," or "Can I borrow the car?"

My focus on my daughters had been so myopic that I didn't even suspect a thing during the three years that my ex-husband had been cheating on me. Only after my daughters were both in elementary school and I received an eight-page fax from his mistress detailing their relationship did anything even resembling professional ambition return. With the compassion and support of a university department chair who made sure I only taught during school hours and the support of a herd of related females, I recommitted to teaching, but even then, my parental aspirations far overshadowed my professional ones.

So, when I saw that woman who was sitting with a chimpanzee dressed like a child on television, I realized I needed to figure out how I was going to deal with my impending transition out of the nest of motherhood that had defined my identity and purpose for over twenty years.

My first reaction was to turn to my partner, The Man I Love, who had come along at just the right time after my divorce. He had been a stable and loving force for my daughters and me. During our years together, I had been happy with our non-traditional romance, but as the time for my daughters to leave home approached, I wanted a proposal of marriage. He wanted his freedom and a downtown bachelor pad. As my daughters pursued lives on their own, so did he.

My next reaction, Plan B, involved my two godsons who were both infants when my youngest daughter left for college. As my own daughters prepared for independence, I decided that my godsons would be the perfect proxies to fill my Empty Nest. Within months of adopting this plan, however, the families of both of my godsons announced they were moving— one to Germany, the other to Boston. Both sets of parents claimed that their decisions had nothing to do with my increased obsession with their children and the intimacies of their family structures, but I'm still not entirely convinced.

Because my dad taught me the necessity of back-up plans, I developed a Plan C. This plan was very simple: I would lose myself in work.

I didn't just let my work distract me, I let it consume me. Not only did I throw myself into my full-time job at the university in a way I hadn't before, I also got a second job at a small private college. I taught six days a week including Saturdays and nights. This work was motivated more by desperation than aspiration. I was exhausted. My health deteriorated. I gained weight. My cholesterol was sky-high, and I looked terrible. When I wasn't working, I was crying. I took better care of the sick cats and damaged birds in my neighborhood than I did of my own broken wings. Plan C was not working out.

The day that both of my daughters moved away was one of the loneliest of my life. I might not have had a Plan D, but I had something even better—a best friend who has known me since kindergarten. Monica came over that day and didn't leave my side until the next morning. We walked down to the beach and after some convincing, I swam with her in the Pacific Ocean as we had in our childhood. We stayed up talking into the early hours of the morning as we had during countless summer slumber parties. Over morning coffee, she asked me, "Why don't you go back to Africa?"

Monica had known me when I was a child who dreamed of going to Africa, and she has known me throughout my career as an unlikely educator who was fortunate enough to have fulfilled that dream by teaching and studying languages in East Africa when I had first graduated from college. Throughout the years of raising our children, I had often talked about how much I longed to return.

The allure started when I was a little girl who loved animals and my set of World Book Encyclopedias. Cross-referencing the sections on "Animals" and "Africa" in the "A" volume of those encyclopedias was one of my after-school hobbies. During summers, I would play school using that encyclopedia, pretending I was a teacher with the neighbor kids while they sat cross-legged in front of my toy chalkboard under our jacaranda tree.

My interest in Africa grew as my love of languages did because Africa is the home of one-third of the world's languages. After earning a degree in Linguistics, I was accepted into the United States Peace Corps and taught in the

Comoros Islands off the coast of Tanzania and Mozambique. There I learned an indigenous Bantu language called Shingazidja that is related to Swahili while refining my French and struggling with Arabic. I taught in the mornings then spent afternoons drinking tea in the medina with my friend Anzize or swimming near the Friday Mosque with my neighbor Fatima. Quite suddenly, however, I seemed to fall victim to a strange condition known as Baby Fever. When the German exchange student from high school whom I had been dating for years showed up unexpectedly on that island in the Indian Ocean and asked me to marry him, it was all over. Before long I was back in California. We married. Two angelic daughters followed. And everything else, including my dreams of living in Africa, faded into the background.

That first night of my Empty Nest, after I cried my eyes out (again), Monica reminded me of all of this. She repeated the question even after I had ignored her the first time.

"Why don't you finally go back to Africa?"

"I can't do that," I said.

"Why not?" she replied.

And I didn't have an answer other than it didn't seem possible.

Providence stepped in weeks after this conversation. Soon after Monica's suggestion, I was recruited to apply for a ten-month long teaching fellowship in Tanzania. A great believer in signs, I could not ignore this one. I asked my university if I could be granted an unpaid leave. Once again, my department chair showed me tremendous support. Administration said yes. I applied.

The project sounded perfect. Through a grant set up by the US Embassy in Dar es Salaam, Tanzania and Georgetown University, the selected candidate would work with local teachers and lecturers at a small teaching college in a place called Bukoba. She would also have a local research partner to study multilingualism in both of our countries.

After a flurry of uploaded letters of recommendation, transcripts, sample lesson plans, questionnaires and multiple Skype interviews, I waited anxiously to hear the final decision. This opportunity seemed like my last hope. *This* was my Plan D, and I felt out of options. Who ever heard of a Plan E?

Seeing how lost I had been after she had moved away and how invested I was in the possibility of going back to Africa, my daughter Victoria assured me that she was proud of me no matter what.

She worriedly asked, "Mom, what are you going to do if you don't get chosen?"

I didn't have the heart to tell her that if I didn't get selected for the project, I would most likely spend the rest of my life carrying around a small primate or a medium-sized reptile dressed in her christening gown. Fortunately, it didn't come to that. The night I found out I was selected, I drifted off to sleep with a smile and a tabby, and I realized how long it had actually been since I remembered any of my dreams.

MIGRATION

Departing from Los Angeles International Airport was a blur. Even before I got on the freeway, I saw several beggars with cardboard signs pleading their cases: A veteran in a wheelchair wrote that "anything helps;" a single mother and her small children needed food; a young man requested donations for his murdered brother's funeral. Underneath the overpasses of the 405 freeway, tent cities quivered with the rush of passing cars as trash swirled in the exhaust fumes.

At the airport terminal, a flock of vulturous paparazzi hovered around the stairs leading to security, flitting back and forth, looking for stars or any hint of celebrity they could find, a frantic pack on a meaningless hunt. During take-off, I wore sunglasses like most of the other passengers then shut the shades to avoid the glare of the sun.

During the first leg of my flight, I tried to sleep. Twelve hours and six Diet Cokes later, I collected my belongings which had scattered on the floor like wood shavings in a hamster cage. During the layover in Zurich, I was disheveled, impatient and tense. This was due to the fact that I only had thirty minutes to make the layover, and if I missed it, I would have to wait twenty four hours until the next flight. Although I had gone through security in Los Angeles, and although I had a mere half hour to make my layover, I had to go through security yet again in Zurich. Actually, I had to go through security again THREE times in Zurich because 1.) I had a water bottle from the plane in my purse 2.) My pen apparently resembled a weapon and 3.) My *Haltung,* my attitude, was suspicious.

Miraculously, I made my connection and slept the entire flight to Tanzania. It was close to midnight when we landed, and the airport was virtually empty. A young father helped me retrieve my luggage off the carousal. The customs agent checked my passport and visa, waving me through with a smile and the word I would hear most often during my year here: *karibu.*

Welcome.

Although I had expected an extended odyssey through baggage claims and customs, I was out of the terminal within 15 minutes.

Once the sliding doors of the terminal opened, I was embraced by 85 degrees of humidity as the young father and his son made sure I got into a taxi safely before waving good-bye.

Thirty seconds into my ride with a taxi driver who introduced himself as Mohammed, the warmth was accompanied by images of a city full of life in spite of the late hour. Two young boys about ten years old wandered the streets laughing with their arms around each other. Small fires were set up along the sidewalks to roast rows of kabobs. Street vendors walked through the middle of the road selling items of all sorts—books, electronics, cleaning supplies, music, toys, ice cream. Bicyclists swerved perilously through the city traffic. Buses were piled tightly with passengers who often entered and exited through the windows rather than the door.

I had no idea where I was going except for the address my new boss had given me. As Mohammed ferried me through the streets of Dar es Salaam, he pointed out various landmarks: the port filled with ships, the Serena Hotel, a massive Catholic church.

As we crossed a bridge, he said, "This is where the rich people live, Oyster Bay." Suddenly, the buildings were more lavish and officious. The ocean views were spectacular and unobstructed. Mohammed pointed out the various residences of ambassadors and investors from around the world, and before long, we were on some lovely palm-lined streets that led to an equally lovely building.

"Welcome home," he said as we pulled into the Sea Cliff Apartments.

The multi-storied complex rivaled any luxury apartment I had ever seen, and it was festooned with Christmas decorations. A stunning woman at the check-in counter handed me my key, and an older man wearing a fez insisted on carrying my two suitcases to my room on the second floor.

The little convenience apartment, which would be my home whenever I was in Dar es Salaam, was perfect. Colorful Tinga-Tinga paintings of African animals covered the walls, and the bed was piled high with pillows and a zebra-print comforter.

I fell asleep in my clothes and was awoken the next morning by a phone call from Rebecca, the woman whose voice I had heard for the final interviews and the person who would be my direct supervisor for this project, my new boss. Listening to her voice through the phone that first morning in Tanzania, I could tell that she was as surprised as I was that I had actually made the connection in Zurich. She told me she would pick me up in a half an hour at the apartment so that we could start working.

In the lobby, I recognized Rebecca right away. A brunette,

lightly freckled cross between a hippy and Lauren Bacall, Rebecca has an informal, casual confidence that offered me an immediate and overall familiarity. Despite the fact that she was quite possibly the most powerful person for whom I had ever worked, I felt immediately comfortable around her. She is fond of colloquialisms like "What's the scoop?" and "bigwigs," and after I climbed into her small SUV, she drove me all around the vicinity of the apartment complex and showed me the nearest ATM, grocery stores, and cafés. She recommended The Slipway (a tourist mecca fashioned in the style of Zanzibar with everything from ice cream parlors to seafront bars) as a good place to go if I ever needed any creature comforts from home. We also drove past the embassy where Rebecca worked, and she reminded me that the previous embassy had been "blown to smithereens." I told her that I really liked her soft touch.

Over lunch at an Italian restaurant filled with Americans and Europeans, she gave me a quick briefing about the project. She told me more about Ocham Olanda Collins who was the head of the Linguistics department at the small college in Bukoba. He would be my counterpart and research partner for the year. She showed me his proposal for the project, which was ambitious: He wanted to share theories about bilingual education, develop a new language curriculum, establish a teacher's resource center and create a portable library.

Before I came to Tanzania, Rebecca had also explained that I would spend the first week working and training with her in the southern coastal region of Kilwa before I left for Bukoba, a small municipality on the other end of the country along the borders of Uganda and Rwanda, where I would remain and work with Mr. Ocham Olanda Collins for the rest of the year.

After lunch that first day, Rebecca dropped me off at the apartment at around 4:00 in the afternoon. I fell face first, and again fully dressed, into a mountain of pillows that I completely smothered in drool by dawn.

The next morning, I was up at 6:00 a.m., still mildly jet-lagged and ready to get to work. Rebecca had sent a driver who then took me to her house before we set off for our week in Kilwa near the Mozambique border. As we arrived, Rebecca was ready and waiting on her front porch. As we drove away, her husband Chris (a dead-ringer for George Carlin) waved good-bye and reminded us about the 6-foot-long venomous creatures that are indigenous to this part of the world:

"Be careful of green mamba snakes!"

My first week in Tanzania was a strange montage. One moment Rebecca and I were speaking formally with high-level administrators who had elephant tusks displayed like trophies on their massive desks. Next we were fetching water, sweeping the floors of open-air classrooms or pulling over to the side of the road and squatting in an open field to relieve ourselves of our morning tea while a group of children came running toward us laughing and pointing. We worked that week near the ruins of ancient mosques and palaces where shadows moved with the wind, where tropical plants grew out of crevices, and vines cascaded over bays of pointed arches. I expected a green mamba snake at any moment.

In order to reach Kilwa, we drove six hours down the coast on dirt roads while it rained, often passing massive buses that had been stuck in the mud like elephants in quicksand. Throughout my time with her, I watched Rebecca not only conduct herself with decorum during the day, I also saw her hike through high grass at night with a headlamp to work with teachers at an all-girls school. We had both been Girl Scouts, but I am sure she earned more badges than I had. She could easily have stayed in fancy hotels during our week in Kilwa. Instead, we always stayed with the teachers. In one place, we stayed in a house with a scorpion in the kitchen and a millipede in the bathroom.

"Whaddaya think we should name them?" she asked.

Not seduced by the enchantment of Kilwa, Rebecca spent every waking moment that we were there talking to or about teachers. Every. Single. Moment.

Kilwa is located about 200 miles south of Dar es Salaam, and it has a rich history. The Kisiwani ruins there are a UNESCO World Heritage Site and are set on a small island, within eyeshot of mainland Tanzania. These ruins can only be visited with a permit and a canoe. During its heyday in the 1300s Kilwa was called "one of the most beautiful towns in the world" by the Arabian explorer Ibn Buttata. The island once had a human population of 10,000 and the only coin mint in all of Africa. It was also once one of the most significant gold trading emporia of its time, accessible to the Arab world, India and China. As part of the Swahili Coast during the great explorations of Shirazi merchants during the medieval period, it was also, painfully, a slave port. Although long since abandoned and, at least until its 1981 recognition by UNESCO, virtually forgotten by the world, Kilwa is gaspingly spectacular. The Great Mosque, founded in the 11th century, is wonderfully well preserved with its ornate ceiling. The cliff-top palace has been leveled except for the foundation, but it is still impressive.

None of this was as remotely interesting to Rebecca as the teachers of Kilwa were. Her sole focus was on them.

When I complimented her on her work ethic, Rebecca was practically aghast.

"What are you talking about?" she asked. "These teachers are the ones you should be admiring. You and I are gettin' paid for this. These teachers are on vacation right now, and *this* is how they're spendin' their time off."

Saying good-bye to those teachers was surprisingly poignant. I was especially sad to leave one woman named Mwana whose daughter would visit us every afternoon.

Halfway through our time in Kilwa, Mwana stopped coming to the workshops due to a bout with Typhoid while her daughter was cared for by the other teachers as she recovered. On our last day in Kilwa, Mwana emerged from her room, a rash still visible on her otherwise flawless skin, her sunken eyes simultaneously expressing disappointment at a lost opportunity as well as relief that she had recovered so quickly.

Mwana handed me a parting gift, a Tanzanian *kanga*, a piece of art as much as a piece of fabric. A *kanga* is a traditional piece of printed cotton fabric with versatile uses. It can be used as a skirt, a wrap or a baby carrier. Not only are *kangas* beautifully crafted and colorful, my favorite characteristic of a *kanga* is its function as a means of communication: Each has its own message, its own *jina*. These messages can be proverbs or riddles, serious or funny and can express the worldview of the wearer or maybe just the mood of the day. Great care must be given in the selection of a *kanga* as a gift to make sure the *jina* conveys the right message for the occasion.

The *jina* for the *kanga* Mwana gave me was *ukipata ushukuru ukikosa usikufuru.*

I understood the literal meaning of the words, but not the nuance. Even after she explained the message to me, it took me most of the ride back to Dar es Salaam to reflect on it: To be ungrateful is a sort of blasphemy.

Mwana and I hugged, and I climbed into the back of the Landcruiser. I rolled down the window and we clasped hands one last time.

It started to rain as we pulled away. Rebecca and I waved through the sunroof and watched the teachers wave back. As the Kilwa Girls School slowly shrank away and disappeared from sight, the jungle swallowed us up, giant palm fronds blinking away rainy tears like giant eyelashes on the meniscus of the rear window.

After that first week with Rebecca, I felt simultaneously

exhausted and invigorated, both physically and intellectually. On our last evening in Kilwa, I had taken a break to swim in the Indian Ocean, but Rebecca summoned me back to shore by mimicking the theme song to "Jaws" through an invisible conch held to her lips.

"C'mon, we've still got a lotta work to do," she declared as she gestured for me to get out of the ocean just as my parents had when I was a child.

Rebecca never stopped. She set the bar very high, and on the long drive back to Dar es Salaam, I wondered if I could meet her expectations for the project that lay ahead.

As we drove home at the end of that week, I asked her if she could tell me more specifically what she wanted me to do once I got to Bukoba. After a brief pause, her answer was straightforward:

"Everything you can."

As we pulled up to her home, Rebecca was first greeted by the unbridled enthusiasm of Addie, a yellow lab. Chris then landed a kiss firmly on her cheeks and wrapped one arm around her waist as he reached in with the other to unload her suitcases.

"Well, hello there darlins!" he said.

Before she said good-bye to me, Rebecca extended an invitation for dinner at their house a few nights later on the night before I would leave for Bukoba.

"You have two days for R and R," she said. "Enjoy yourself, and I'll see ya in a couple a days."

It was 8:00 p.m. when I dragged myself out of the Land Cruiser and up the two flights of stairs to my apartment. I dropped my bag in a corner and fell into bed, once again fully dressed. I slept for 20 hours straight. When I finally woke up, the mid-afternoon sun was starting to fade, and my pillow was once again drenched in drool.

It was Christmas Eve.

WINTERSONG

I had been so busy that first week in Tanzania that I barely had time to miss my family nor to even think about Christmas. It is usually one of my favorite holidays, but as I woke up, I suddenly felt lonely and melancholy again. I missed home. I especially missed my daughters, and I didn't feel festive at all. This was the first time in my entire life that I had been alone on Christmas.

By the time I had woken up and showered, it was still too early to call anyone back in California. I headed alone down to the shores of Coco Beach, a popular location in Oyster Bay. I walked down the street in front of the apartment, and I passed a group of mothers with their babies and children whom I had seen before, all resting under the giant roots of a mangrove tree. Sometimes the mothers would respond to my greetings. More often, they stuck out their tongues at me. I can't blame them.

After a short walk along the beach, I returned to the apartment where someone had left me a small succulent plant with a red bow around it. Wanting to kill time until I could call home, I foolishly watched the news on TV, and it was nothing but bad. Two churches were attacked by Boko Haram in Nigeria. A young woman was sexually attacked by a group of men on a bus in India. In America, twenty young school children and six teachers had been gunned down in one of the worst mass shootings in U.S. history. I turned the television off.

When I finally reached my family, my daughters placed their phones on the coffee table of my mom's living room, and I could listen to and participate in the conversation and watch everyone open their gifts.

Eventually we signed off as my family prepared to go out to celebrate. I went downstairs to the restaurant and ate dinner alone by the swimming pool, grateful that I did not have any dishes to wash.

On Christmas Day, I slept a lot, read by the pool and answered e-mails. I also walked over to the Slipway to do some light shopping. In one of the small stores, the sales clerk, a statuesque and passionate Russian woman, told me her life story which included salacious details about her Italian husband and his young mistress. She told me how her husband even flaunted the affair, often bringing his mistress past her shop on the way to one of the local bars. Halfway through one of her sentences, something outside caught her eye, and she abruptly ran out of the store and began screaming, her muscovite voice echoing through the faux souk. She returned and said, "Sorry about that."

"What was that?" I asked her.

"Didn't you see them? That was *him!*"

Grateful that I did not have to deal with a cheating husband anymore, I returned to the apartment to get ready for a dinner organized by one of the other workshop facilitators I had met in Kilwa.

Rachel had conducted computer training workshops in Kilwa with me and Rebecca, and she had invited me to a

Christmas dinner. She had organized the dinner for her American, Swedish and French friends even though she did not celebrate the holiday herself, a gesture I found extremely thoughtful. Eating *al fresco* next to a French oil executive and a Swedish diplomat, I felt as if I were in Europe rather than Africa.

The group offered some suggestions about how I should spend my last full day in Dar es Salaam:

"You should go scuba diving!"

"You should go to one of the beach lodges."

"Or maybe the spa at the Sea Cliff Hotel."

"Have you been to any of the islands yet? Maybe a day trip to one of those!"

As the tanned Frenchman drove me back to my apartment that night, he told me that when I had time, I really needed to go to Zanzibar Island. "Zair eez so much to zee zair!" he effused.

No one had suggested what I really had in mind: to go to the National Museum.

I took a quick swim, showered, put on a nightgown and climbed into bed. I exchanged some final texts with my daughters, then put on my headphones and fell asleep listening to the Christmas playlist they had made for me: *...the weary world rejoices...here to stay is a new bird...there must have been some magic...above thy deep and dreamless sleep, the...silent...stars...go...by...*

THE CAVEMAN OF MY DREAMS

Fossil evidence of hominids dating back nearly two million years was discovered in Tanzania, making it one of the earliest known sites of evidence of mankind's origins, and anyone who knows me knows that I have a certain, how can I say it, *fascination* with our cavemen ancestors. I am inclined to pause in the middle of some quotidian activity and ponder, "I wonder how the cavemen did this?" In trying to understand myself and my fellow humans (especially the men in my life), I often speculate about how some of our peculiar and confounding behaviors might have some evolutionary roots.

I credit, or blame, my mom for this curiosity. She would often do the same: "I wonder what they used for toys/ toilet paper/ beds/ during 'the cavemen days?'" She would ask such questions usually while she observed me in the middle of some mundane, daily activity that required a gadget or accessory.

I never outgrew this curiosity. In fact, it grew along with me, thus contributing to my attraction to East Africa. On my last free day in Dar es Salaam before leaving for Bukoba, I decided to follow my own inclination and visit the National Museum of Tanzania to see some of the famous fossils instead of following some of the suggestions of my Christmas-dinner companions.

Online reviews of the museum by foreign travelers were insulting and harshly judgmental (e.g., "there is a lot of room for improvement" and "do not expect very much"), and the throng of American tourists coming out of the museum as I arrived protracted the rude behavior toward our host country by complaining that the museum lacked air conditioning. I was neither discouraged nor disappointed. How could I be? There are cavemen bones in that museum!

I asked my cab driver Juma about the museum. He said he had never been inside, so I invited him to be my guest rather than wait in his taxi. He accepted, and together we explored the halls of the museum, a massive white building that housed not only an exhibition of "the cavemen days" but also documents, artifacts, paintings and photographs of Tanzanian history.

There were little wonders of the Natural World. There were ethnographic displays of tribal ornaments and witchcraft apparati. There were paintings and sculptures including a depiction of shackled and enslaved Tanzanians carrying the giant tusk of a slaughtered elephant for a porcine white man who was also being carried.

Lingering over a beautifully-organized and classified collection of shells and a sea creature cadaver floating in formaldehyde, Juma gently laughed at my effusive reaction to such curios.

"Why do you *mzungu* like to put things in museums?"

"To protect and preserve them I guess," was my response.

"From what?"

"From people."

His response was either "hmmm" or "hmmpf."

Standing in front of a ragged corpse of a taxidermied lion and a gallery of mounted animal heads, he then looked at me with a quizzical look that could only be translated as "WTF?!!"

Then he asked, "Why do you *mzungu* prefer to see these things in a museum instead of... out there?" waving his hands toward the windows like a magician.

I couldn't come up with a decent answer fast enough.

He shook his head, gestured his hands in surrender then sat down on a bench near the front entrance where he said he would remain until I was done. I wondered if he would still be there when I was finished with my tour.

As I continued through the museum, I was glad that he was not witness to my observations of the sepia-colored photos that covered the walls chronicling the history of this place through the images of humiliated tribal leaders in chains alongside portraits of German and British colonialists (including a photo of another porcine white man being carried this time on a large hammock). I felt like a guilty co-conspirator because he was a fellow *mzungu* and foreigner.

German colonial history in Tanzania, although not as obvious as British colonization here, had a powerful impact that was documented in those photos. From the late 1880s to the end of World War I, Germans regulated the existing slave trade, planted coffee and rubber trees, mined for gold, created a formal education system and generally claimed this area as theirs: German East Africa. Protests and uprisings by the indigenous people were overpowered by fire power and brute force. When the Sultan of Zanzibar objected to German occupation, Otto von Bismarck himself sent five warships in 1885 and ordered the guns to be aimed directly at the Royal Palace.

Despite this historical legacy, throughout my time in Tanzania, I never heard a single bad word spoken about the Germans by Tanzanians. Not one. Such criticism was reserved for "the colonizers." The British.

This is probably due to the more recent and oft-mentioned

impact of British colonization of Tanzania and its lingering linguistic impact, which occurred after the German colonial era. When the Germans were defeated in World War I, this part of the world was ceded to the British by European powers who named it Tanganyika. The lingering and profound British influence here, particularly in the official language policies (English remains an official language alongside Swahili) would consistently trouble me throughout my year in Tanzania.

I observed and contemplated the history of Tanzania as I moved further along the halls of the museum, and eventually the photos transformed from brown to full color. Vibrant pictures following independence showed the faces of the presidents of Tanzania. Most compelling is that of the beloved first President of Tanzania, Julius Nyerere who is nicknamed *Mwalimu*, "The Teacher." Nyerere's success at creating a new and independent country after years of colonization has earned him reverence and respect. School children and adults alike stood in front of the paintings and photos of Nyerere in the museum the day I visited, and it was clear that he was the man many of them had come to see that day at the museum.

But the man for me, the man I had come to the National Museum to see, was the intriguing and brutishly handsome *Paranthropus Boisei* aka "Nutcracker Man." Mary Leakey discovered the bones of "Nutcracker Man" (so named because of his specialized jaw for chewing nuts and seeds) in the Olduvai Gorge in central Tanzania on July 17 (my mom's birthday!), 1959. This hunk was part of the first hominin species to use stone tools, and he lived in what is now Tanzania 1.75 million years ago.

As I entered the hall dedicated to the origins of humankind, I felt a teenaged tingle of anticipatory excitement. The room was full of ancestral homage. Evolutionary charts and human family trees contextualized each species. There were the skulls and bones of *Homo Neanderthalensis, Australo-pithecus Africanus,* and *Paranithropus Boiki* among others. One skull of a *Homo Neanderthalensis* seemed to have its jaw fixed in a smile of joy, and I couldn't help but smile back. Pieces of ribs and femurs, phalanges and vertebrae were laid out under glass cases. With all these beautiful body parts around me and the sight of "Nutcracker Man's" skull before me, my knees trembled. Who needs Chippendale's? I felt more intrigued by the mystery of these appendages than I ever did by the fleshy tissues of anonymous young, hard bodies.

What were all those online complaints about? How much more from a museum could anyone expect?

I lingered quietly in the hall while a few people walked past me and "Nutcracker Man," shockingly oblivious to our enchanted romance across the millennia. It was hard to pull myself away, but eventually I did and found Juma smoking a cigarette near his car around noon.

"Finished?" he asked.

I nodded.

"I know of some great places to show you. Much better than this." He frowned as he looked at the whitewashed building.

I explained to him that I would be leaving for Bukoba the next day and thanked him for the offer.

"Bukoba?" he asked as he wrinkled his forehead. "Well, I hope you are able to see more...and that you like bananas."

We spent the rest of the 10-minute drive to the apartment in silence. Parking briefly, he handed me his card and said, "If you ever need a driver..."

I thanked him and handed him a 100,000 Shilling note in return, wondering what they used for currency back in the cavemen days.

FLEDGLINGS

After my visit to the museum, I went to the embassy to do some work with Rebecca. After we finished for the day, we drove to her house for dinner. Luckily, after working with Rebecca in the office that afternoon and receiving official briefings there, I felt better prepared, and I looked forward to some final thoughts and guidance from her over dinner.

During our time in Kilwa together, Rebecca had only given me several unofficial briefings that went something like this:

Me: "What are the health protocols?"

Rebecca: "Don't get sick."

Me: "What are the safety protocols?"

Rebecca: "Don't do anything dangerous."

Me: "What should I do if there is a problem with ...?"

Rebecca: "Handle it."

"Everything's gonna be just fine," she often assured me.

Rebecca and Chris's home wasn't far from the embassy and was situated in a compound of six other two-story homes occupied by various foreign government employees and their families. The compound was encircled by a ten-foot wall, and ingress and egress were regulated by two guards at all times.

Rebecca dropped some bags on the sofa and announced that she would go change.

"Make yourself at home," she said.

Chris offered to take me around and show me the house which was somehow simultaneously comfy and well-curated. Rebecca and Chris have spent most of their lives living and working around the world in places like Greece, Egypt, the United Arab Emirates and Morocco, and their home was adorned with mementos from those regions: bejeweled sabers, magnificent Persian rugs, vintage art deco prints, traditional drums. Local Tanzanian craftsmanship was also well represented: face masks hung on the walls; traditional Zanzibari carved furniture was intermingled with European furniture, and animal carvings sat proudly on the ubiquitous bookshelves.

Photographs lined the staircase, and one in particular transfixed me. In the photo, a young Rebecca sits cross-legged on a carpet, her long wavy hair cascading across her shoulders. She is dressed in a peasant blouse and djinni pants. Using her right hand, she is taking food off of a brass platter, her shining eyes looking off camera. The look on her face is pure elation. As I stood there staring at the photo, Chris handed me a glass of ice water.

He explained that the photo was taken when Rebecca was in the Peace Corps in Morocco during the 1970s. Just then, Rebecca emerged from the bedroom dressed in jeans and a T-shirt.

"You were in the *Peace Corps*...in *Morocco*...in the *seventies*?!" I marveled.

"Yes, indeed I was," she replied with a mischievous laugh, her eyes shining just as they were in the photo.

She turned to Chris and asked, "What's for dinner, babe?"

Dinner included vegetable soup with homemade bread, and we ate in the dining room while the masks watched silently. The conversation was easy and animated. Rebecca and Chris told stories about how they met and fell in love, about their experiences on a Greek Island and in Dubai. Rebecca and I had already finished all talk about work while Chris had been preparing dinner, and she and I both seemed glad for the reprieve from work talk.

As Chris brought out ice cream sundaes, I noticed what looked like a nest in the corner of the dining room. A semicircle of twigs and leaves was lodged in the corner where two walls intersected with the ceiling.

"What's that?" I pointed.

Rebecca and Chris laughed.

"It's a nest," Rebecca confirmed nonchalantly as she flipped her spoon upside down in her mouth and held it there.

I stared, waiting for more of an explanation.

"What?" she shrugged and asked, like there was nothing unusual at all about having a family of birds nesting in one's formal dining room.

She and Chris explained that one bird kept flying into the house when the back door was open for Addie, and slowly but surely that little bird built a home. By the time Rebecca and Chris noticed the nest, they didn't have the heart to remove it. By the time they saw the eggs, they really knew they couldn't remove it. Now that the hatchlings had emerged from the shells and were learning to fly, Rebecca and Chris had surrendered completely to sharing their formal dining room with a family of birds.

As she licked the chocolate off her spoon like a kid, Rebecca told me how she and Chris let the birds out every morning at dawn when they took Addie out for her first walk and how they let the birds in every night when they came tapping at the window. Rebecca explained all of this as if it were the most natural thing in the world.

As the evening was winding down, Rebecca took down

several books that she had placed in a neat stack on one of the bookshelves. She momentarily took a judgmental tone with me for the first (and as it turns out only) time.

"I notice that you talk a lot about cavemen," she said.

"Yes."

"Why only cave*men*?" she indicted. "Ya know, there were cavewomen too. In fact, they were probably even more important than the cavemen."

Rebecca is, and probably always has been, an unapologetic feminist. Earlier in the evening she had shown me photo albums and a childhood scrapbook that had a piece of paper in child's writing. On the paper was a list of rules for The Girls Only Club, a club that Rebecca had founded when she was seven years old. (Rule Number 1: No boys! Rule Number 2: We make the rules!) I should have known that my cavemen references might have been objectionable.

"Here, you should read this," she commanded as much as she suggested while handing me a book entitled *The Descent of Woman*.

"And this," another book.

"And these," she said as she continued to pile several other books into my arms so fast that I couldn't even see the covers.

Eventually Rebecca, Chris and Addie all drove with me back to the apartment, my stomach and arms full. This time Chris didn't warn me about green mamba snakes. I was too busy worrying out loud about details over my upcoming project.

"When should...?

"How will I ...?"

"What if....?"

Rebecca was quiet as I rambled. As I exited the car at the apartment complex, I leaned through the open window to hug Rebecca good-bye.

"Don't worry," she lilted: "Ya know what's going to happen

out there this year? *Something*, that's what. Something will happen, and that's all we know."

Before bed I took one last swim in the apartment pool. A bat swooped amid the oleander trees as I drifted back and forth. I climbed into bed with wet hair and fell asleep contemplating what Bukoba would be like, and when I awoke it was still dark outside. At the airport, I boarded a small plane after I had checked my two suitcases. During lift off, I realized Rebecca was probably letting the birds out, and I noticed how suddenly the dawn had arrived.

BROUGHT TO MY SENSES
IN BUKOBA

During the first week I had spent in Dar es Salaam I did not meet a single Tanzanian who had been to Bukoba, a city in the far western region of Tanzania where I would make my home for the next year. When I told Tanzanians where I was going, the response was universal:

"I hope you like bananas."

I had read about Bukoba on the internet or in travel guides, but the information was limited and questionable: Bukoba is a green and mountainous municipality of 30,000 inhabitants located approximately 3,000 feet above sea level. Coffee, tea and bananas are the main cash crops. Bukoba boasts several hotels, one of which has a swimming pool. The first recorded cases of AIDS were documented very close to this region, and this is still a significant health concern which was unfairly attributed "in part to the promiscuity of the Haya women" according to one Western guidebook. The author of the same guidebook also states, "Everyone who comes to visit here [Bukoba] seems to like it, even though it's a little hard to put your finger on exactly why." What a jerk.

There were no direct flights to Bukoba from Dar es

Salaam, so the first leg of my journey was an hour and a half flight to Mwanza, the second largest city in Tanzania. From my view above the clouds, I could see the sweeping expanse of the country: miles and miles of undeveloped nature. Below lay the Ngorongoro crater (the scene of the largest animal migration on Earth), Mt. Kilimanjaro and the Serengeti Desert.

Between long glances out the window and short conversations with fellow passengers, I looked through the books that Rebecca had given me. Among the titles, were both *The Ascent of Woman* and *The Descent of Woman* which give a pretty accurate indication of Rebecca's interests. I briefly skimmed through the first pages of *The Ascent of Woman: A History of The Suffragette Movement and The Ideas Behind It* with moderate interest, but even after the first few paragraphs of *The Descent of Woman: The Classic Study of Evolution,* I was fascinated. In this book, the author describes the role of women in human evolution and also discusses Sir Alister Hardy's "Aquatic Theory of Evolution" whereby ancient human ancestors sought protection from man-eating cats by living in the four-foot shallows of the ocean shores.

This book challenged my laser focus on cave*men*, explaining that evolution is driven much more by the survival needs of infants—and by extension their mothers on whom mammals and primate babies so powerfully depend—than by the hunting or sexual arousal needs of males (the latter, let's face it, don't seem too demanding). The book uses this Aquatic Theory of Evolution to explain why we are hairless mammals (like aquatic mammals) and why we have saltwater tears, subcutaneous fat, and webbing between our fingers and toes.

As I tried to imagine such a possibility, the sight of Lake Victoria tore my attention away from the book and my possible ancestral past. Just as I saw the water, the pilot announced our preparation for landing in Mwanza. We disembarked briefly into a small terminal that offered afternoon tea during the brief layover. When I boarded the plane to Bukoba, I discovered that it was the exact same plane I had just arrived on. I was greeted by the same crew and directed to the same seat I had previously occupied. The flight from Mwanza to Bukoba was short but exquisite. The entire flight path was over Lake Victoria at an altitude so low that I could see the ripples in the water.

As our small plane prepared for landing on the dirt runway of Bukoba, I saw layers of green trees bordering the expanse of the lake (which incidentally lives up to its majestic reputation). Through my small window, I saw a nun and a man I recognized as Ocham, waiting for me just outside the tiny terminal.

My new colleague, Professor Collins Olanda Ocham, is the man responsible for the grant that brought me to Bukoba. Having navigated byzantine layers of paperwork, he cleared the way for this project and my safe arrival. We had already been writing back and forth enthusiastically about our shared interests and ideas, and I recognized his quick smile and skinny frame right away from his Facebook photos. It was his thoroughly formal cadence that was the surprise. As we walked along the misty runway toward the nun's car, talking excitedly, I couldn't help but think this was the beginning of a beautiful friendship.

As happy as I was to finally meet Ocham, I was slightly distracted. All of my physical senses were immediately and thoroughly overwhelmed by the place that would be my home for the year. The guidebooks did not do it justice.

Bukoba looks like an evergreen forest wrapped in a tropical jungle, like a thousand shades of emerald dripping with breadfruit, mango, papaya and banana. It looks like hilly dirt roads that turn into red clay when it rains, with people moving in all directions carrying firewood, charcoal, the day's harvest and water balanced impossibly and perfectly on their heads. It looks like men walking hand in hand as Lake Victoria winks through the thatched roof fringes of stalls along the shore. Bukobatown looks like the Wild West with its dusty roads, wooden storefronts and cars winding through the streets like outlaws. It looks like pale lizards, monkeys, frogs, goats, chickens and birds of extraordinary shapes and colors. From the hilltops, Bukoba looks like Eden.

Bukoba smells like charcoal, pine trees, the sweat of hard work, fire, fresh air and bananas.

Bukoba tastes like rice and beans, and eggs with curry, and spinach and cassava. It tastes like giant bananas that remind me of potatoes and bananas that are small and sweet. It tastes like warm tea with ginger, sugar and masala spices. Bukoba tastes like papaya and cinnamon. It tastes like Mexican Coca-Cola made with cane sugar instead of corn syrup. It tastes like *ugali*, a mixture of flour and water served with sauce and vegetables. Bukoba tastes like traditional African cooking, using the gifts of the earth, the trees and the lake prepared over an open fire.

Bukoba sounds like monkeys outside your window and like the mating calls of feathery creatures. It sounds like the songs of a thousand people rejoicing on a Sunday morning from the Lutheran, Methodist, Anglican and Catholic churches, the music floating up to heaven like helium balloons. It sounds like the call to prayer on a Friday afternoon, and it sounds like the horn of a ship called Victoria as she returns from Mwanza every other morning at 7:00 a.m. Bukoba sounds like the silence of bananas. It sounds like languages that worship the rhythm of staccato. It sounds like vintage American country songs that blare in taxis while the drivers sing along. It sounds like the wind through the trees and the grass.

Bukoba feels like cool rains and warm sunlight. It feels like mud between your toes and passionfruit nectar running down your fingers. Bukoba feels like warm hands holding yours, like women embracing you every time they meet or leave you. Bukoba feels like the soft flesh of banana in your mouth. Bukoba feels very ancient—a place where ghosts still live peacefully among us. It feels simultaneously very close to, and very far away from, home.

DESIRE

As much as Bukoba felt like a place I could call home for the next year, the house where I would be living did not. After picking me up at the airport, Ocham, along with his wife Pauline and one of the nuns from the university, escorted me the short distance up a steep hill to my new housing. I had already been told that I would be living in a hostel-like house that could also accommodate other professors and lecturers, most likely nuns. That sounded perfect because I love communal living. Unfortunately, although there were indeed four other bedrooms, they were completely empty. I was the only one living there.

Although situated down the road from Rugambwa Girls Secondary School, the house was remote and lacked a kitchen. My room contained a bunk bed with a mattress on just the lower bunk and a half-finished bathroom with a squat toilet and no shower-head. Such relatively sparse conditions were to be expected: During my final pre-departure interview with Rebecca, she had asked me if I was prepared to take bucket showers. The shower wasn't the problem for me. The isolation was.

"They are in the process of finishing this," Ocham explained as he embarrassingly gestured towards the "water closet."

Pauline shook her head and said something like "tsk-tsk."

Feeling sorry for me, Pauline invited me to dinner at their home and also offered to accompany me into town the next day to help me find some provisions. Ocham mentioned that I was welcomed to take my meals with "the priests," an invitation so vague and casual that, although intriguing, didn't seem like something I was going to follow up on.

After we dropped off my baggage and looked briefly around the house, Ocham, Pauline and I took a taxi back to their home. Two things were immediately apparent: Ocham and Pauline loved their family, and they both loved to read. Four children, from a toddler to a teenager, ran to greet us at the threshold. The bookcases in the living room were filled with books by their favorite authors and also some of mine: Langston Hughes, Ralph Ellison, Ernest Hemingway, F. Scott Fitzgerald, and Dylan Thomas.

Dinner with Ocham and his family was comforting. His older children, Isabelle and Eugene, were home from school for the holidays, and the younger children, Hellen and Dylan were clearly happy to have their older siblings there. I was surprised to hear that many school-aged children like Ocham and Pauline's attend boarding schools.

"Isn't it hard to be away from them?" I asked Pauline plaintively.

"Of course, but I want them to have a good education."

"How often do you get to see them?"

By now, six-year-old Hellen was sitting on my lap, and three-year-old Dylan was asleep in Pauline's.

"They come home for holidays, and I go see them a couple of times a year."

My questions continued to the point where my incredulity

was palpable. To me, Pauline seemed so cold and detached about being separated from her young children. Sensing this, she clarified in her thick Kenyan brogue.

"I cannot afford for my children to be dependent upon only me. They must know how to fend for themselves. They must know that there are other adults like grannies and aunties or even you who can love and take care of them. I need to be sure that if something happens to me, they will be fine. If they are dependent on me and if something happens to me, then where would that leave them?"

Humbled and appropriately put in my place, I apologized.

Shifting the conversation, Pauline reminded me of her offer to take me into town the next day. We agreed to meet at my place at noon, and then we called a taxi to come take me back to my lonely abode.

I didn't sleep much at all that first night, and although I did finally fall asleep, I was awoken early and suddenly at sunrise. Someone, or as it turns out some*thing,* pounded against my window at dawn so violently that I bolted up and hit my head on the bunk above. I didn't have the courage to open the curtains to see what it was. I just laid there silently for over an hour until I thought it was safe to get up.

True to her word, Pauline met me at noon to show me around Bukoba. When she asked me how my first night was, I lied. As our taxi descended the hill into town, Pauline said, "*karibu Bukoba.*"

Welcome to Bukoba.

Located on the Western shores of the largest lake on the continent of Africa, Bukoba is the homeland of the Haya people, one of Tanzania's most culturally influential tribes. The formalized town of Bukoba as it looks today traces its roots back to the German Colonial Era, and most of the colonial-era buildings are near the lakeside of town.

The oldest building is the *Duka Kubwa,* (The Big Store) an

utterly unremarkable building except that it was built in 1898. The Lake Hotel is nearby and once hosted its most famous guests, Grace Kelly, Ava Gardner and Clark Gable who filmed *Mogambo* in the area.

Across from the Lake Hotel is an abandoned German colonial cemetery with granite headstones and wrought-iron gates covered with cobwebs. Up Jamhuri Road looms the most prominent and imposing landmark in Bukoba, the Mater Misericordia Cathedral where Cardinal Rugambwa, the very first Roman Catholic Cardinal from Africa, is buried. There are also Lutheran, Evangelical and Anglican churches, a mosque and even a Sikh temple across from a Toyota dealer. Like most villages and cities around the world, there is a large central marketplace, and it seems that most of the buildings around the market were erected in the mid-twentieth century, with dates ranging mostly from 1953-1959 adorning the cement facades of stores and government buildings.

The market itself is a hub of human activity: men sit drinking tea; women work the stalls, some so tired that they sleep on top of or underneath the tables, covered with or cuddled up with giant banana bunches, mangoes or water-melon. Children run around with toys they have hewn from plastic bottles or tin cans.

Streets here have wonderful names like Barongo, Kawa-wa, Kashozi and my favorite, Zamzam Road. A clock tower and a distinctly non-round "round-about" with a sculpture of banana trees lead to the ELCT Tea Room and Bookstore where Pauline and I would eat lunch together that first day.

As we drove around, I noticed that everywhere throughout town, from the "Welcome to Bukoba" sign to store fronts, red and white signs advertised Coca-Cola. A massive bottling plant that challenges the cathedral's pre-eminence looms over the port of Bukoba. A massive inflatable Coke bottle, with its curves puffed out like a bully's chest, overshadowed the small bodega next to it. Everywhere I looked, that unmistakable logo was painted on the sides of walls, fluttering on plastic banners, plastered in buildings and practically commanded us to have a Coke and a smile.

But even this ubiquitous conquest of American commercialism was no match for the natural beauty of Bukoba. Magnificent birds like the giant Marabou stork abound. The Kanoni River runs through town, its shores packed with papyrus plants. Vervet monkeys play on the grounds of the ELCT Hotel. And splendid Lake Victoria reigns over everything with her expanse of hydraulic grace while Musira Island, once a prison island in the days of Haya kings, is the closest of her crown jewels.

Before lunch, Pauline took me shopping at the market to buy a few items to make my life more comfortable: a teakettle, a cup, assorted baskets for storage, a broom, and some fruit. She was a formidable negotiator, accusing the vendors of charging me *mzungu* prices. I quickly learned her haggling catchphrase: *"Eh u kaka wewe."*

Heh, my brother!

The exchanges were lively and intense, and I felt embarrassed that she negotiated so intensely over a dollar or so here and there because that didn't really make a difference to me, but it sure did to the merchants.

One of the most pressing orders of business for me was learning how to access technology, especially the internet. Cellphone use involved purchasing a phone and a SIM card (which must be registered) and then purchasing vouchers that are scratched like lottery tickets to reveal codes that I needed to input into my phone in order to add minutes. "Pay as you go" was the only plan at that time. I could also buy a modem or dongle for internet use. Eventually I figured out that I also needed to refill this device by removing the SIM card from the modem, removing my phone's SIM card, replacing it with my internet card and reloading minutes onto that card, then removing it again, placing it back into the internet device and then clicking a few buttons. That took me weeks to figure out. *Weeks*.

After Pauline and I explored the town, we had lunch at the ELCT Tea Room. Just outside sat two elderly men crippled by polio, a disease that had also harmed my paternal grandfather. Inside, we enjoyed an all-you-can-eat buffet with rice, boiled banana, wild eggplant in peanut sauce, and a salad of cucumbers, onions and peppers called *kachumbali*. We talked more about motherhood and our dreams for our children. I apologized again for coming across as judgmental the night before with all my questions about how much time Pauline and her children spent apart and tried to clarify.

"I just can't even imagine being away from my children at such a young age," I said.

I explained to her that one of the reasons I had left my life in California and come all the way to Tanzania was that I was having such a difficult time adjusting to life without my daughters. I confessed that I had spent a significant amount of time crying about it and trying to figure out what to do next. I explained how I just really didn't know quite what to do with my life now.

"I'll tell you what you should be doing," Pauline said with her precise diction.

"You should be counting your lucky stars, *that's* what you should be doing," she scolded.

Half-heartedly, I responded:

"Yeah, I know."

"No—you don't," Pauline admonished, leaning in closer to me.

"Listen to me." Her eyes locked with mine. Then she repeated herself, her Kenyan accent louder and slower than before, her index finger poking me just above my heart, each jab keeping beat with each syllable:

"YOU... SHOULD... BE ... COUNT-*ING*... YOUR... LUCK-*Y*... STARS, I TELL YOU!" She leaned back in her seat and shook her head.

"Okay. Okay!" I laughed.

She shook her head and, once again, expressed a very audible "tsk-tsk."

We then talked about work. Pauline was working on her Master's Degree in Education at the college where Ocham taught. She was planning on opening her own school one day and was particularly interested in the education of girls.

We bonded over our shared faith in the transformative power of education for all children and a specific hope that our own children would be able to pursue their educations in order to fulfill their potential, dreams, and desires.

Exiting the restaurant, we, along with the other customers, offered a few coins to the paraplegic men who spent their days here on the sidewalk, often chatting with children on their way to and from school.

Returning home that afternoon, I felt optimistic about living here. Pauline was great company, and Bukoba more than exceeded my expectations. After unpacking and arranging my room, I decided to venture out for the first time alone and walked a kilometer or so down the hill to the Waalkgard Hotel.

I tried to have a more positive attitude about my housing. After arranging it with some of the items I had purchased, the room seemed a little cheerier, and I appreciated that I would be in close proximity to the Waalkgard Hotel, a place that would become very important because it was the hotel that had the only swimming pool in all of Bukoba.

The way to the Waalkgard is simple and direct. A narrow footpath leads through banana trees to a larger dirt road upon which bicycles, motorcycles and the occasional car could pass.

This road connects to the paved Kanazi Road, a narrow and steep hill of a transport corridor that leads not only to the Waalkgard but also to downtown Bukoba. On that first walk, and almost all subsequent ones, children followed me, laughing, asking for candy or trying to touch my strange-looking skin and hair.

Where the dirt road and Kanazi Road intersect, there is a small market that sells drinks and sundries. As Kanazi Road descends, a compound of four round brick homes with beautifully tiled roofs appears on the right side. Inside the walled compound, I could see an explosion of bright yellow lantana, white roses and cascades of pink bougainvillea lining gravel pathways just beyond the massive iron gate that was manned by security guards. I walked nonchalantly past and noticed the proscenium hanging above the gates, reminiscent of an English country manor, a sign that announced the intriguing name of this place: DESIRE.

As I stopped to admire the gardens of this oasis in semi-defiance of the security guards, an elderly gentleman emerged onto his porch from within the walls and asked me if I was the "visitor from America." I responded cheerfully in the affirmative.

"Where have you been? We were expecting you at dinner last night! *Karibu!*" he kindly exclaimed as he waved me in.

The stern-looking face of the guard suddenly transformed into a kind, smiling, laugh-lined one.

"*Karibu DESIRE,*" he said.

Welcome to DESIRE.

I felt like Dorothy Gale entering the Land of Oz. This seemed like a different, wonderful world. And indeed, that's exactly what it was.

The man on the porch was Monsignor, one of the founders of the university where I would be working with Ocham, and he was also one of the priests Ocham had said I was invited to dine with.

I never made it to the Waalkgard that day, lingering instead at the table with Monsignor, as teatime became dinnertime. Monsignor explained that DESIRE was a former restaurant and nightclub that was now being rented by the Diocese of Bukoba as a temporary rectory for the fathers who worked as professors, administrators and village priests. He showed me around the compound which included a now-obsolete bar area that still had signs advertising Serengeti and Kilimanjaro beers. There were three small cottages and the small former restaurant had been requisitioned as the dining hall. Gravel pathways led through gardens, and there seemed to be plenty of room to dance. Monsignor explained that the other fathers who lived at DESIRE were away for the holidays. Monsignor was kind, gentle and a great storyteller, and on those days before the other priests of DESIRE returned, I enjoyed the quiet company of a wise and gracious man.

I returned to DESIRE every evening for dinner with Monsignor, escorted back home each night by a security guard whose name was Edson and whose age could not have exceeded nineteen.

"Be sure to lock your doors," Edson reminded me each night after he checked the foyer and gave me the all-clear. After I locked the door, I would sit by the window listening to Edson's footsteps gradually disappear into the darkness.

The silence in the house haunted me. After my fourth night in that lonely and empty house, I not only walked to the Waalkgard Hotel, I checked in. It wasn't just the lonely isolation that banished me, but the early morning loud knocking at my window continued. Then on the fourth night, a stranger came pounding on my door around midnight, drunkenly asking for some money. Not even the recent addition of the showerhead in my bathroom could keep me there one more night.

Besides, it was New Year's Eve.

AULD ACQUAINTANCE

Situated atop a hill, the Waalkgard Hotel has a sweeping view of Bukoba. From the driveway at the base of the white, Arabesque four-storied building, a pageantry of luscious foliage leads down to the expanse of Lake Victoria in all her glory. As I stood there trying to catch my breath from the walk and from the breathtaking panorama, a woman descended a staircase from the reception area and introduced herself.

"You are most welcome here," Beatrice said, and like almost everyone I have ever met in Tanzania, she meant it.

Beatrice was the manager of the hotel. Like me, she was a single mom. I asked her about her children, who she said were "big." Her daughter was studying in Uganda, her son in Mwanza. We stayed outside until the sunset, and by the time we walked into the reception office we were holding hands. As I checked in, I noticed that amid the smaller-than-life-size mahogany carvings of hunters with animals and women carrying gourds of water, a massive cage housed a fantastic yellow-eyed, gray and white-feathered parrot.

"That is Kasuku." Beatrice told me as I reached out my hand towards the cage, and the bird stuck out his head so that

I could scratch it.

I told her how much I loved animals.

"You are in the perfect place. I am sure that one day you will come face to face with a monkey in our gardens."

Beatrice led me to Room 28 (my lucky number), a small chamber with a bed that connected to a bathroom with a sitting toilet and a shower. After thoroughly enjoying the oft-previously unappreciated sheer luxury of warm water, I dressed myself in a strapless black jumpsuit that I delusionally imagined made me look like one of Charlie's original Angels. Then, I went to the gardens for dinner.

By the time I exited the back of the hotel and followed a series of steps up into the gardens and pool, it was dark. The path led through a veranda of liantha vines, visible only as deep purple silhouettes against a pale violet sky. A few well-dressed couples dined on pilau and butter chicken or drank Kilimanjaro beer from bottles at candle-lit tables situated around the pool, a light steam emanating from the neon greenish glow as if from a giant cauldron. I sat alone eating vegetable soup and rice, occasionally and futilely checking my phone for messages.

As I stared into the pool, an early memory, the very first memory of my life actually, appeared. I can remember when I was less than two years old sinking slowly to the bottom of a swimming pool, gravity's force challenged by the weight of the water. Instead of being afraid, I remember being delighted in the slow process, aware that I was falling, but in slow motion. I instinctively held my breath and looked upward to see the rays of sunlight, dancing and bending through the water. It was pure joy. Suddenly, the smooth surface of the water was shattered as my father invaded my aquatic nirvana, diving in, kicking furiously towards me and finally taking me into his arms just as I had bounced gently on the pool floor. With my first breath back at the surface, I let out a gasp of deep laughter. The laughter lasted only until I saw the look on my mom's face—a look of sheer terror clouding her usual cheery countenance. Although I had been a baby when I almost drowned in that Los Angeles pool, I can remember it vividly.

After that moment, I learned how to swim. More specifically, great measures were taken to ensure that I learned how to swim. My family insisted on it, and I loved it. My mother spent long afternoons at the local school pool while I took hours of swimming and eventually diving lessons. My grandmother regularly took me to the pool at her apartment complex and stood in the shallow end while I swam through her legs or floated next to her on my back. My dad taught me to swim in the ocean, carrying me out past the waves on his shoulders, showing me how to safely navigate powerful surf and explaining how to escape riptides. It wasn't until I was an adult that I learned that neither of my grandmothers knew how to swim and that my dad was actually terrified of the ocean.

The sound of a phone ringing transported me back to the pool at the Waalkgard Hotel in Tanzania. It was Pauline inviting me to spend the next day, New Year's Day, with her, Ocham and their children at a lakeside spot to celebrate both the New Year and Ocham's birthday. Without hesitation, I accepted.

I finished my tea then paid the bill without talking to anyone except the waitress. Walking down to the short stairway from the pool to the hotel I could see the lights of the city below—Bukoba by night. Near the bottom of the staircase, I almost tripped over a magnificent tortoise who shared a striking resemblance to my childhood pet, Tom, a Mexican Desert Tortoise who used to eat lettuce and tomatoes out of my hands. I stopped to pick up the Waalkgard tortoise and placed him safely under some bushes. We lingered silently and alone for a few moments until he emerged from his shell and lumbered off into the bushes, and I nestled into my tiny room where I fell in and out of sleep listening to the celebrations at the bar below until they accelerated to a dramatic midnight crescendo.

The next day I met Pauline, Ocham and their children at a lakeside establishment called the Kiyoera Beach Resort. The resort consisted of a lean-to restaurant with seats placed intermittently along the lake. Ocham's family was sitting in an old, beached boat that had been converted into a seating area. By the time I arrived, the kids had already enjoyed many of the treats being sold by vendors walking along the shore: homemade popsicles, popcorn, chocolates. The children greeted me lovingly, already calling me "Auntie," and before I could sit down, Pauline had ordered me tea that was delivered by the smiling waitress whose equally happy toddler followed her to our boat and then climbed into Pauline's lap where she spent the rest of the day.

I poured my tea, placed it to my lips and then lifted my eyes to behold a rich pageantry. All along the shore, what seemed to be the entire citizenry of Bukoba passed back and forth dressed in their finest attire. Little girls regaled in long dresses and scarves carried babies on their backs or in their arms. Young boys dressed in tuxedoes and suits strutted with their arms around each other's shoulders. One young boy came running up to me and placed a grey and iridescent shell into the palm of my hand, then without a word ran back to his buddies and disappeared forever into the crowd.

Men and women of all ages, shapes and sizes paraded up and down the shoreline in an apparent New Year's Day tradition, each a vision of fashion decorum. Some women wore their hair in extravagant braids, chignons or updos. Others had natural hair or shaved heads, each with eyes and smiles as the centerpieces of their physical beauty.

As I sat there with my hair falling out of place and dressed in a cotton sun-proof shirt and khaki skirt, I looked like I'd just come out of a month-long camping trip.

Ocham, Pauline and I sat back and watched appreciatively.

"We call them little women," Ocham laughed and pointed out a group of self-composed toddlers dressed in miniature ball gowns.

Ocham, Pauline and I talked all day long while the children ran around, splashed in the lake, cartwheeled on the grass and paraded around with the other children.

As the sun faded and the winds kicked up, Pauline and I returned the waitress' sleeping daughter and paid the tab. We all piled into a taxi without any seatbelts. Pauline and Ocham's son, Dylan, sat on his mother's lap, and the whole ride up the hill his sugar-covered fingers grazed my white, freckled skin and auburn hair. We sang "Happy Birthday" to Ocham at the top of our voices, and I could see the driver's wide smile in the rearview mirror.

Suddenly, we pulled up to the Waalkgard, and I extracted myself from the tangle of Ocham's family. As I stood there, waving good-bye until I could no longer see Dylan's tiny waving hand, I realized that this was about as new as a New Year could be.

HONEYMOON AT
A RECTORY

It took my ex-husband seven years to ask me to live with him. It took the last man I lived with eight. It took the priests of St. Augustine University in Bukoba exactly one week. I wish I could say that this was the result of some improvement in my feminine charms, but the truth is that in my experience Tanzanian men do not waste any time. And this would be no ordinary love story.

The week after New Year's Day, the other priests who lived at DESIRE gradually returned from their Christmas visits home. Each night, a new man was at the dinner table until there were five of us.

I had a very clear arrangement with the men with whom I eventually cohabitated in Tanzania. It would be a temporary situation. I had to respect their personal space, and it was clear by their chosen professions that they had absolutely no intentions of ever marrying me. In other words, the arrangement was the dream of most of the men I have loved. Unlike in my past relationships, this time I could hold no illusions. I could not deny the basic facts of the situation. And that was more than fine with me.

For the first week in Bukoba, I had been living all alone in that house reserved for the nuns and female lecturers like me until I eventually started staying at the Waalkgard. There were indeed nuns who would eventually come through and stay in the house from time to time, and these nuns were, as my sole neighbor told me, "always coming and going," but that was the occasional exception. I was spending most of my free time at the rectory of DESIRE with the exception of where I actually slept. I practically had a toothbrush there.

I had felt immediately at home with these priests who did not suffocate me with the Irish Catholicism of my ancestors. Their theology was love, and they exemplified the words often attributed to St. Francis of Assisi. "Preach the Gospel at all times, and if necessary use words." Only in church did I hear them preach the Gospel, but I witnessed their faith every day.

We ate all of our meals together. Monsignor drove me to and from work most days, and we all lingered after dinner amicably discussing subjects that would be controversial or heated at most dinner tables like politics, philosophy and religion. Imagine having dinner and lively, intelligent and thoughtful discussions every night with four men who have PhDs, absolutely no untoward intentions and who offered their sincere respect and undivided attention. It was heaven!

I quickly learned that these four priests were fully engaged in the community and in life outside of the walls of the church and the rectory. These are Tanzanian men of the world, and they told the most vivid stories about their travels, about riding around Rome on Vespas when they were young men, about their lives in their villages and boarding schools, about their travels to the U.S. which included vivid descriptions of San Francisco, New Mexico and Philadelphia. Between the four of them, they have been practically everywhere and did not cloister themselves like Benedictines. They are Jesuits, humanitarians, teachers, philosophers. They were the most engaging group of dinner companions I have ever had. What's more, they even laughed at my stupid jokes that had been heretofore unappreciated.[1] What more could a gal ask for?

I was simultaneously nervous and curious when Father Mgeni, the director of the university, called me to his office one day. His assistant, Cesilia looked quietly up at me as I passed through the short hall to his office and offered a kind smile. Abandoning the relaxed informality that we enjoyed at DESIRE, Father Mgeni formally invited me to sit down with a sweeping gesture of his right arm as soon as I entered his office. He then took the chair across from me, leaned forward, and, without any small talk leading into the business at hand, began a series of questions.

"I am informed that you have been sleeping at the hotel," he said, as much a question as a statement.

Embarrassed, I tried to politely explain why I hadn't been sleeping at the lonely house the university had provided for me, aware that this could be seen as an insult.

"Yes, that's true," I admitted before trying to lie about the reasons. "I just thought I would stay at the Waalkgard for a little vacation until classes started."

Father Mgeni leaned back and crossed his fingers, pressing his clasped hands into his chest. He was quiet for a few moments, probably trying to find soft words for getting to the truth. Eventually he leaned forward again, stared directly into my eyes and asked a simple yet piercing question.

"Do you feel safe at that house?"

I tried to think of a culturally-sensitive answer but instead started to cry as I shook my head "no."

At this point, Father Mgeni explained why he had called me into his office, and soon my tears of fear would be

---

[1] e.g. How did the philosophical sweet potato describe his existence? I yam what I yam.

transformed into tears of joy.

"That's what the other fathers and I at DESIRE have been worried about, and we have had some serious discussion about the situation," he explained in his deep and gentle voice.

He asked if I would be amenable to the idea of moving into Father Charles' little house at DESIRE. Father Charles had agreed to move into one of the rooms at Father Mgeni's massive house which was big enough for an entire family.

Even before he finished the proposition, I was nodding my head "yes," tears of joy now flowing down my cheek as if he'd just proposed.

"Great," he said. "Pack your things, and I will pick you up at 6:00."

"Today?" I asked.

"Yes, today."

I got home from work that day at 4:15. I was packed and ready to move out by 4:30, Peter Gabriel's "Solsbury Hill" playing in my head ("Pack your things, I've come to take you home") until Fathers Mgeni and Charles pulled up to take me to my new home: DESIRE.

From the moment Fathers Charles and Mgeni carried my bags (if not me) across the threshold, I felt immediately at home.

But I also felt a little peculiar because I did something with these men that I hadn't ever really done before (and something I do not generally like to do) with most men in my life. I actually listened to them.

When Father Charles advised me not to touch frogs or lizards because they might be poisonous, I heeded his warning, repressing my urge to handle the little critters who populated the gardens.

If one of the fathers suggested that I might need a sweater, I took their word for it. I listened to and followed up on their suggestions about books I should read. I didn't give them a single ounce of what my dad calls "push back" (a strategy that he paradoxically taught me). I did not act, as one or two men in my past may have called me, "impossible." And I did not drive these men (as I have almost all others who get this close to me) to such a defensive stance of perturbation that they would erupt into a flurry of profanity that would make Charles Bukowski blush.

Those weeks after I moved to DESIRE were like a honeymoon.

The men would not let me lift a finger. When I was hanging up my clothes outside to dry one afternoon, Father Joseph shook his head and directed me to Asimwe, Irene and Doreen who worked at DESIRE.

"Stay in your lane," he explained. "Do not insult their work, and do your own."

I offered to cook several times, but Irene was a masterful cook. Once I tried to make pasta over an open fire for us, and it came out like a matzah ball.

"Just focus on your work," Father Joseph reiterated after that meal.

After my time with these fathers, I came to develop a sense of compassion for the men in my life back home who have also sincerely supported and loved me. I realized a truth. I am too much for one man. I might even have been too much for the Fantastic Four with whom I lived, but they never showed it, and each one of them always seemed to know just what to say and do.

Monsignor was the first one to welcome me into DESIRE. After that first lonely night at the empty house when I was walking down the hill, he asked me to join him and the fathers for dinner. I had jumped at the chance, and the poor man was stuck with me ever after. He has a PhD in Philosophy and a very gentle disposition. Often sitting quietly, sometimes even with his eyes closed, while the rest of us engaged in lively conversation, Monsignor would occasionally interject a one or two sentence comment that hit the mark so perfectly that it often silenced us all.

One night he sat there listening to one of our discussions with his eyes closed, then briefly opened them and said something like "...only the one wearing the shoe knows where it pinches." During the first few days when it was just he and I sharing meals at DESIRE, we talked about Viktor Frankl, Nietzsche, Kant, Schiller and St. Thomas. Monsignor is a stickler for punctuality and decorum, so I had my work cut out for me. Monsignor showed me through his kind example and gentle words how to be a more considerate and thoughtful human being.[2]

Monsignor is the man who showed me how to truly listen.

Father Mgeni was the director of St. Augustine University and the man who invited me to come live at DESIRE. With a gentle nature and playful spirit, Father Mgeni has a Doctorate in Education. My first impression of him on campus was that he seemed to be a wonderful leader and administrator who understands firsthand the value of education. Plucked from his childhood school by teachers who recognized him as an exceptional student, he was sent to schools on scholarship and lived for years in Rome. Originally from Iringe, Father Mgeni speaks his mother tongue in addition to Swahili, English and Italian. He is affable at work and demonstrates great respect for his position. At home however, he was light-hearted and enjoyed teasing me, often by grossing me out while describing all the different types of animals and insects he has eaten throughout his life including monkey brains. After dinner each night, he invariably chivalrously opened the door of the dining room leading outside and insisted:

"Ladies first...there might be lions out there."

---

[2] This is all I have ever wanted in a man.

Ha. Ha. Ha.

Father Mgeni made me feel safe, made me laugh, and would never let me take myself too seriously.[3]

He is the man who, like my father, reminded me that I am tougher than I think.

Father Charles, who graciously gave up his cottage for me to move here, was the bursar, which means he controlled the money not only at DESIRE but also at the college. He has also made a vow of poverty, which is a perfect combination: unlike my ex-husband's habits, Father Charles' constitution ensures economic integrity. He operates within the budget, never overextends financially, the bills all get paid on time, and there is no chance of him squandering money on sports cars or secret paramours. Father Charles has a Magic Johnson baby face and the heart of a medieval knight. At first, I nicknamed him "Charles in Charge," but eventually the nickname that stuck was "The Scientist" because of his degrees in Material Chemistry (a discipline he's still trying to explain to me). He knows so many facts about the environment and often provided such ornate descriptions of animals and natural history that I would listen for hours over tea as he meticulously described the perfect order of the Natural World. He organized his time into four quadrants of time management which demonstrates his affinity for classification systems.

As I mentioned, he is the one who moved out of his awesome bachelor pad for me; he also regularly offered to wait for me to drive me to or from work if I was ever running too late for Monsignor (which may or may not have happened once or twice). Sometimes he joined in with Father Mgeni to tease me, but mostly he was attentive to my every need.

---

[3] Oh, and this too. This is also all I've ever really wanted in a man.

Sometimes it was as if he could read my mind.[4] If I wanted more potatoes at dinner, he passed them to me before I even had the chance to ask. Father Charles was not just the man who paid the bills; he was always there for me even before I knew myself what I needed.

Father Charles was the man who, like my own brothers, showed me the beauty of true, brotherly love.

And finally, there was Father Joseph, the most unique character and well-educated person I have ever met in my entire life. Father Joseph is a cathedral of a man: he towers above us all, his arms floating vaults above the columns of his legs with eyes radiating like stained glass windows the color of Tanzanite. There is no way to completely and accurately describe him. He looks like a Haya Paul Newman with those intense blue eyes. I told him one night that he is like two men in one:[5] He is a man of the western world with his impeccable Dr. Henry Higgins British accent, a Burberry raincoat, an Omega watch and an impressive and extensive education (two PhDs). He is also—first and foremost—an African man who embraces his deep tribal roots. Father Joseph's second PhD (from Oxford) was in Sociological Anthropology, and his dissertation explained the ancient beliefs and customs of the Haya people of this region. He was born and raised here in the Kagera Region, and although he had in many ways become a "man of the world," he is proudly connected to this area. When he speaks, his long fingers point and wave like an Italian conductor's baton, but I have no doubt that he could also do some serious damage with those elegant hands if he needed to.

I once told him that I thought he might be able to wrestle

---

[4] Also, this! This too is a critical ability that I've always wanted in a man.

[5] I believe that I have also asked for this quality in a man before.

a leopard with those hands. He looked at me askance and with a raised eyebrow replied, "Whatever do you mean, you *think* I could?" He loves California too, having helped establish the African Studies Department of a major California university. He often made me laugh so hard that my stomach hurt, and he also often comforted me by bringing me treats when I felt homesick.

He is the man who showed me how to navigate his world.

Between the four of these men, my bases were finally covered. Collectively they made sure I felt safe and protected. They made me laugh and not take myself so seriously, and they were kind and patient with me. They respected me as an equal, letting me be an independent woman and ensuring that I could focus on my own goals while also doing kind gestures for me. They challenged me intellectually, and simultaneously took care of me and gave me my freedom.[6]

---

[6] And *this* is all I've ever really asked for in a man. Well, just about.

REVELATION

The semester didn't start for a few weeks after my arrival in Bukoba, but I wanted to see the campus and get to know my colleagues as soon as I could. Located about four miles away from DESIRE, the Bukoba campus is a small, but well-kept compound surrounded by banana plantations. The first time I went there, Ocham and I traveled together by taxi. Security guards in olive green shirts opened the large iron gates and waved us through to a dirt road that inclined at a 30-degree angle. Scattered about the manicured lawns and gardens were several buildings of various sizes, slightly resembling organized and tidy military barracks: cinder block buildings, a canteen, a flagpole with the Tanzanian flag waving in the wind.

Apologetically, Ocham showed me to my new office.

"I'm sure this isn't as nice as the one you have at home," he chagrined as he opened the door to an eight-foot by twenty-foot room with an entire wall of windows framing a breathtaking view of rolling hills, giant palm trees and a turquoise sky. I laughed.

"Ocham, this is *AMAZING!*"

Throughout my year in Bukoba, Ocham often thought that I was just being gracious in moments like these. He never quite believed me when I tried to convey just how lovely I thought it was here.

"You are just being polite," he often disregarded.

Later on, I would tell him about some of the offices I had been given back home in California. Some didn't have windows. One had a window, but it was too smoggy outside to offer much of a view. I was once given an office of a teacher who had passed away, and most of her belongings were still in the desk and bookshelves. I was told to go through her personal property by myself and clean the office on my own. Little effort at all was made there to make me feel welcomed, and the office itself was in a portable building placed onto asphalt.

As Ocham showed me my new office in Bukoba, I wanted to cry with joy as I tried to assure him that I was most definitely not just being polite as I expressed my delight.

I unpacked my books and photos of my daughters. Then I opened the windows and enjoyed the view and fresh air.

My office in Bukoba was located in the academic block with several other faculty offices. To my right was the Dean of Students who, although the university was technically not in session, already had a line of over 30 students deep waiting to see her. Down the corridor to my left were several offices for professors of History, French, Geology, Sociology and Education. Ocham's office was located down the slight hill at the lower end of campus in the administrative block near Father Joseph's office and the offices of the other English professors, Peterson and Felix.

Peterson and Felix greeted me in classic Tanzanian professional fashion: extremely formally. Standing at well over six feet tall and hailing from Kenya, Felix extended a hand from a perfectly pressed suit. He spoke to me in the impeccable

English of the Kenyans, and I felt self-conscious about my twangy accent. In his signature leather jacket, Petersen had a James Dean grin and motorcycle. Having just finished his Master's Degree in Indonesia, his English was more relaxed than Felix's and Ocham's. Upon our introduction, Petersen and I fist bumped.

While Ocham went to his office that first day, I walked the campus exploring the classrooms. Each was a giant lecture hall with fixed rows of desks, open windows, chalkboards and concrete floors. I noticed that the lecture hall where I would teach was equipped with computer hookups, and I excitedly looked up to see a projector hanging from the ceiling on top of which sat a small, grey monkey looking casually down on me.

At mid-morning, Ocham and I met for morning tea break at the canteen. Several fires smoldered behind the canteen where women prepared roasted cassava, eggs and fried doughy pastries like *andazi* or *vitumbua*.

Teatime in Tanzania is serious business. Tea is often served with masala herbs or ginger and is almost always served with lots of sugar. The morning tea break would soon and thankfully become a ritual for Ocham and me. On this first day, we talked freely and excitedly about ideas for our work together.

"You are lucky," he told me. "You will have a small class size here."

Accustomed to "small class sizes" of 15-22 students in California, I knew to expect large classes in Tanzania. When I asked him how many students to prepare for, Ocham said, "one hundred and eighty six."

Gulp.

That is more students than I ever had collectively in all my classes combined in a single semester. I had never taught a class that large before, and I began to realize some of the challenges for teachers in Tanzania if one hundred and eighty six students in one class was considered small.

One of the many ideas Ocham shared with me that first tea together was his idea to establish a portable library for the most isolated rural schools in the region.

"Ocham, you have the best ideas," I said.

"You are just being polite," he responded.

Politeness is *very* important in Tanzania, and I did my best to follow this cultural value, but on my third day preparing at the university, I failed. Miserably. After walking past a certain woman whom I often saw around campus (I will call her Jurani), I waved to her, greeting her with an enthusiastic, California "hi!" She turned around quickly and followed me to my office.

"I must speak to you," she insisted.

"Of course," I said and invited her to sit down. She declined.

"I must tell you that you degrade me every morning with that dismissive greeting!" she derided and then mimicked my wide smile and "hi!"

I was speechless.

"You should stop to greet me properly," she demanded.

Aware of the elaborate greeting system in Tanzania courtesy of Father Joseph's dissertation and coaching, I thought I had done a pretty good job of making sure to "greet" my colleagues and neighbors "properly" by stopping to speak with them. But this woman had never even spoken to me before, not even when Ocham introduced us. She hadn't even smiled. It hadn't even occurred to me to stop to talk to her on campus. That just seemed awkward, but here she was in my office telling me how I had degraded and insulted her. I felt terrible.

Throughout my time in Tanzania, Father Joe would be my greatest cultural guide and advisor. When I sought his advice and recounted the story of Jurani later that evening, he listened quietly, his enthrallingly long fingers interlaced and resting on his chest. On this point he clarified that the extensive greetings in Tanzania are not just for friendship but also to show respect and consideration. The exact rules concerning the recipients of greetings were elaborate and slightly obscure.

"It is best to greet all of your neighbors and colleagues properly," he advised. I worried about how I could make amends to the woman I had "degraded."

"I wouldn't worry too much about her," he assured me.

I apologized to Ocham for any insult I may have caused.

"I don't know what you are talking about," he said.

I told him the story, and then he responded, "I don't believe it!"

Like Father Joseph, he also encouraged me not to worry too much about it.

After that day, I made sure to stop and greet all my colleagues properly. This meant asking about their families, their homes, their work, and their recent journeys. When my greetings extended to the groundskeepers, cleaning staff and security guards, Jurani came by my office again to tell me that such behavior was also insulting: I should show her more respect than those in a "lower position." After that visit I continued to greet everyone properly, but I reserved more extended greetings for her. Some were so elaborate that she extricated herself from conversations with me on two occasions.

My greetings for her included not only inquiring about her family and home. I also asked her the news of her breakfast, her computer, her grading, her animals, her mode of transport for the day, her clothes, her hair. By the time classes started, she no longer stopped when I approached to greet her. Instead, she just walked by, waved, and then offered me a quick smile as she said "hi."

I spent my days on campus during those first few weeks preparing to teach one hundred and eight six students and getting to know my colleagues. Faculty and staff all ate lunch together each afternoon. Lining up to heap spoonfuls of rice, beans, boiled bananas and fish from the lake onto china plates, we joked and relaxed. With the exception of Jurani, I felt welcomed and embraced. From that first faculty meeting, I felt included and part of the team. I listened as the professors discussed some of the same challenges I faced in California: limited resources, unprepared students, lack of funding. Compared to California though, the challenges were even more daunting. Just when the conversation turned almost hopeless, Felix said in his calm and metered delivery:

"But we shall persevere. We shall not give up, and we shall carry on and do the best we can for our students under these circumstances."

This man endeared himself to me forever with this single comment, and throughout my year there he stayed true to that declaration.

After work those first few weeks, I walked down to the Waalkgard in the afternoons to swim, and this too would become a daily ritual. For about twenty dollars a month, I bought a pool membership which provided unlimited access to swim and have an afternoon tea. The lifeguard at the pool was a young man named Egbert who also helped construct the pool of which he was, justifiably, proud. Sitting behind the bar as I swam laps, Egbert listened to the radio and watched over me with the concern of a parent.

"No one should swim alone," he explained.

After my swims, Beatrice usually joined me for tea in the gardens next to the pool. Surrounded by passion flowers, liantha vines, palm fronds and ancient trees we would sit at a white table on the grass and talk intimately about our personal lives, mostly about our children, our lost lovers and our mothers.

We are both single mothers, working hard to educate our children. We both worry about our mothers. We both have dreams of our own. Beatrice was the first friend I made on my own in Bukoba, and even if she had been the only friend I ever made there, that would have been more than I could have asked for. She gave me a safe place to stay and made me feel at home that first week. She continued to give me sanctuary throughout my time in Bukoba, not just providing a beautiful space to relax but also by providing a loving, warm and generous friendship.

I asked her about the sign that hung in the lobby, thinking that the owner of this hotel must be some kind of megalomaniac:

In Swahili it says that we must give all the glory to *Bwana*—"boss."

Beatrice laughed, revealing a missing bicuspid.

She explained: "We must always thank God for his gifts."

She explained that *Bwana* is another word for God.

Religion is ubiquitous here. In Bukoba, there is a Sikh temple, a mosque, the cathedral as well as Seventh Day Adventist, Anglican, Episcopal, Methodist and Lutheran churches. There are also temporary, makeshift revival structures. Traditional African Religion abounds, unconfined by physical structures. The first question I was usually asked upon first introduction in Tanzania was "what religion are you?"

"Undeclared" was not an acceptable response, and after a while people stopped asking because of all the time I spent with the fathers. It didn't take long for people to assume I was Catholic, and sometimes they even assumed I was actually a nun. Every Sunday I drove to the campus with the fathers who delivered Mass in the largest lecture hall. I listened to their homilies, sang along with the choir, felt grateful and gave offerings to my community. These were contemplative mornings, and I could often hear choirs of birds or the hymns from the services of other denominations scattered through-out the campus through the open windows. I spent a lot of time singing hymns in Swahili and saying "thank you" to the cosmic universal life force and calling it *Bwana*.

The imposition of outside forces, including religion, in Tanzania is complicated and horrifying. When one of the fathers lovingly mentioned "the white fathers" who established Catholicism here, I felt uncomfortable and ashamed. When I expressed this, he delineated the positive role that religious missionaries had in ending slavery and colonialism here, and I still felt uncomfortable and ashamed.

One of the nuns I became friends with, Sister Clara, told me one day that while Tanzanians are indeed very religious, they are also very understanding of human behavior.

"Ah, the reproductive system is very active here. What can we really do to stop that?" she once said in reference to the apparent profusion of romantic and sexual activity.

Despite the significance of religion in almost every aspect of everyday life, I found that religions in Tanzania were, as Sister Clara said, generally non-judgmental, with one exception.

American fundamentalist Christians have had an increasingly significant impact on religion throughout Africa, including Tanzania. With a focus on spreading "the Word" which seems to include the infallibility of the Bible and an emphasis on sin, evangelicals have brought a very specific brand of religion to this part of the world. I came across a lot of these types of Americans in Tanzania.

I met one American couple on the flight from Mwanza to Bukoba who seemed friendly enough. They first assumed that I was also there as a missionary and asked me what organization I was with. When I explained my educational "mission," they seemed disinterested. Instead, they told me—with great self-reverence and righteousness—that they were here to train other missionaries and future preachers. I asked them about their studies of theology or divinity.

"Oh, we didn't have to *study* those things," the wife said. "Because we have accepted Jesus as our Lord and Savior, He works directly through us."

When I asked them what had brought them to Tanzania instead of spreading the Gospel back home, they explained that they had come here to get away from the "homosexuals and abortionists" in America. The force of their hatred was so strong that I felt as if I had been kicked in the stomach.

The wife talked to me about "sin" and "perversion" as we retrieved our luggage, and her husband tried to look down my dress as I bent over to lift my suitcase. I left quickly and hoped to never see them again.

While I spent Sunday mornings at church, I spent Sunday afternoons going downtown to shop and walk around town. One such afternoon not long after I arrived in Bukoba, I saw the American couple I had encountered on the plane from Mwanza having tea at an outdoor table near the bus stop. Before I could escape unnoticed, they waved me over. Not wanting to be rude I asked them what they were up to.

"We're working."

They must have noticed my quizzical look because they explained that they were working in a supervisory capacity and then directed my attention to a woman standing on a bench and preaching, a Bible gripped in her right hand. It was Jurani! Not wanting to commit another *faux pas* I decided to greet her properly. I approached the bench at the center of the crowd. As I got closer, I could hear that she was not just preaching to the crowd, she was condemning them. In English. As passengers were boarding buses to Mwanza or Luanda, Jurani shook her fists at women, calling them prostitutes. She damned the entire crowd to hell for being sinners. Even children were the source of her wrath.

"Repent or you will burn in hell!"

With the same anger and disgust with which she had chastised me for improper greetings, she lashed out at one group of travelers, condemning them to hell. She screamed out, "God *HATES* you!"

I walked closer and closer to her, wondering what names she might call me. Eventually, she saw me approach. After only a few seconds, she blinked and averted her gaze from me. I changed my mind about greeting her, and I turned and walked away, brushing past that American couple offering nothing but a scowl, never again worrying about how to greet Jurani, wishing Ocham were there to see that I really was not so polite after all.

USEFUL WORDS AND PHRASES FOR CALIFORNIANS WORKING AT A CATHOLIC UNIVERSITY IN WESTERN TANZANIA

Although I stopped worrying about Jurani, I still worried about "degrading" anyone here due to my lack of cultural or linguistic understanding. True, I had plenty of training and orientation before my arrival. I had Father Joseph's cultural guidance, and I also spoke a dialect very similar to the Swahili spoken here. Still, I knew that I had a lot to learn. Thinking that some of the local bookstores would have a better selection of information than what I had brought with me, I decided to go dictionary shopping one Saturday. Local churches own the only bookstores in Bukoba. The smaller, Bible bookstore is run by the Catholic Church and sells the Bible, books on the saints, and guides to the Holy Catechism. The ELCT Bookstore has more variety: in addition to the Bible, Bible stories, school books and art supplies, they also sell some fiction books as well as dictionaries and phrase books.

At the ELCT Bookstore, I picked up a small, apparently self-published phrase book written by "white missionaries" who had lived in the Kagera Region. The introduction promised to give useful phrases and tips for any foreigner working in this particular area. I purchased the book along with some teaching supplies. After I arrived home and put away some fruit I had bought at the market, I sat down to read the book. It was informative, but as it turns out, not very useful.

Some of the phrases included "this is overcooked," and "I don't like this." I don't think this is how Tanzanians speak. I know it's not how I want to speak. Some of the words and phrases in the book were also followed by instructions like, "work faster," or "no, you may not take the day off," and were followed by shameful explanations like "to be used when speaking to your inferiors." Based on many of the phrases in this book, that condition seemed to apply to anyone with whom the "white missionaries" who wrote this book might have the need to use Swahili. This book and the ones I had brought with me were inadequate, so I turned to the world around me for direction. I quickly learned that learning the local languages in Bukoba is much easier for foreigners than learning English is for foreigners back home.

Growing up in Southern California, I often heard the critical refrain: "why don't they just speak English?" The "they" included any number of speakers of Spanish, Vietnamese, Tagalog, Farsi, Khmer, Hmong or Chinese who came to my hometown—once a sanctuary city—in search of a "better life." Those launching the accusatory question in response to the voices of newly arrived transplants were ubiquitously monolingual English speakers. This question has guided my career path, and I have spent my entire adult life trying not only to understand *why* so many struggle to speak English but to address *how* to support them. The more I work overseas and learn new languages, the more I realize a big part of the problem for anybody learning English is the very people who ask the question, "why don't they learn English?"

The conditions in California for learning a language are much different from those in Tanzania where the linguistic capacity of the inhabitants baffles the mind. Most people speak Swahili, English and a local, vernacular language. Every time, and I really mean *every* time, I speak Swahili or attempt one of the local languages, no matter how I struggle with my words or say something completely incomprehensible, my fellow interlocutor will say, "ah, you are speaking so well," or "you see, Swahili is an easy language."

Swahili is logical, but hardly easy with its nine noun classes that make Latin noun declension look manageable, as well as a Byzantine configuration of syntactic affixes. It's not so much that Bantu speakers don't know how complex their languages are. It's that they are welcoming me into their dialectal homes, encouraging me to speak in the same way parents and grandparents around the world do with babies.

Only when I overcame some of the grammatical challenges of Swahili and made myself comfortable did my conversational partners admit the truth about just how difficult this language really is. But they still said things like, "eh, you will be speaking like one of us in no time."

Everyone in Tanzania was my language teacher. The cook at my favorite roadside stand where I often ate lunch pointed to the food (an omelet mixed with potatoes) and tells me what it's called (*chipsi mayaii),* and then had me repeat the words until I said them correctly. The librarians taught me academic vocabulary. The women who sold me fruit taught me to count, even drawing pictures in the red soil. The young men thrashing grass for their cows outside my office window helped me practice greetings in three languages. Every day people repeated words, explained etymology, sent me texts and wrote notes so I could see how something is written. They even explained figurative language to me. After my swims at the Waalkgard, the lifeguard, Egbert gave me homework.

But it isn't only Tanzanians who are great language teachers. I have been lucky enough to pursue work that has allowed me to learn several languages, and the first language I learned after English was Spanish. I could speak it before I ever even left Southern California, and it wasn't because I memorized verb conjugations in high school. I learned Spanish because every time I even *tried* to say something in the language of Neruda and Cervantes, Spanish speakers encouraged me: they listened, corrected, pretended to understand and answered me back in Spanish even if they spoke perfect English.

"Ah, you are one of us!"

Perfecto.

I have never seen that type of collective behavior from native English speakers at home. We are not known for being as patient and helpful with English language learners as people around the world have been with me. We are more like the French. Anyone who has studied French at school and then gone to Paris to practice knows what I am talking about. Parisians will usually scoff and sneer at the first insulting mispronunciation, excommunicating you linguistically, banishing you from their francophone kingdom by sweeping your dreams down the sidewalk and into the gutter along with the baguette and croissant crumbs. You imagine they are thinking "why don't zeh learn French?"

And that is usually how we treat those who speak other languages trying to learn English in California. Some of my most cringe-worthy moments back home involved someone being rude to an English learner: the Texan berating a server at a fast-food restaurant for speaking with an accent as he himself mispronounced the Mexican food he ordered, the well-dressed woman who called a Cambodian holocaust survivor the "r" word, the all-too-common general impatience and dismissive interactions culminating in that loaded and oft-heard question: why don't *they* learn English? If the people in Tanzania treated me like that, not only would I fail to learn the local languages, I would also probably fail to believe in humanity.

Instead, the first word I heard was *karibu*: welcome. I heard this word repeatedly each and every day. Welcome to my home. Welcome to my office. Welcome to join our conversation. Welcome to sit next to me. Welcome to eat breakfast/lunch/dinner with me. Welcome. WELCOME! And so now my Swahili is pretty good, not because of what I have accomplished, but because of what everyone around me has. They have made me feel welcome.

And I realized that this was probably going to be the most valuable professional lesson I would learn in Tanzania, even with all of my research questions, observations and theories. Language attitudes, motivations and opportunities are very powerful. The way language learners are treated by speakers of those languages is as powerful as, if not more than, any teaching strategies, any hours of studying or any policies that Ocham and I might explore.

I was inspired every day by Tanzanians. There was a generally positive attitude towards language learners. I wish that I could help change Californians' general negative attitude towards those who are learning English as a second, third or fourth language. Although as an educator I may not be able to affect this change throughout society, I do believe that change is inevitable. There is a new global English language emerging, one that has little to do with the British upper crust or non-distinctive regional American dialects. This global English allows a professor from East Africa to communicate with a scholar from Europe or for a businessman in Southeast Asia to negotiate with a client in South America. This global English allows for variations and forgiveness in pronunciation and lexicon. This English demands just a little more patience, work and attention on the part of the listener than many native English speakers are accustomed to.

I often think about the many people I observed in my hometown. Those newcomers *were* speaking English—at least they were trying to, just like many all over the world are trying to. Maybe the problem isn't so much that "they" are not speaking English as it is a problem of us not listening very well.

That phrasebook from the ELCT bookstore was not only obsolete, it was offensive. Thanks to my experiences in East Africa and to the patience of Tanzanians, I learned more about language from them than any book could teach me. By no means an exhaustive list of the words and phrases that I found helpful, the following expressions were more relevant to me than that ELCT store phrasebook with its discussion of how to speak to one's "inferiors"—a group I have never encountered during my lifetime, let alone during my year in Tanzania.

Here is a short list of some of the most important and useful new words and phrases for a Californian living and working in Tanzania based on my experiences.

Asante: This means "thank you" in Swahili, and is the second-most used word after *Karibu* (welcome).

Asante kwa umshakuru: This is what people say after you say "thank you." It means "thank you for the thank you." This is how polite Tanzanians are—they express gratitude when you express gratitude.

Clandie: An abbreviation for "clandestine," this is the term used for, as one man told me, " a honey on the side." Apparently accepted by some partners here as a way of life, clandies and spouses may be in communication with each other.

Dress Code: Apparently outside of coastal Southern California where it is acceptable to wear pajama bottoms in public and jeans to work, there is something called "The Dress Code" which limits one's clothing to items which are deemed "presentable" and "appropriate." Pajama bottoms and jeans apparently do not fall into such categories. Neither do flip flops or bare feet.

Food Security: Ocham didn't believe me when I told him that about 14% of U.S. households are food insecure and that there are children who go to bed hungry each night. I had to explain American food deserts. Tanzania in general and Bukoba in particular are relatively food secure because this area produces enough food to meet the needs of its population, and Bukoba's rainfalls and proximity to Lake Victoria mean a plenitude of not only bananas, but avocadoes, mangoes, jackfruit, potatoes, carrots, cucumbers, nuts, tangerines, rice, beans and, of course, fish.

Gratitude: While I have heard this word before, only now—thanks to Tanzanians—do I truly understand what it means. The philosophy around here seems to be "See the good and appreciate it." Showing gratitude isn't just something people do the fourth Thursday of November like we do back home. Each day seems to be Thanksgiving. I hear people express apprecia-tion every single day for the seemingly most mundane graces of life: fresh air, the sun, seasonal crops, friendship, family, and the mere wonder of being alive and healthy. Not only during my first weeks in Tanzania, but during the entire year, I can't recall ever once hearing anyone complain about anything. Really, not one single thing.

Matoke: A type of banana.

Mzungu: A white person. If you happen to be white, you will hear people shout this at you wherever you go.

Njoge: Another type of banana.

Ndezi: Another type of banana.

Orphan Creation: Inevitably each time I go to Africa, someone has asked me if I am going to bring back a child, as if African children were souvenirs, as if adults in Africa did not take care of the next generation. Just like every other place on the planet, children in Africa are indeed very vulnerable. Just like every other place on the planet, there are adults who love and worry about those children. Because Western media— from literature to commercials for donations to celebrities— has done such a powerful job of convincing us that African children can best be "saved" by outsiders, the demand for African adoptions by foreigners has in many places outpaced the "supply."

Pharmaceutical Dumping Ground: One afternoon Father Charles came home with copies of an e-mail that contained a list identifying over twenty different over-the-counter drugs that were available for purchase in Tanzania. These medications had been rejected for approval or banned in the countries where they had been developed and produced but were for sale in Tanzania. I learned that many of the drugs that are deemed unfit or unsafe for human use in my home country are sent to places like Tanzania.

Poverty Pornography: A lot of Westerners seem to like to come to places like Tanzania, find the poorest, most down-trodden spots and then take pictures, often selfies. Just like women in fashion magazines are not representative of the way most women look, the life of most East Africans does not look like the images we have been traditionally presented with. I see more poverty just driving down Beach Boulevard in my hometown, but I've never seen any foreigners come and take a picture of the men and women begging or sleeping on the street corners or posing with them.

Privilege (also see White Privilege): According to the Cambridge Dictionary, the word "privilege" means "a special advantage or authority possessed by a particular person or group." In many cases, like mine, the receiver of these "special advantages" has done nothing whatsoever to earn such advantages like where and how I am able to live, travel, eat, speak and work. This privilege is particularly apparent during my time in Tanzania.

Protocol: I am still seeking a clear definition of protocol in Tanzania; however, protocol in Tanzania is *extremely* important and formal. There are both personal and professional protocols which need to be followed. Violation of protocol often results in unintentional insult. Any truly useful phrase-book in Tanzania for foreigners needs to give a clear definition and explanation of Tanzanian protocol. Examples would help too. This is most likely where misunderstandings will occur.

Shagalabagala: There is no direct translation of this phrase. It is slightly onomatopoeic, meaning cockamamie, ramshackly, wonky and disorganized. This phrase is generally helpful in describing many roads in rural Tanzania.

"Speak in such a way that people love to listen to you. Listen in such a way that people love to talk to you:" I never actually heard anyone say this exact phrase during my time in

Tanzania; however, I did observe and hear it demonstrated daily.

Takatifu: This word means "holy." Usually you will hear it repeated three times as an expression of gratitude. This is a particularly useful word if one is living amongst priests. Expect to hear it often. Expect to hear it repeated three times.

Tonsure: This is a word used in the English language with Latinate etymology, and I had to look it up in the dictionary when Monsignor told me that is where priests have ashes placed on Ash Wednesday. It is the top part of the human head in roughly the same place as a yarmulke.

Tumainaletu: This is the response to the greeting *"Christu"* and means "We praise his name." This is a particularly useful word if one is living amongst priests. Expect to hear it often.

Ululation : Another English word coming from Latin, this is the trilling of the tongue that is characteristic of African and Middle Eastern singing or chanting.

Vitumbua: A delicious Tanzanian treat made with rice flour, coconut milk, cinnamon and cardamom fried in coconut oil. These taste best when Father Joseph brings them home fresh and warm on Thursday evenings after he has heard confessions at the cathedral.

Watoke: a type of banana

White privilege (also see privilege): These two words have become a lightning rod for misunderstanding, miscommunication and misanthropy, but this concept is impossible for me to deny, especially in this part of the world. My race actually gives me distinct advantages in places like Tanzania. Simply because I am white, I can go almost wherever I want and do whatever I want. I can walk right past security guards who just wave me through at hotels. I am invited to linger in a shop after closing time while others are kicked out. Tellers at the bank move me to the front of the line. They don't know if I'm American or French or Swedish or South African. All they know is that I am white.

This privilege became particularly glaring when I was training a group of U.S. teachers working in Tanzania. These teachers represented the ethnic and cultural diversity of America, and stereotypes in Tanzania about Americans became apparent when one villager questioned one of the teachers about her "American-ness," insisting, "if you're not white, then you're not a real American."

At lunch I broached the subject with her by way of apology. Her response reminded me that white privilege is not restricted to this part of the world. First, she looked up at me, pausing briefly over her plate of *chipsimayai.* Staring blankly for a second at me, barely able to resist rolling her eyes at my naïveté, she said:

"Don't worry. Unfortunately, I'm used to it," she responded quietly. "I've been dealing with it my whole life," swiftly clarifying that such words and expressions were not foreign to her at all.

MORE THAN WORDS:
IN A SMALL LIBRARY IN EAST AFRICA ON MY SECOND DAUGHTER'S TWENTIETH BIRTHDAY

Over twenty years had passed since I came to East Africa for the first time. Despite experiencing my life-long dream to live here as a young woman right out of college, I left earlier than planned because I was called by an even more powerful siren's song: my daughters were screaming to be born. I left the Comoros Islands, abandoning a life-long dream along with the fragrance of ylang-ylang and the melodic words of Bantu, Arabic and French.

For all the words in all the languages I have ever heard, a single word—a name—eclipses all others as my favorite, and to this day it still reigns supreme over all the words in all of the world's languages. If I had to choose one word to hear the rest of my life, it would be the one that took me away from East Africa all those years ago. "Mom."

I am a lover of words, and luckily, I do not have to choose only one word in one language; however, there are two words I can go the rest of my life without hearing: *shikamo* and *mzungu*. Although meant as a greeting of respect, the word *shikomo* literally means, "I kiss your feet," its etymology linked directly to Arabic and the slave trade in East Africa.

While most of the citizens of Bukoba greet one another with a *"habari"* or a *"jambo,"* I am invariably greeted with *"shikomo."* Seriously? I don't want anyone here kissing my feet—can't we just have a cup of tea together? I'm never quite sure what I've done to garner this level of reverence and respect. It is often used for those who are older or in a higher position of status than the speaker, but many of those who greet me this way are much older than I am. Do they say this to me simply because I am *mzungu*?

One day, just when I had given up hope of ever being greeted like everyone else, I was greeted by a silhouette of a man coming up the hill while the sun was directly in my eyes. I was overjoyed when he called out a friendly and informal *"mambo"* to me. Thinking that I had finally established myself as an accepted member of the community, I smiled...until I came face to face with my greeter and realized that the explanation was much simpler than that: he was blind.

The perception of *wazungu* offers ample evidence of the white legacy here, and let me tell you (from the Captain Obvious Files), it's not one to be proud of. From the physical, political, economic and emotional abuse of colonialism to the damage of neocolonialism and the embarrassing White Savior Complex, the legacy of foreigners here has left its mark. (Ocham describes this so powerfully in his poetry: "philanthropists whose pity is...costly and binding like Uncle Tom's chains.")

When most people saw me in Bukoba, they often tried to figure out which one of the basic white groups I belong to. Strangers in town would ask me for money or ask me what missionary group I'm with. Others would ask me what volunteer organization I am with. Others asked if I had come to climb Mt. Kilamanjaro. Someone even asked if I was a spy.

Although I felt welcome and included from the beginning, only after three weeks of being on campus every single day and working alongside the very accomplished faculty on the Bukoba campus did I finally stop being self-conscious about the color of my skin. But they still called me *mzungu*. I guess that's only reasonable. For the majority of my time in Bukoba, I was the only white person on campus.

By the time classes started, I knew most of the faculty and staff of the college by name and had prepared what I hoped would be a reasonable syllabus for my "small" class. While I typically try to learn the names of all my students by the end of the first day of class back home in California, I knew I would be lucky if I knew the names of all my students in Bukoba by the end of the semester. The night before the first class, I read through the several-paged roster that Ocham had given me, and I saw some of the most amazing names: Boniphace, Fidestu, Mwesiga, Balthazar, Zubeir, Goodluck, Godhelp, Devotha, Gladness, Manpower, Socrates and Livingstone. I was so overwhelmed by the sheer size of the class that I didn't even bother taking roll call the first day of class.

Each student in my class was preparing to be a teacher, so in addition to supervising their class work, I would also be observing and evaluating some of these students as they completed their student teaching. Luckily with decent resources in the library, students had access to quality books. For any handouts, I left assignments in the copy center on campus where students would pay a few coins per copy, and in this way, I tried to teach.

No matter what I assigned, the students did it. Despite my liberal attendance policies, students rarely missed a class. During office hours, there was always a line outside my door—sometimes for hours. In this spirit of deep dedication, the students inspired me and once again reinforced my faith in the power of education.

One challenge was trying to understand the role English plays in education in Tanzania. While Swahili is the language of instruction in primary schools, English is the language of instruction for secondary schools and beyond. Still, many students (even my most dedicated) resisted using English.

"It's a colonial language," they often reminded me. "It represents the vestiges of a terrible legacy."

And this legacy is apparent throughout the schools in the region, not just in the language itself but in the way it is used. Whenever I went to observe one of the student teachers, I cringed at the way English behaves in Tanzania:

"SPEAK ENGLISH ONLY"

"NO LAUGHING IN THE HALLS!"

Meanwhile, Swahili gets to say things like "welcome!" and "enjoy these books!"

English acts like a bully around here because that is exactly how the language arrived. After the first week of classes, I realized that my syllabus was all wrong: instead of teaching new ideas on how to learn English, I needed to create a seminar to present new theories and philosophies on *why* to learn English. A few weeks into the semester, after I had spent hours organizing groups, creating handouts, grading papers, working in the library and revising curriculum with Ocham, I also realized another critical mistake: I hadn't yet learned the most important words for my work here—my students' names.

This oversight was glaring, not only because it was the cornerstone of my teaching in California but also because of my own frustration at being referred to only as *mzungu*. When talking about a particular student in my class with Ocham, I referred to her simply as "student." I should have been more sensitive. It was so frustrating being called by a word that only described me superficially, a word that quite frankly, made me feel left out.

When the librarians at the college agreed to let me help them process and catalogue an impressive shipment of books from an organization called "Books for Africa, USA," I was very happy.

For over a week we unpacked hundreds of boxes filled with some of the most beautiful books sent from universities all across the United States, and for that whole week no one in that library offered to kiss my feet.

The librarians, Ocham and I all love books, and we share a love of words. As we unpacked, the librarians and I discussed the nuances of some of the words and expressions we came across:

"Madame, what is the meaning of "I love you to pieces?""

I explained the idiom, and quickly their linguistic panache played with the words, and we started saying "I love you three pieces," and this would become our daily greeting to each other.

"Professor, what do 'symposium' and 'queer' and 'stoic' mean?" Devotha asked me as she processed some books for sociology.

And finally, the word that stumps me:

"What is the meaning of 'post-modernism'?"

Something happened during those days in the library. We bonded during our collective, professional nesting as we unpacked the books, organized shelves, catalogued inventory and tidied up.

Luckily, this was how I spent my daytime hours on January 18, my youngest daughter's birthday. That night, she and I Skyped. I saw my daughter's sweet face on my computer, and she asked me in a hushed voice, very close to tears, sounding much like she did as a toddler.

"Please tell me you are happy, so I know it is worth us being this far apart."

I paused and thought for a moment before I answered. "I am happy."

And then I realized that for the first time in a while, I

actually *did* feel happy.

And despite the sadness I felt at being separated from my daughter on her birthday, I smiled to myself as I walked the slight incline from the library towards my office the next day. The librarians had called out to me. After practicing with words like "Professor" and "Sister," they had settled, unknowingly, on my favorite name, a name that soon became adopted by some of the students as well:

"Good afternoon, Mom!"

And after that week with the librarians, nobody on campus ever addressed me as *mzungu* ever again.

A FIELD GUIDE TO
SPIRIT ANIMALS

In addition to being addressed as "Mom" throughout most of my time in Bukoba, I was also often called "Sister." This was due in part to the company I kept. Except for Pauline and Beatrice, most of my female friends were nuns, and despite my attempts to clarify that I was a layperson, the ease with which I seemed to have blended into my community of priests and nuns only reinforced this perception.

The nun I spent the most time with was Sister Charlotte, the visiting lecturer who came from Mwanza from time to time. Whenever she came to Bukoba from the main campus in Mwanza, we shared the little cottage at DESIRE.

Sister Charlotte was born and raised in The Democratic Republic of the Congo, and we are the same age. While I spent my youth traipsing around in a bikini, she had begun her preparation for a life of spiritual devotion.

At night, we slept in adjacent bedrooms. At work, our classrooms were next to each other. At meals, we sat side by side.

The first night we had dinner together, she noticed that I did not eat meat, not even the fish that was a mainstay of our meals. When I explained my lifelong struggle to eat anything with a mother, or a face, she replied:

"Mangez les têtes en première et tu ne verras pas les visages!"

(Just eat the heads first, and you won't see the faces!)

Everyone laughed.

Et tu, Charlotte?

The teasing was always kind-hearted and made me feel like part of the family, but Monsignor did not tease, and he often checked in with me to make sure I did not have my feelings hurt.

After dinner one night after Monsignor and I spent almost an hour watching a lizard stalk a moth, crouching like Spiderman on the ceiling, we stepped outside to see the moonrise. We saw multitudes of birds flittering and flying in the fading light.

"There are so many beautiful birds here," I marveled.

"It is true," said Monsignor. "Do you know why?" he asked gently.

I shook my head.

"Because we do not eat birds here," he joked.

We both chuckled quietly.

Most of the individual bird species are totems for various tribes and clans. Another example of the genius of traditional culture, this works as an ancient way of animal conservation, and the birds here merit conservation efforts: the Birds of Bukoba are some of the most abundantly rare in the world. Serious birders come here to find unusual species to add to their life lists.

Discovering this, I decided to learn more about identifying some of these treasures of the animal kingdom, ordering several field guides from my favorite bookstore in Dar es Salaam. On my very first bird watching expedition in Bukoba (which encompassed a full two block radius from DESIRE), I was overwhelmed. Here is what I saw, identified to the best of my burgeoning ability:

One Goliath Heron was observed perched on an electrical post just across the street from my house. A bird with a long neck curved in the shape of an "S" and impossibly long, skinny legs, this creature was MASSIVE! Towering above the street on the pole, the appropriately named bird eventually spread its remarkable wings and like a small plane, soared off toward Lake Victoria, casting a shadow on the road below.

Just outside the kitchen window, a Yellow Grenadine nestled in the hibiscus bush. A sweetheart of a bird, she looked like something you would want to put in a cage just so you could stare at its green feathers and chubby cheeks.

Monsignor and I spotted three White-Eyed Slaty Flycatchers sitting on the electric wire hanging across DESIRE, and we would continue to observe them again several times in the coming weeks, the three of them inseparable. These little birds could fit into my palm, and are the kinds of birds you might find ceramic replicas of to sit on your nightstand or coffee table. Although their name isn't too flattering, these flycatchers are adorable.

In a nearby field I spotted a Great White Egret, much larger than the relatively common Cattle Egret that you see on cows. Also, with an elongated S-shaped neck, the Great White Egret is all white except for its black legs, toes and beak. To watch it fly is a marvel. Its flight action looks as if it is taking off in slow motion with gentle, ponderous wing beats.

At the entrance to the Waalkgard Hotel, there is a veritable village of Forked Tailed Drongoes that have claimed the palm trees through some sort of avian eminent domain. Shining with glossy black wings, and longish and very striking forked tails, these little acrobats are noisy and proud. Their spherical, igloo-shaped nests adorn the trees like woven Christmas ornaments, with each bird seeming to try and build a more elaborate one than her neighbor.

Along the dirt road near my old, lonely house near Rugambwa Secondary School I saw an African Mourning Dove who, despite its fancy name, looks (I don't want to say this too loudly for fear of insulting anyone) well, a lot like a common pigeon.

Near the Kagera River I observed an African Darter, also a large bird but with a C-shaped neck and a puffy breast sticking up just under her beak. While she was swimming in the river, I could only see her head and neck, with her long, pointed bill angled upwards towards the sky.

The most obvious birds in Bukoba are the child-sized Marabou Storks who dominate the lakefront beaches, particularly around the Bukoba Club and near the bridge crossing the river. Standing about three feet tall, they look (and act) a lot like giant vultures, and I wouldn't trust any of them to deliver a baby. They stand around like old-timey businessmen in grey and black suits with puffed up chests and aloof demeanors. All that's missing are small top hats, walking canes and monocles.

I also saw Grey Crowned Cranes, African Grey Hornbills and birds I couldn't identify like the suave shiny black bird who vainly opened his wings to fly and revealed a bright crimson underwing. I called him Dracula. Starlings and swifts abound in this region. Tiny little birds, too small and fast to observe without binoculars, often sped in front of Monsignor's windshield. Birds with chubby blue hamster cheeks and smiling eyes sat on the pathways near the library.

Bukoba is an open-air aviary, and after many months I began to understand why of all the majestic abundance of animals here, it is the birds which draw people from all over the world. While living in Bukoba, I spent time each day contemplating the wonder of these animals, the living, breathing descendants of dinosaurs.

One day I watched a flock of splendid starlings fly away to such a distance that they turned into nothing but tiny flecks floating in the air.

One day I found a feather on the ground, held it up to the light and saw an entire opaque world within a single filament.

PART 2

Spirits

Thamani ya taa ni giza kilingiapo

"The value of light is seen when darkness falls."

— Tanzanian *kanga*

THE DANGEROUS VANITY
OF BIRDS AND OTHER
CREATURES

That very first morning in Bukoba, when I lived alone in the lonely house and before I lived at DESIRE, I was awoken by a violent pounding on my bedroom window. Too afraid to open the drapes to see who or what had frightened me like that, I cowered in my bunk until the sun was high above the trees. The next morning the same violent "thud" startled me out of my sleep. By that time, I had hidden a machete under my mattress, but I was still too afraid to even look out the window.

Once the sun was high at mid-morning, I would survey the area outside the window. All I ever saw were cadavers of passion fruit laying burst open on the ground just under the window, the sweet juice having dried before it could bleed all the way down the glass. Someone—or something—had been throwing them at my bedroom window.

After moving away from that lonely place, I had almost forgotten about the early morning pounding at my window until one morning while sleeping peacefully under the protection of life at DESIRE, I was startled awake once again by the exact same sound: a sudden and violent pounding at the window.

Emboldened by my newfound sense of security, this time I opened the drapes to see a massive bird flying at full speed, hurling itself, along with a passion fruit, directly against my window. At breakfast I brought this up to the fathers.

Monsignor explained that as the sun rises, it causes a reflection in the windows, creating a mirror, and the birds—so enamored with themselves—were chasing their own image as if chasing a mate.

"How do you know they don't think it's an enemy that they want to fight?" I asked.

Monsignor then pointed out the stains of passion fruit that the bird had left on the window.

"You see. They are bringing offerings of affection...to *themselves!*"

The narcissistic symbolism was not lost on any of us.

When I expressed my concern for their safety, the fathers started to tease me. Again.

"Do you want us to put warning signs on the windows for them?"

"Knowing you, you probably want us to put up signs in several languages so no one is excluded."

"Do you want us to cover up the windows?"

Actually, I thought that last one was a decent idea.

I seriously felt bad for those birds, fooled by their own reflections, falsely seduced by their own beauty. Growing up near Hollywood, California I know how dangerous that can be.

Hollywood casts a long shadow, even reaching some of the most remote parts of the world like Bukoba, but that shadow is particularly unavoidable in Southern California where looks matter. A lot. In hindsight, it is fortunate that I lacked the archetypal beauty that most of my friends had in our youth. On weekends or slumber parties, my girlfriends would spend hours looking in the mirror, applying makeup, shaping eyebrows, applying skin treatments. They often tried to give me a makeover.

"What's the point?" I often thought.

I couldn't bear to look at myself in the mirror. I thought I looked like an alien compared to my friends. Most of my high school social life involved boys coming up to me at parties asking me to introduce them to one of my girlfriends.

"She's hot!" they'd say about Laura or Beth or Chrissy.

Yeah, I know, dude. And I'm *not*.

I remember riding my bike along the beach boardwalk during summers, and a group of paunchy, middle-aged burnouts with beer bellies would park their beach chairs then put up signs between 1 and 10 to score the looks of the girls riding by. The highest I ever got was a 6. One time, one of them yelled out to me, "Keep riding that bike, babe and lose those last five pounds."

I was five feet and five inches tall and weighed 112 pounds. I had just turned fifteen.

So, unlike the birds of Bukoba, I never much liked looking at myself in the mirror. Even when my friends would give me a beauty makeover, I thought it was a colossal waste of time. Now that I am older, I am glad that my sense of worth was never tied to the way I look.

There is a lot of pressure on women all around the world to be young and beautiful, and Bukoba is no exception. My very first day at the downtown market when Pauline told me I needed to count my lucky stars, I chuckled at the small kiosk selling Chinese cosmetics, no doubt laden with unhealthy chemicals. The two salesgirls were appropriately gorgeous, slightly condescending to the "lesser" beauties, the women who were contemplating spending a week's wages on hair weaves or wigs.

Up and down the roads of Bukoba, pretty young girls sat sidesaddle on the motorcycle taxis in order to "ride in style" only to show up at my classes with skid marks and scrapes all over their bodies because few drivers can keep balance like that on a windy, hilly road.

Beauty contests are a big deal in Tanzania, so there is a certain emphasis on looks here too, just like everywhere I suppose. But there isn't the dangerous proximity of Hollywood's sirenesque allure that beleaguers too many beautiful women from around the world.

Wherever I travel in my life, once people discover that I live close to Hollywood they are fascinated. Imagining the glamour and wealth deceptively spread around the world through movies and awards shows, people seem shocked and incredulous when I tell them that, in my opinion, Hollywood is one of the most depressing and degrading places on earth.

Hollywood is a magnet to thousands and thousands of beautiful young people, many teen-aged girls, from all across the world who come banking on their good looks to make them stars. Only a statistically insignificant portion achieves this "dream." Instead, many end up homeless or virtually homeless. Many are also recruited into the pornography industry or become victims of human trafficking. There are plenty of beautiful people strung out on drugs or alcohol.

When I lament Hollywood and its obsession with fame, people like to point out the good deeds done by stars, the money donated, the causes supported. True enough, millions of dollars have been donated to various causes around the world. But many organizations I have worked with in Africa find this type of "Glam Aid" challenging. Often, the celebrities want their charitable acts to be publicized, often claiming that they are trying to raise awareness. But often, the high profile of the celebrity overshadows the awareness that experts and those who are actually trained in the Hollywood cause du jour want to convey.

I heard one African activist lament on television that his voice could not be heard over an electric guitar.

There are different kinds of vanity, and just because I am

not particularly vain about the way I look doesn't mean that I am not guilty of vanity myself. Watching Pauline, for example, made me realize how vain I am as a mother, holding on so tightly to my daughters, wanting to be the most important adult in their lives. I am also overly prideful and vain about my work, resulting at times, especially here in Tanzania, in the impression that I am like those hotties at the Bukoba makeup kiosk, looking down my nose at those who do not work the way I do. I see classrooms as almost sacred places and have been unintentionally rude to those who tried to visit with me while I swept the floor of a classroom or otherwise prepared my workspace. I have at times been so focused on a work-related task that I was worried more about completing the task to near perfection than to the feelings of my colleagues.

How can I explain to them that this is really just a defense mechanism to counter the low score I got on an involuntary bathing suit competition when I was 15 years old? How can I explain that I am trying to prove that although I am not a "10," I want to feel valuable and desperately hope to contribute something beautiful to the world? How can I explain that I must leave something else behind when I die than what one poor bird did, an animal who was so gorgeous that one morning she flew with such fervent and arduous force into Monsignor's window that she left nothing behind except an exquisitely beautiful corpse?

THE SUNLIGHT IN YOUR UNIVERSE
IN A CHILDREN'S HOSPITAL ON MY FIRST-BORN DAUGHTER'S BIRTHDAY

When the little boy from the neighborhood sneezed, the women at the corner store said, "*Kua na utaona.*"

"Grow and you will see..."

I understood the words, but I had no idea why they were spoken in this context. The women explained. When a child sneezes, they ward off sickness and death and remind him to grow so that he can see what life is like.

Later, I asked Father Charles about it. He told me about his grandmother and how every time he visited her as a young boy, she placed her hand on his head or shoulder repeating the same mantra, even if he wasn't sick:

"Grow and you will see...

What life is like...

What it is like to have a best friend...

What it is like to fall in love...

What it is like to have your heart broken...

What it is like to become a man...

Grow and see what life is..."

He explained how there was nothing for a young boy to do in those moments but to accept the benedictions of his grandmother. I think of my own grandmothers—how one would rock and sing me to sleep whenever she could and the other would write me long letters trying to tell me what her life was like.

I think about how my Aunt Linda's first child died in infancy, an invisible and undetectable thief stealing his tiny breaths in the middle of the night. I think about how my aunt then tried to climb into the tiny casket with her silenced child, and I tried to imagine the pain of my aunt and my grandmother who were powerless despite all of their wishes for little Tommy to grow and see what life is like.

They surely would understand the sentiment behind the words of the women at the corner store without any need of explanation.

Charles said he was lucky that he had a grandma who had grown old (although he wasn't sure of her exact age) because the life expectancy in Tanzania is only 57 years. One of the reasons the life expectancy here is so low is because the infant mortality rate is so high that it affects the actuarial tables. Those mere months of life placed into the calculations of life expectancy bring the averages down significantly.

The increased vaccination rates and clean water efforts in Tanzania have recently reduced the infant mortality rates which range (according to sources) from 50-85 deaths per 1,000 births (in the United States it is about 6 in 1,000); however, Tanzania still has one of the highest infant mortality rates in the world.

I thought about these statistics one day as I was leaving the hospital near Bukoba after visiting a colleague who had been admitted after being sick for several days. The wind carried the cries of little children and mothers across the courtyard from the children's ward to the small chapel where I sat alone.

Exactly twenty two years ago that very day I too was in a hospital with my baby daughter who was crying, for the very first time. That was the day I became a mom. That was the day that she changed the world, my world. The center of my universe became her welfare. The orbit of my life permanently shifted to rotate around her survival. The laser-beam focus of my *raison d'être* was to keep her alive. How many nights did I beg that cosmic universal force to keep her safe? How many nights did I worry? How many nights did I sneak into her bedroom just to hear her breathe?

By the time she went off to college, I had forgotten those early nights when all I asked from the universe was for her to be safe and healthy. The years had been wonderful, but not what I had intended for my daughters: an absent father, divorce, the loss of our home, betrayal of friends, and financial ruin. When people lamented, "what else could go wrong?" I stopped them because I knew what else could go wrong.

As long as we were healthy, I could endure anything.

But I had stopped appreciating what a gift my daughters' health was. The memory of my second daughter Victoria's in vitro misdiagnosis of hydrocephalus had faded after she was born healthy after all, and the years had kept her safe and sound. Thanks to a stable teaching job with good healthcare along with nothing but sheer luck, my daughters avoided the dark specters of the The Misdiagnosing Doctor, The Breath Thief, The One-Ton Falling Armoire, The Car That Crashed Into The Garage Mere Moments After My Daughters Were Playing In The Exact Spot of Total Demolition, and The Home Invasion Robbery Thankfully Thwarted By A German Shepherd Named Louie.

While some children around the world suffered incomprehensible and fatal illnesses, my daughters were spared. After a while, I began to take their health and their lives for granted, distracted by concerns of quotidian cares. By the time they were preparing for college, I really had forgotten to recognize how fortunate we had been.

After those first days of my Empty Nest in California, a friend of mine from Nigeria overheard me talking about how sad I was. She set me straight.

"Do you mean to tell me that your daughters survived infancy, had no childhood illnesses, had access to a first-rate education and are now going to college on a scholarship and you are *CRYING?* In my village we would all be *CELE-BRATING.* Woman, you are *spoiled!*"

And I knew she was right. But I didn't really *know* she was right until I sat there alone on my daughter's birthday at the small hospital chapel in the village of Kagondo near where both Father Joseph and Monsignor had been born and raised. The cries I heard that day were nothing like the cries twenty-two years earlier from a hospital room with a team of doctors and a cache of medication that literally saved my life as my blood pressure soared, and I began exsanguinating. The tears on the night that Alexandra was born were tears of joy: the tears of a new grandmother, a new uncle, of a woman reborn, of a child taking her first gasps of breath. The tears I saw at the hospital that morning in Tanzania were tears of utter despair: a father could not afford his daughter's surgery; a mother wrapped in a *kanga* rolled on the grass outside in anguish.

I left the hospital chapel to see about the mother rolling on the grass. She couldn't stand. When Father Charles drove me back home later, he explained that many people in Tanzania become temporarily paralyzed due to emotional trauma. He said that eventually the mother I had seen would be fine. I knew that although she would eventually be able to stand on her own, she most assuredly would never be truly "fine."

Eventually, some nurses carried the mother away on a stretcher. Soon after, a doctor I had met from Scandinavia walked brusquely past me to the parking lot. I followed her and found her under a tree. Crying. Someone had died. I couldn't understand a word she was saying through her hyperventilation. I just held her as she sobbed. What else could I do?

(Un)fortunately I have plenty of experience consoling sobbing females. My daughters have both experienced the challenges of life, and the three of us have survived and endured so much together that they actually believe that I can change the world. But this is the world, the mortal one, that none of us can alter.

That day at the hospital was the anniversary of the day that my life truly began. I wanted to acknowledge the occasion in some way. The only thing I could think of was to buy some candy for the children at the corner store, join in the *"kua na utaonas,"* and take a moment to be thankful and to readjust the central axis of my orbit just a tiny bit. My worst fears never materialized. Despite all of the tough times, my daughters survived childhood and became healthy, strong, independent women.

They have grown, and they have been able to see what life is like.

WHAT'S LOVE
GOT TO DO WITH IT?

My visa status was a source of much confusion during my time in Tanzania. Although I contacted the Tanzanian embassy in Washington D.C. months before arriving and sent in my passport and all other documents, I was told that my visa was "temporary." The woman at the embassy said that I would "have to take care of it" once I arrived in country.

Arriving in Dar es Salaam that first night, the customs agent looked at my passport and told me everything was in order.

However, one of the first things Father Charles asked me to do when I arrived at the university was to give my passport to Cesilia, the director's administrative assistant, to make sure I/we were in compliance with immigration. I went directly to see Cesilia to give her the required documents right away.

Cesilia is one of those strikingly beautiful and elegant women who also happens to be incredibly warm and kind. Most days when Father Mgeni was out of the office, she was listening to Tina Turner, songs like "I Might Have Been Queen," "Show Some Respect" and "You Better Be Good to Me," as her personal soundtrack.

Cesilia comes from a tribe known for politeness and patience, which is really saying something because just about everyone in Tanzania is polite and patient. When I told her that I was not a very patient woman, Cesilia responded, "I can teach you."

I laughed and explained some of my character deficiencies.

"Yes, I have seen," she said kindly. "But I can teach you."

I explained the extent of the problem.

"O.K." she laughed. "Maybe I can teach you to be *selectively* patient," she promised.

I adored Cesilia from the moment I met her. We occasionally shared a cup of tea or a quick greeting as we passed one another on campus.

During my office hours one morning, she entered contritely, apologizing for the intrusion and for the fact that she had not been able to sort out my visa.

I hadn't even known there was a problem.

"Madame, tomorrow we must go together to the Immigration Office to sort this out." Cesilia was unnecessarily apologetic.

"This is fantastic," I said, looking forward to some girl time.

Father Charles confirmed with me over our afternoon tea that Cesilia (or Cesi as I soon called her) and I would meet on campus the next day and then proceed together downtown.

Knowing me so well already he added, "But no playing around. Once you're finished you need to come back to the university immediately."

Ah, man.

Cesilia and I met at my office at 9:00 a.m. and then took a taxi down the hill to the Immigration Office. Inside it looked like a 1940s Perry Mason courthouse with waist-high wooden swinging doors between the various seating areas for which I could find no particular purpose. While Cesi presented my paperwork, I got down to serious business and found a mother who was willing to let me hold her baby.

After Cesi and I sat next to each other for about twenty minutes playing with the baby, we were called into an office with a very serious looking man who shut the door behind us as we sat down on a rickety bench. He looked at me suspiciously over his bifocals (perhaps because I was still holding the baby), then at Cesi, then back at me. He enjoyed his power a little too much. I wanted to ask him if he was part German.

He explained to us that there was a "problem" with renewing my visa. Apparently, the solution to this problem was simple. I needed to pay more money. As I was about to either push back or cave in (I hadn't decided yet), Cesi, very calmly and very politely, refused. She gracefully stood up, simultaneously dignified and indignant. When I started to acquiesce, she, very calmly and very politely, stopped me. Some words were exchanged in a mother tongue that was unfamiliar to me. There was a staredown, and Cesi won. Handily. Soon, the officer left the room, then quickly re-entered with a form. He told us to get some pictures and return with them and the form. Cesi, very calmly and very politely, took the form.

"Oh, well," I said. "I guess we'll have to come back later."

I looked for the mother of the baby and found her in another office, totally unfazed that I had taken her child for an extended period of time.

Cesi guided me to a small business across the road where I could pay about two dollars to have the required photos taken. I filled out the form, and we walked back across the main road to the Immigration Office. I handed in the paperwork along with my passport, and the receptionist told us to come back in about an hour or two for everything to be processed. Cesi respectfully expressed her gratitude while I got one last cuddle with the baby. Then we walked back out into the bright early afternoon sun.

"Can I please treat you to lunch?" I asked.

"Oh, Mum, that is very kind of you," she said.

"Please call me Lee Anne," I requested.

Cesi was too shy and unassuming to pick a restaurant, so I suggested the fancy and curiously named Victorious Perch Restaurant, just about a block down from the Immigration Office.

Cesi hesitated. "But that is so expensive," she worried.

"Please, Cesi," I insisted, "it's my pleasure."

The name of this restaurant, although strange, did make a little sense, paying homage to the Nile Perch, which I suppose could be considered "victorious."

The Nile Perch, a whale of a fish, was introduced to Lake Victoria in the 1950s by the British in an effort to remedy overfishing and to mitigate the decline in catch sizes in the lake. One of the unintended consequences of the introduction of the Nile Perch, is that it has turned into an ecological nightmare: the voracious and "victorious" Nile Perch has annihilated the species diversity of the lake by devouring half of the population of the indigenous population of cichlids, little bony fish like the one Sister Charlotte decapitated the first night I met her.

The Predatory and Victorious Perch sometimes grows up to six feet long and 200 pounds thanks to its appetite for cichlids, this appetite creating, according to one scientist "the greatest vertebrate mass extinction in recorded history." While this has been a disaster ecologically, for many business-men and government officials, the Nile Perch—hauled by the ton from the open lake and served on our table at DESIRE every night—has been an economic victory.

So, I wondered if the owners of this restaurant had probably benefited somehow from the introduction of this non-indigenous species into the lake. I also suspected that they didn't really care much about the fate of the poor cichlid.

Rich investors seem to be involved with the Victorious Perch and not just because of the name of the restaurant. Besides the massive life-sized statue of a Nile Perch dominating the courtyard, overdressed men brandishing gold watches, cell phones and computers sat there as well.

Excepting the waitresses, Cesilia and I were the only women in the restaurant.

We entered through the clean tile patio, where giant palms emerged from massive pots and daylight strings of light crossed over our heads. Each table had a linen tablecloth and fresh tropical flowers. Between the two of us, Cesi was the only one who was really appropriately dressed in spite of my efforts to conform to The Dress Code. Heads turned to look at Cesi as we were brought to our table.

Cesi was always impeccably dressed, and she even designs and makes her own clothes. That day at the Victorious Perch, she wore a long skirt made of traditional African fabric that went down to her ankles where there was a little pleated flair on the left side. Her blouse was made of matching material and revealed her elegant collarbone and arms. Even without such fine garments, Cesi is an absolute knockout. Her almond eyes penetrate, her plaited hair impresses, and her smile slays. Even though all eyes were on her as we walked in and even as we ate, her attention never wavered once from my companionship.

Looking at the menu, I was astonished at how much more affordable food was at the Victorious Perch than at a comparable restaurant at home or even in Dar es Salaam. Fresh fish, chicken, salads, rice and noodle dishes were all about ten dollars. Granted, a meal at a roadside *mamalisha* in Tanzania where workers and students go for some Mama-style home cooking costs about two dollars, but still according to my standards this was a steal.

"Madame..." Cesi demurred and practically recoiled at the prices.

Again, I begged Cesi to call me by my first name.

She continued and blushed. "This is too expensive."

For Cesi and most people in Bukoba, this lunch is indeed an extravagance. Ten dollars can go pretty far here, and as I said, the price of this meal could pay for about five guests at a more typical eating establishment. I worried that I was making her uncomfortable, so I asked if she wanted to go somewhere else.

"Oh, no. This is so beautiful here; I just worry that this is too much money."

I insisted that it was my pleasure, which indeed it was, particularly because it allowed me some time to "horse around" with Cesilia before going back to campus. I reminded her that I could write it off as a business expense.

Cesi has her Bachelor's Degree in Economics, so in addition to being on a Tanzanian budget, she also tends to see the world through the lens of cost analysis. I told her we were just a couple of successful gals out for a business lunch just like all those dudes around us.

"Please relax and enjoy this, Cesi." And for the next hour and a half she did.

We talked about our families, about her plans to one day get her master's degree, maybe open up a small business of her own. We talked about work and about the people we love.

Eventually we talked about marriage. As a very religious woman, she said she does want to get married one day, but she clarified: "I must choose *very* carefully, because the wrong choice would be too costly."

Discussing widow inheritance, dowries, marital property rights and domestic violence laws in both of our countries, I realized how much more informed Cesilia is about the implications of marriage than I ever was. Cesi was so thoughtful, so smart. She is risk-averse and fiscally literate. She explained the cultural consequences and norms about divorce in Tanzania.

Divorce is stigmatized in Tanzania. Wherever I went there, people asked me if I was married, and during my first weeks in Bukoba I explained that I was divorced. The response to this was universal:

"Oh, that is just *terrible!* I am so sorry!"

I tried to explain that I am far better off, but to no avail. Sometimes I would just say that my husband died. That seemed less terrible.

Cesi is too polite to have asked me about my marital status although she knew that I have daughters. As affirmation of her wise and thoughtful attitude about marriage, I told her my story.

When I got married, I was twenty four, just three years younger than Cesi. I didn't think at *all* about the emotional, economic or objective cost benefits of my choice. I mostly just reacted to *feeling*. Never mind that one of my best friends warned me he was a cheater, never mind that even *his* best friend told me, "Nice girls like you should not be hanging out with guys like us," never mind that my father forbade me to date him when I was in high school, never mind that he was a verified lothario. He had declared his unequivocal love to me, and, once I succumbed to Baby Fever, marriage seemed like the most practical next step.

Unlike the wise Cesi, I never even bothered to avail myself of knowledge about marital laws and obligations. Despite my years of formal education and a complete freedom of choice about whom I could marry, I was an utter and complete fool. After almost ten years of marriage, not only had I been cheated on, I was liable for a debilitating debt that I had known nothing about. It didn't matter that he had forged my name on loan applications. It didn't matter that I had not been informed of some debts (much of that money going to support a love nest and a German mistress), California Law not only recognizes community property but also community liability. The law was the law. As his wife, I was responsible for his financial choices.

I explained the marriage laws and customs in my country to Cesi as she explained those of hers. I explained that, unlike her, I had learned the hard way.

"I'm so sorry, Lee," Cesi consoled me, using the name that my closest friends and family call me.

I explained that at this point in my life, all I could and can do is shrug, let it go and feel grateful.

"If I hadn't married him, I wouldn't have my daughters."

We talked non-stop, and the hour and a half flew by quickly. Cesi loved her chicken and potatoes, and she kept saying how beautiful the dining room was.

"I wish this day would never end," she said as we both agreed it was time to return to the Immigration Office and ultimately campus. Cesilia practically gasped when the bill arrived, and she peeked at the total.

As I paid the tab, exorbitant by Cesilia's standards, I thought about how lucky I am that so many things in my life are worth the high prices that I have been willing, and able, to pay.

A LEGACY OF MONARCHS

While I was a young girl in California pretending to teach in Africa under the jacaranda tree in my front yard, Ocham was a little boy in Kenya reading American storybooks under the jacaranda tree in his.

Both of us enjoyed sharing stories with each other, and during our breaks from work, we spent a lot of time telling each other stories about our lives. The best stories Ocham told me were about his childhood village, and one of the best of all was his recollection of a hippopotamus who had fallen into a massive hole near his home. When I asked him how they helped the hippo out, he laughed at me and said,

"Um, we *ate* it!"

Throughout our year together, we spent hours and hours talking and working together. It was like having a new child-hood friend who shared my curiosity about the world, especially a love of language. I had someone who really under-stood me.

During our tea break one day, Ocham told me that he was re-kindling one of his childhood hobbies. When he told me how he used to collect stamps when he was younger and was thinking of returning to his childhood hobby of "philately," I thought I might be able to tell him about my renewed interest in one of mine as well.

He showed me an infinitesimal piece of art stuck to an envelope.

"I wish I knew what happened to my old stamp collection. It really was quite lovely," he lamented.

I too was longing for the trophies of my childhood, collected and kept like a treasure trove until I became a way too-cool teenager. Like Ocham, as an adult, I felt a bit embarrassed about unusual, lingering childhood pastimes, but I trusted that he wouldn't judge me because he himself was being vulnerable.

So, I told him.

I told him about my wondrous insect collection and how I used to spend afternoons collecting tiny flying and crawling creatures, finding them in the gutters of my neighborhood and under the bushes behind my school. At one point, I became a poacher, catching and killing even the *de facto* protected butterflies to round out my collection. I would classify each one, attaching a tiny calligraphed label identifying the genus and species to the pin impaling each one. I explained to Ocham how I too missed my childhood collection. I told him how just the day before I had found a monstrous dead dragonfly on the road near the Waalkgard Hotel and brought it to my cottage to place it on the bookshelf.

It felt so good to have someone to share these things with.

Ocham looked across the small table, the corner of his mouth curled just like his son Dylan's and said:

"You know, Lee, that is *very* weird."

Thanks, Ocham.

And so, the conversation shifted to insects. He told me when he was a little boy, he used to catch grasshoppers (which are the size of Pixie Stix here) and keep them in a miniature corral of twigs, pretending that he was a great Maasai chief, and they were his cattle.

He told me about the beautiful butterflies he used to chase as a child and how sad it was to see that same species of butterfly on the verge of extinction and mounted in a museum in Nairobi.

"You can no longer see them floating in the wild. Now my children can only see them preserved in that museum. How sad."

As we talked over tea, I felt really bad about killing those beautiful butterflies in my youth. I had simply wanted to capture the ephemeral beauty of those hypnotic fairies forever.

Inevitably our conversation returned to language, a safe topic for us where Ocham wasn't so judgmental. He and I always spoke in English. Thank goodness we also speak a common figurative language because the versions of English that he and I speak are as different as *Danaus Plexippus* and *Anomalochromis Thomasi*.

Ocham comes from (or as he would say "hails from") Kenya, where English and Swahili are co-official languages. He also speaks several vernacular languages as well as German due to his studies in Europe. When we talk, he uses words like "bespoke," and "invigilator," words that I thought could only be found preserved in parchment in word museums, but in Tanzania they flutter around as common as can be.

Most of my Tanzanian students and colleagues also used many of the same words and pronunciations as Ocham does. My friends from London sound like Elmer Fudd by comparison. Ocham told me about his education, how strict the teachers were about the "proper" pronunciation of English words, reducing me to tears of laughter one afternoon as he recounted the time he gave a presentation in school about malaria, and the teacher made him repeat the correct diction of "diarrhea" over and over again in front of a room of hysterical classmates.

Like his native Kenya, Tanzania also recognizes both English and Swahili as official languages, and I quickly learned that for most people in Bukoba, English is actually their third or fourth language which is one of the reasons that I love this part of the world. I am absolutely besotted (it's contagious) with the linguistic diversity in East Africa.

"We better be careful or people will think we're Pentecosts!" Father Mgeni said one night after a dinner conversation that morphed from English to Swahili to French and Italian with smatterings of German, Latin and Haya. I swear, sometimes I didn't even know what language we were using. I'm not even sure that I spoke all of the languages that we conjured at the dinner table, but the swarm of words swept me up so that I was completely immersed. Father Charles asked me to teach him Spanish one day. Two days later, we discussed the day's timetable...in Spanish!

One thing is sure. The Curse of Babel never touched this place. Languages live and breathe freely here.

Whenever children in the village asked me what my "mother tongue" is and I tell them it is English, they often shared a rolling-on-the-ground, holding-their-sides, tears-streaming-down-their-faces laughter in the same way I imagine the students in Ocham's childhood class had once laughed with him.

"No, your MOTHER tongue, your first language!" they try to explain, thinking that I had misunderstood.

Amongst the children in Bukoba, the idea that English could be someone's first language often seemed tantamount to the idea that someone would wear an ermine fur cape and a jewel-encrusted crown to a family dinner while holding the royal orb and scepter.

I often wanted to explain that my "mother tongue" bears little resemblance to the English I teach both overseas and back home in California. My cultural identity is reflected not so much in the specific language that I speak but rather in my lexicon, words that come down to me from my parents, grandparents and great-grandparents through the songs and stories they shared with me when I was little. My words also come from the region where I grew up. I use rustic phrases from my grandmother and my mom like "womp up some vittles" and "hitch in yer giddyup." I have incorporated words passed down from my dad who grew up in a family and a neighborhood where he learned colorful nouns like "shenanigans" and "gob." Having grown up in Southern California, I also have a highly intricate vocabulary for freeways, vibes, and drought-resistant plants.

I often wanted to explain to the children in the village that my mother tongue is a very rare language called Califappaliddishian (a hybrid of Southern California slang, archaic Midwestern and Hiberno-English) or that my daughter, Victoria, claims that she actually speaks Cat as her first language. That would have stopped the laughter for sure.

Ocham too, has a unique linguistic identity, and we spend hours discussing our work in the context of how our childhood experiences have shaped our work in adulthood, how our students face challenges navigating their own unique linguistic, cultural and racial identities in the English language classroom and world. We know why the world has adopted English as the *lingua franca*. We cherish the human tendency toward multilingualism but bemoan the concomitant tension between social languages and academic languages. We both know how valuable education is, and we also know how valuable those vernacular languages and dialects are for our students' senses of identity. We mourn the fact that some of those languages are dying out like the butterflies of Ocham's childhood, and in some ways, we are trying to preserve a very old version of English just as I once tried to preserve the butterflies of mine.

We spent a lot of time over our daily tea breaks denouncing the influence and effects of colonialism, from East Africa to California to Ireland. Both of us idealists, and perhaps naïve, we express gratitude to be past all of that. We often discussed how this new English we see emerging around the world seems to have a life of its own, a non-colonial identity, and we often declared that the language we teach has little to do with any colonial heritage.

But during a short pause in one of our conversations at that tiny college on a hill above Lake Victoria, we each reached for our Earl Grey tea and started laughing as we both noticed that our manners (as well as the names of our children) belied our declarations: With napkins placed regally in our laps, Ocham and I were both sipping our tea "properly," holding our delicate china cups using the ultimate British affectation, with our pinkies up.

CHAIN OF FOOLS

April 1st doesn't hold any social significance in Tanzania, but it holds a special place in my heart: The Day of Fools. On the first day of April that I spent in Tanzania, I awoke missing my daughters' early springtime hijinks and shenanigans. Alexandra, usually so serious and dignified, fools me every year with some elaborate prank. But personally I never need anyone's help being a fool, especially while in Tanzania. I did a very nice job of that all by myself.

The first day I came to Bukoba on the layover in Mwanza, I smiled sweetly at a woman in the small airport bathroom, and it was a good thing too. I emerged from the restroom and walked into the waiting area without knowing that the back of my dress was tucked up inside of my "slip" (read: Spanx). People were laughing, I thought because I was *mzungu*. The woman I had smiled at came over and gently untucked my dress, the satiny fabric falling slowly down my derriere like a theatre curtain. But not before a gorgeous young priest who (I would later discover) happened to be a good friend of Father Charles (along with some other passengers headed to Bukoba) got an eyeful of my hindquarters.

The first day Monsignor took me to meet the Mother

Superior in charge of the church schools within the Bukoba Diocese, I received an early call from a certain monthly visitor. While wearing a white skirt. And driving in the front seat of a car with beige upholstery. I waited until Monsignor got out of the car, wrapped a sweater around my waist and hightailed it into the convent. Let's just say that the nuns and I bonded very quickly.

The first time I went to mass at the university I tripped over a step and fell, nearly knocking the offertory basket over. The children in the front row giggled.

The first day Sister Charlotte came to stay at DESIRE there was no toilet paper in her *choo*. I couldn't find any in our storeroom, so I did what anyone would do: I knocked on Monsignor's door at 10:00 at night and asked to borrow some. He came back with an armful of toilet paper rolls and a look that said, "Let's please not do this again."

The first time I went shopping downtown by myself, I asked the fathers if they wanted anything from the store. Father Joseph asked for a specific meat product, but then added, "Ah, it's a dead animal—you will most likely forget!" I was so proud that I had overcome his predicted absent-mindedness that I called out to him upon returning and announced roughly the equivalent of "I am so happy! I got my hands on your sausage!" His response was also something like, "Let's please not do this again."

Some of my friends and family back home think that I have grown into an elegant woman of the world, but the truth is that I am just as awkward as I was in middle school. In addition to various social ungraces I exhibited in Tanzania, my general composure (or rather the lack thereof) elicited plenty of chuckles. On sunny days I walked around with my rain umbrella to avoid withering in the sun and heat, and the students politely tittered at me as I walked past. If I didn't have my umbrella, I often draped a scarf over my head or wore an old hat that had distinctively cowboy features.

While female students and colleagues navigated the rocky paths of the university gracefully in their high heels and perfectly pressed dresses, I often stumbled and even fell while wearing the most sensible shoes possible, a pair of flat-heeled, knee-high boots. Again, cue the laughter.

Tanzanian culture is a teasing culture, which suited my personality just fine. Unlike those who laughed at my awkwardness in middle school, I had the comforting feeling in Tanzania that people really were laughing *with* me even when they were indeed laughing *at* me.

Ocham remarked one day that while he was studying in Germany he noticed that people didn't laugh at each other when someone fell down (which is quite often during the slippery, icy months of winter) like they do in Tanzania.[7] In Tanzania if I fell down, many within observational distance would laugh at me, after seeing that it was not a serious fall. This was not *Schadenfreude*; it was more like hahaha-aren't-we-a-peculiar-species-trying-to-think-we-are-in-control-freude.

Back home in California, people may not laugh at you if you fall down, but there is a tendency to be pretty hard on each other's imperfections. Strangely, we seem to be more forgiving and compassionate about the folly of the conduct of other species. We see the trials and errors of other animals as normal, even endearing as evidenced by likes and views on social media: The chimpanzees falling over each other or missing a branch while swinging are just adorable; the big cats tripping and tumbling during a failed hunting attempt are still impressive. But back home we have such a culture of unrealistic expectations and even shame about basic biological functions that if I even pass the bathroom back home and my

---

[7] Actually, we both remarked that people in Germany tend not to laugh much at all.

cat is in the litter box, she will most likely climb out, shut the door with her back leg and give me a look over her furry shoulder that says, "Madame, have you no sense of decorum?"

In California, we are often overly self-conscious which, ironically, makes us even more awkward. I don't know why we think we are cooler than we are. I don't know why we don't laugh about how bizarre it is to be a *homosapien* the way most of my Tanzanian colleagues and friends can.

Tanzanians seem to prefer to laugh directly and collectively at our oft-strange and foolish hominid behavior. During the course of even those first few months in Bukoba, I came to value my own absurd humanity more than ever.

In addition to my awkwardness, I have also made some ridiculous choices in life that I cannot hide from the world. Most notably, I let my ex-husband make a complete fool out of me by ignoring the signs of his infidelity and disrespect even before I married him. But I came to realize, through conversations like those I had with Cesilia, the value of not trying to project some false image or hiding who I really am. The more that people in Bukoba laughed at me, the closer we became.

The undergraduate who heard the story of my unfaithful and ultimately destructive ex-husband and my subsequent divorce came to my office hours to get advice about leaving her abusive husband.

The male graduate student and secondary school teacher consulted me about the cultural taboos and serious social consequences of not discussing puberty and menstruation with teenaged girls here.

The colleagues who gradually felt less self-conscious when talking to me invited me to their homes and shared the rich and imperfect stories of their lives.

The little girl who accompanied me on one of my daily walks demonstrated a dance which is familiar to parents everywhere, and rather than running away she simply walked over to a bush, squatted down and evacuated her bladder the way we all do. She didn't even avoid eye contact with me, she just finished her business. We had a quick chuckle and continued our walk as she finished telling me a story.

There was something very comforting about it all, knowing that I am not alone in my ridiculous, foolish bipedal physical condition. In Bukoba it seemed understood that humans are subjugated to the same laws of biology and imperfection as the other creatures of the animal kingdom are. What is often embarrassing at home—falling down, biological functions, fashion or verbal faux pas—is just normal here. When that woman in the airport in Mwanza untucked the dress from my undergarment (while laughing, of course) I think she was inspired more by my condition than by the sweet smile I had given her earlier. With that lovely pink hemline stuffed inelegantly into the elastic waistband of a piece of lingerie designed to make me look slimmer than I am, I not only showed her my haunches, I also revealed my own foolish nature.

SPRING BREAKERS

When I tell the priests how much I love my walks in the "forest," they laugh.

"That's not a forest!"

"It sure looks like a forest to me," I say. "Then what is it?"

"Oh, that's just the countryside."

A few moments later Father Charles said, "We will take you to see a real forest."

And, over Spring Break, they did. The fathers who had already done so much for me by taking me in after my housing arrangement had not worked out were also going to let me accompany them to Mutukulu, the border town between Tanzania and Uganda. On the way there, we would be passing through the Minziro Forest, a "real" forest.

The Minziro forest is just a small part of the larger Malabigambo Forest that crosses over into Uganda. It is mostly swamp and wet acacia woodlands with over 600 native butterfly species, more than in any other African forest. I'm not sure what I was more enthusiastic about—seeing the forest, crossing over into another country or being invited to take a road trip with these two men who guarded their free time and privacy like Brink's truck drivers.

In my teen years, my friends and I would take similar road trips crossing the border into Mexico from California during Spring Break, going to places like Tijuana and Rosarito for inexpensive Lobster Thermidor and margaritas. My most vivid memory of those times involves my friend, Lisa, behind the wheel of a red convertible looking like Princess Diana with abs of steel and a contagious laugh. Rockwell's "Somebody's Watching Me" was on the play loop of the only AM radio station we could get. All these years later, every time I hear that song, I am immediately transported back to that era when we were carefree, with the salt air whipping through our hair, the companionship of best friends, the hope of youth and Pacific Coast Highway open before us.

This time, decades later, on my Spring Break road trip to the border with Father Mgeni and Father Charles, it was the Dolly Parton and Kenny Rogers version of "Islands in The Stream" that was on a play loop.

The fathers liked to hear me sing, so I belted out:

"And we rely on each other, uh huh."

"And you just walk through the night, slowly losing sight of the real thing."

For modesty's sake, instead of singing "making love with each other," I sang "cause we love one another."

Uh huh.

The three of us shared a more restrained joy than that of my youth, but it was a joy nonetheless, with the tarmacked road wide open in front of us as if anything were possible. Within minutes, Bukoba was far behind us and around us there was nothing but green valleys and hilltops far off into the horizon. We rolled on, with American country music blaring, punctuated by Father Mgeni's old school Tanzanian jams. On both sides, thick and apparently authentic forests spread out, the homes of huge butterflies and elusive animals. I could almost see the giant dinosaurs that had roamed this land and the pterodactyls that had flown through the trees and over the once-undisturbed caches of granite and gemstones.

About 20 miles before we reached the border town, we stopped at a roadside vendor, and Father Charles bought us giant cobs of roasted corn like the ones I get from the *eloté* men in Los Angeles. I got out to stretch my legs and looked around.

It was so peaceful and lush that it was hard to imagine that this was once the theatre for the Uganda-Tanzania War in the late 1970s when Idi Amin declared war on Tanzania and sent troops in to annex the Kagera region. But the closer we got to the border, the easier it was to find traces of this bloody conflict. The skeleton of a burned-out church, just one victim of Amin's attack, still stands atop a hill near the border, a mummified and silent witness to history.

Amin's atrocities are notorious. For men like Father Joseph who call this specific region home, these atrocities are also part of the fabric of his life and his hometown. Memories of corpses floating down the Kagera river still cause some around here to stop, give pause and pay momentary homage. Despite Uganda's invasion of Tanzania, as well as Amin's well-documented and brazen violations of human rights, Tanzania received no assistance from other countries in the African Union. Tanzania's fight against Uganda led to the overthrow of Amin and his terrifying regime. Tanzania alone, despite its own struggles with poverty, foot the entire bill. Without Tanzania, who knows what else Amin would have been able to destroy?

With peaceful relations nowadays, border security at Mutukula now consists of a simple iron gate that can be lifted by hand. The day we crossed, the arm of the gate was open; the guard just waved us through. Like many border towns, Mutukula is a place of commerce and exchange, of barter and deals. The Fathers had come to shop.

Hoping myself to find some traditional African goods, I was stunned to see shop after *shagalabagala* shop filled with Chinese goods, mostly made of plastic or synthetic fiber. The houseware stalls eventually gave way to clothing stores.

The dusty alleys were filled with customers, merchants and unsupervised children. I stayed close to the fathers who had asked me not to wander off, as I am prone to do. As they were looking at shirts and ties, they asked my opinion on colors and fit. Men's dress shirts were wrapped in thick plastic boxes, folded perfectly with coordinating ties and cufflinks, and practically every other stand sold them. Looking for traditional fabric per Cesilia's request, I had a harder time. Imports dominated the inventory. I couldn't find a single hand-made basket, not even a scrap of fabric that wasn't made out of polyester, nylon or acrylic. After a while, I stopped looking. I don't really enjoy shopping anyway, so I decided to enjoy my time with Fathers Charles and Mgeni instead.

"Don't you want to buy anything?" Father Mgeni asked.

When I told them what I was looking for, Father Charles suggested we stop off at a huge traditional marketplace on the way back home.

After just over an hour in Mutukula, we were back in the now-dusty RAV4. After a few twists and turns, we stopped and parked in a field with dozens of other cars and hundreds of bicycles.

"If you can't find what you're looking for here, it doesn't exist." Father Mgeni declared as we walked towards the sprawling market that looked more like a village than any-thing else. My companions explained to me how the market was organized: a section for fruits and vegetables, one for meat, one for fabric, one for housewares, one for moonshine.

As we entered the market, we stopped so that Father Charles could survey the watermelons and tangerines. We heard a piercing shriek and turned around to find a woman pointing and staring at me, the only *mzungu* around. The shrieking turned to a cruel, cackling laugh. In fact, she laughed so hard that she finally had to sit down on the ground. Father Charles graciously directed us to another section of the market. I, not so graciously, directed my suspicions to a home brew called *waragi*.

Avoiding the butcher section of the market where animals in various stages of dissection hung unrefrigerated in the sun, we meandered through rows and rows of hand-made baskets in all shapes and sizes. Swaths of Tanzanian high-quality cotton fabric and *tangas* of the most intricate patterns and vibrant colors distracted me until I found just what I wanted.

Walking past the illegal hooch tills that ferment bananas into an obviously potent spirit, we observed patrons on the verge of either nausea or unconsciousness sitting on the woven mats in the makeshift saloons. The customers looked a lot like my friends and I did at one point or another during our road trips to Tijuana when someone inevitably had to be hoisted up off of the Talavera and Saltillo tile floors.

In addition to the fabric, the fathers and I also bought barrels of fruit and vegetables to bring back home. By the time we drove away from the market, the back of the car was filled with baskets of tangerines, cassava, potatoes, spinach, carrots, mangoes and papaya. There were four giant watermelons at my feet and two meters of fine hand-woven Tanzanian fabric in my lap.

After that, we stopped for lunch at a nearby lodge that catered to tourists on safari. The food was salty and lavished in heavy sauce, and I indulged in a mid-day glass of red wine, an extravagance or perhaps a tribute to my earlier Spring Break road trips. Conversation over lunch was easy and light-hearted, and as the wine started to take effect, I worried that I might be assuming too much familiarity by revealing parts of myself that I am not proud of. These two men would have *never* used a place like Tijuana as a personal playground as I once had. No, their Jesuit sensibilities are so profound that they seem to be the result of nature as much as nurture, and I have no doubt that these two men who treat me as if I am a better human being than I actually am would have been volunteering at an orphanage, school or sanctuary center if they had ever gone to Tijuana as teenagers.

Detecting my self-consciousness over lunch, Father Charles gently encouraged me. "Feel free to be yourself. We are family, Lee."

Father Mgeni proclaimed his catch phrase to me in perfect Italian, "*Viva la libertà!*"

Long live freedom.

After teetotalling for so long, the wine had a strong effect, and by the time we were back on the road, I was in a semi-altered state—peaceful and happy and singing:

"We start and end as one..."

I could see Father Mgeni's smile in the rearview mirror as Father Charles joined me in the chorus:

"Sail away with me

To another world..."

I knew then that every time I heard this song, I would be transported back to these moments driving with Father Mgeni and Father Charles through the beautiful landscape of their homeland. I laid my head back as we sang and watched the forests and countryside fly by, eventually noticing that we had taken a different way home, down a road with no border to cross.

THEY WOULD LIKE TO
HAVE US FOR DINNER

After work one day, Father Mgeni informed me that there would be no dinner served at DESIRE the following evening due to some kind of reception at the Bishop's house for all the priests and nuns. After thanking him for the notice, I told him that I would make other plans.

"No, you won't!" he admonished. "This is a *family* dinner."

So, it was settled.

One advantage that nuns and priests have for occasions like this is they know exactly what to wear. I, on the other hand, had no idea what to wear to a party to honor the outgoing Bishop where all of the celebrants, except me, would be people of the cloth.

The truth is, I really didn't have much to choose from. The clothes I had brought that would conform to The Dress Code were already showing signs of threadbare wear and tear due to the harsh nature of hand washing. Cesi was making some skirts for me, but they weren't ready yet.

"Wear your best clothes," Father Joseph said.

I didn't even know exactly what that meant, nor could I even distinguish what my *best* clothes were anymore. They all looked pathetic.

I became a MacGyver of fashion. I didn't have much to work with, but I assembled anything beauty-related I could find: the dredges of some hair products, an almost empty bottle of nail polish, a stub of eyeliner, some perfume vapors and the pale pink dress I had accidentally tucked into my Spanx in Mwanza that now had a ripped hemline. I scrounged it all together and even hand sewed the hemline of my dress. For an extra layer of modesty, I wrapped a pink scarf around my shoulders, and I met the fathers precisely at the agreed-upon time so that we could all go together, in their words, as a family.

As we pulled up at the gate of the sprawling compound and imposing house, I felt something that I hadn't felt in a while now.

I felt guilty.

The driveway up to the gates was lined with locals, mostly women and children. As I emerged from Father Mgeni's SUV with my pink dress (now seeming like a fine garment) flowing glamorously in the wind, the children rushed me, handing me handfuls of wildflowers or touching my hand.

"Children really love you," Father Mgeni said.

I think they just mistook me for someone important.

"OK, have fun. We'll see you later," Father Joseph said, as they all melted into the crowd leaving me standing in the foyer alone.

So much for family dinner.

Inside, the house was adorned in colonial-era finery. The tables and chairs were set up outside in such a way that it resembled a royal banquet. At the head table, or throne as I later called it, sat the guests of honor including Father Mgeni and one woman—the Mother Superior who probably would have been happy to sit with the rest of us. On the right side of the courtyard sat the men (aka priests). On the left side sat the women (aka nuns...and me). I was the only one not wearing a habit, and I felt as out of place as I did when I was ten years old at a slumber party where all the other girls had matching pajamas except me.

But the feeling of not belonging was fleeting. Sister Florida, the nurse from the university, sought me out, and before I knew it, I was introduced to numerous amiable Sisters. We were soon drinking sodas, talking like old friends, and then dinner, or rather, the feast, was served.

I hadn't seen so much food in one place since I'd been in Tanzania: platters of chicken, goat, beef, pork, samosas, pilau, rice, beans, salads, fruits of all types, including, of course, bananas. While I was stuffing my face with pilau and *katchumbali,* the nuns all started dancing. They all knew the steps to what looked to me like a version of the Electric Slide. They were all having a good old time. So was I.

At one point it seemed that there was an acceptable co-mingling of male and female. During this cross-gender communication, Father Charles found me. I smiled as he approached, but he looked pretty serious.

"Lee, I need to talk to you." All I could think was, "Uh oh. What did I do this time?"

Earlier in the day Father Charles had told me he had to leave campus early and could not drive me home as usual.

"I have to pick up something for the Bishop's present."

I offered to go with him, but he declined saying, "No, this isn't for you, Lee." My friends and colleagues in Tanzania had adopted the shortened version of my name that was also used by my closest family and friends.

I figured his afternoon errand had just been another excuse for Father Charles to have his "Man Time," a solitary temporal dimension that I have learned, the hard way and thanks mostly to my own dad, is precious to many men in my life. I had forgotten all about his afternoon errand until he brought it up again at the Bishop's dinner.

"It's about the gift," Charles said.

"What about the gift?" I asked.

"We would like to present it as a family, and we would like you to be the one to give it."

I was touched and didn't bother to temper my enthusiasm.

"That's great!!" I said with a smile that Charles did not return.

"Well, you might not think it's so great when you hear what it is," he said.

"What's the gift?" I enthused.

Charles paused, and then said,

"It's a goat."

"A what?"

"A goat."

"A goat?"

"A goat."

Never wanting to miss the opportunity to make a bad pun, I said, "Are you *kid*ding me?"

Silence. He was in no mood for my levity.

"Get it? Kid, like a baby goat..."

More silence. I re-focused.

"A dead one?" I worried.

"No, a live one. Follow me, I'll show you."

So, we snuck off to a dark part of the compound. Near the car park, hitched to a wooden post, was a wide-eyed, camel-colored goat who looked at me with a sense of betrayal. I stood there quietly for a minute until I found the words.

"We got the Bishop a *goat*?!"

Attempting to secure my cooperation, Charles explained that animals are traditional gifts, that this was a female who would most likely be used for breeding or to supply milk.

"Can you guarantee she will not be slaughtered?"

Silence.

Father Charles gave me a look. More precisely he gave me

The Look that men in my life often present to me when they are trying to say, "Can you please not make a scene right now?"

Then, as if she could understand, the goat started tugging on her tether, bucking up a storm. My eyes started to well up, and I feared that Father Charles and I were on the verge of our first fight. He had me. If I didn't cooperate, I would not only insult our host, the Bishop, I would—and this was more crucial—insult the four Fathers who had been so generous and kind to me these past months. I started to think that all that talk earlier in the day about "family" was nothing but sweet talk so that I would comply with this request.

"What do I need to do?" I succumbed, futilely holding back tears.

"All you need to do is...," he started, and I stopped listening because every time a man has started a sentence to me with those words, there was nothing simple at all about the instructions that followed.

Charles explained further, once he knew I was actually paying attention. After dinner, there would be some entertainment and then presentations of the gifts. Each order, diocese, convent or, in our case, family would walk up to the main table, offer some words of tribute and hand the gift to the Bishop. The fathers would like *me* to physically hand the goat to the Bishop.

"Is this some kind of cruel joke?" I asked Charles, but he was dead serious.

"All you need to do is..." Yeah, yeah. I know. What could go wrong?

Sure enough, after dinner the guests performed a series of songs and skits. Some were funny, some serious. Sister Florida's contingency sang a haunting and hypnotic melody in Swahili so beautiful that it entranced me so much that I stopped being nervous about the next phase of the evening.

Not long after that, Father Joseph came up to me, gave me an authoritative pat on the shoulder and somberly said, "Let's go."

A short line for the presentation of gifts had started to form, not far from where the goat was. I asked if she and I could avoid the line as long as possible and stay in the little corner near the car park until it was our turn. It was more of a statement than a question, and Father Joe gave me a look like, "You better not try any funny business and mess this up!"

Just about the time the goat seemed to trust me and let me pat her little, wooly head, it was our turn. With great fanfare, we were announced and approached the grand table with our gifts. There was also a giant card we had all signed as well as an assortment of fruits and vegetables.

She seemed relatively calm as we approached the table, but she must have gotten wise because as soon as we were in front of the Bishop, she started bucking and thrashing again. Before I knew it, she had encircled my legs, entwining them with her rope, hogtying me like a rodeo pro. I couldn't get control of her. Heck, I couldn't get control of myself. Father Joseph gave me a scowl like I was doing this on purpose, but the crowd just howled. Grateful, once again, to be in a teasing culture, I somehow untangled myself. This was not the image of dignitary grace the Fathers had hoped for, I'm sure. Finally, I just handed the goat's rope to one of the nuns who magnanimously received her on behalf of the Bishop.

I went to the restroom to clean up and wash my face. I was a mess. That little stump of eyeliner was now just smudgy debris in the rivulets of my silly tears. After cleaning up, I went back out to the front courtyard near the gate where we had entered. There were still some lingering children just outside the gate, listening to the singing of the sisters, once again drifting through the night air. As I sat on the front step, a nun came over to me, took my hand and walked me over to the goat's new home—a small pen with several other animals. The goat was happily chewing on some grass and let me pat her head again. The nun smiled. Then she started laughing. And then I did too.

When it was time to leave the party, we couldn't find Father Joseph. This, it would turn out, was a pattern for him and for us. Father Joseph seems to be an extreme extrovert, and we would invariably have to seek him out at the end of a party/wedding/funeral/mass and tear him away from some intense conversation with some very important friend/ family member/ colleague/ former student. Eventually we found him ensconced in such a conversation, and after about a half an hour he was ready to go.

Everybody laughed and sang as we drove home. They laughed mostly at that goat and me, and I laughed because I realized that we truly were a family.

"Will you come with us from now on to these family events?" Father Mgeni asked.

"Yes." I said. "But from now on I'm choosing the presents."

A MAN'S WORLD

Not long after the Bishop's departure, party preparations were underway for the installation festivities for the new Bishop of Bukoba. Father Charles let me know that DESIRE would soon have an abundance of visitors. Priests from all over Tanzania would be arriving in droves, and some of them would be dining with us. Several of them would also be staying in the large house where Father Mgeni and Father Charles lived. I offered to give up my cottage for the weekend, so they could have the place all to themselves, but the fathers wouldn't hear of it.

"Don't you dare," said Father Mgeni. "We have a deal. We are family. We will all have dinner together Friday night."

Other than that, plans seemed pretty fluid, except for the installation ceremony at the cathedral on Saturday.

The week before the grand celebration, tables, chairs, linens, plates and cutlery were requisitioned from the dining room and carried across the road to Father Mgeni's and Charles' house by Irene and Asimwe. Trucks arrived carrying baskets of all types of food: green leafy vegetables, tiny eggplants, and a bounty of fruits. One day a man on a bike delivered two live chickens and a massive fish. I watched all of these comings and goings with great interest as I peeked through the curtains of my cottage.

Asimwe and Irene started cooking Thursday night for the arrival of guests on Friday evening. Probably remembering my efforts to cook, they declined my offer to help. They worked late into the night.

"What time is everyone coming for dinner tonight?" I inquired at breakfast so that I would be ready to greet everyone properly.

"Whenever they all get here," was the response.

Around sunset, the cars started arriving into the compound. I peeked out my window to see the guests. Some of the priests wore their collars; some wore more traditional African shirts like Monsignor does sometimes. They arrived several to a car or truck, their lively and friendly conversations flowing out of the cars with them.

Around 7:00 Asimwe knocked on my door and told me it was dinnertime.

I entered Father Mgeni's house, now filled with laughter and the booming voices of African men of all ages. This time I was not only the sole lay person, I was also the only female guest. Everyone was friendly and welcoming. Everyone it seems had been a student, at one time or another, of Father Joseph or Monsignor.

There were a lot of stories beginning with "Remember when..." and many of them detailing the impressive and oft-intimidating power and intelligence of Father Joseph. Even then amongst all of these accomplished men, he held a certain command. His sparkling Tanzanite-colored eyes could turn Arctic cold in an instant, and he could quiet a room without saying a word. Some of these priests, powerful in their own right, still seemed to show a trace of deference, almost fear, to this force of a man.

I was introduced to several high-ranking university administrators. I also met parish priests, students, monsignors and other variations of priestdom that I couldn't keep track of.

Eventually, we all formed a giant circle, Father Joseph leading us in prayer. "As it was in the beginning, is now and ever shall be. World without end. Amen."

Dinner was served buffet style with dishes I had never seen before at DESIRE: eggplant cooked in peanut sauce, green vegetables sautéed with onions, bananas cooked with bean and corn, pilau with fresh cardamom, and an assortment of roasted animals. The sole refrigerator at DESIRE was also stocked with ice cold drinks including all the brands advertised on the old placards still posted around DESIRE from its old days as a nightclub.

With my plate piled high with no effort to hide my gluttony, I was guided to a seat. At first, I thought this was a place of honor, but I soon realized that I was in exactly the seat I did *not* want to sit in. As soon as the next conversation started, I realized that I was sitting in The Hot Seat.

I sat in a configuration of chairs placed in an oval with me sitting at one end of the oval, and one of the honcho administrators at the other end. Other priests filled in the oval, engaged in conversations with their neighbors. More chairs and similar configurations were spread throughout the house in such a way that guests could call across the room to one another if they wanted. Before I knew it, the honcho, who led with the fact that he had been "properly educated" began pelting me with questions:

"What do you think is the main problem with education here?"

"What is the main difference between your country and Tanzania in terms of education?"

"Don't you find the students here lazy?"

Like many of the guests at this dinner, he had been educated in Europe. Like many people I met in Tanzania, he also seemed to think that the United States was superior to

Tanzania in all matters including education. I was shocked at how condescendingly he spoke about the students whom I had found to be overwhelmingly hard-working and bright.

He dismissed my position that students between the two countries were not that different, that I had found more similarities in education than I had expected. I didn't mention that one of the main similarities was how out of touch university administrators like him can be and how they consistently wasted money on vanity projects.

"Don't be ridiculous," he said, "You are just being nice. Tell everyone how much better the system is in America. Go on. You can speak freely."

By now, this conversation had caught the attention of Father Joseph who was chewing on a mutton bone and watching silently like he was ready to pounce. But I didn't know upon whom. I didn't want to disgrace him.

I was very sensitive about being the only woman in the room.

I acknowledged my concerns about the extremely large class sizes here, with a delicate reminder that this could be mitigated not by students or teachers but by administrators like him. I also acknowledged the outdated and unfortunate colonial system that still seemed to be revered throughout Tanzania, again with the onus on administration, not students. I told him that I had found students here to be anything but lazy. I found them to be extremely motivated.

I looked up, my eyes meeting Father Joseph's whose smoldering embers seemed to have cooled.

The honcho continued, now with more than a hint of challenge and condescension in his voice. I had noticed his elitism earlier when he had addressed our students and told them that they should all have "an iPhone, an iPad AND a laptop" if they were serious about their educations.

I told him that most of my students in California could not

afford all of that technology.

Ignoring my critique of administrators and my commen-dation of students, he continued with what suddenly seemed more like an interrogation with the intent to degrade his countrymen than an effort to listen to my opinions.

"What do you think about our language policies?"

"How do you use technology in your classroom in California?"

He guffawed and pshawed me when I told him, and the other dozen or so priests now listening, that I actually didn't like to use technology during class time. My students back home will verify that. I am saddened that we are losing the human connection. I told him that one of the reasons I came to East Africa was to learn more about traditional, informal and natural ways of learning.

He smirked and went on a diatribe about lazy Tanzanian students, the virtues of technology and the superiority of education in Europe while perfectly exhibiting an all-too familiar hubris at his own, infallible, patriarchal authority.

He finished, then looked at me to respond. I looked at Father Joseph who knew what was coming. A Father to my right tried to change the conversation, but such conversations are all too familiar to me: I grew up in a family of men. I am the only female in my generation, and my father is a domineering, Type A, self-made man whose charge to me throughout my life has been "Take No Prisoners."

So, when the honcho kept pushing, I held my ground. Careful to be respectful, I challenged many of his assertions, particularly the "laziness" of students and faculty. After I finished, one older priest even clapped. The honcho tried to interrupt me, but I wouldn't let him. When he realized that I would not support his claims in front of the rest of the group, he stopped.

I visited with some of the other guests, all of whom were

polite, gracious and wonderful company. Some sang hymns and told more stories. I excused myself early and wished everyone a wonderful visit.

The contingency spent the rest of the weekend attending the installation ceremony at the cathedral on Saturday, visiting the seminary on Saturday night and then attending Mass on Sunday. As some of them prepared to leave, I said good-bye. As the afternoon grew late and I saw the guards carry the tables, food and cutlery back from Father Mgeni and Father Charles' house, I felt relieved to have life at DESIRE return to normal. I hadn't spoken to any of the family here since the Friday night dinner, and I honestly worried that I may have crossed a line.

Sitting alone at the dinner table after the weekend was over, I waited for the fathers to come join me. I saw Father Joseph as he walked towards the dining cottage, crossing the courtyard with his elegant hands folded piously in front of him looking very contemplative. He entered, his baritone greeting me powerfully.

"*Habari za leo?*"

How was your day?

After we exchanged greetings, I thanked him for including me in the Friday night dinner.

"Of course," he said.

I broached the subject that had caused me just a slight pang of discomfort.

"I felt a little uncomfortable that I was the only girl there," surprising myself by calling myself a "girl" in spite of my age and stature. "You were not obligated to invite me," I said, opening the door for any comments he might have about the awkward conversation I had engaged in with the honcho.

Father Joseph smiled. "My dear, you were delightful, and we agreed that you are the best type of 'girl,'" he said, and I was not a bit insulted that he too called me this.

"Oh, yeah," I said, my eyes meeting his. "What kind is that?" I asked.

"The kind who is able to speak for herself."

HERE COMES THE SUN

Hours passed into days that turned into weeks that turned into months. I stayed connected to loved ones back home through the wonders of technology. I spoke frequently with my daughters, and I was able to stay abreast of their lives. My daughter, Victoria, sent me letters. The parents of my godsons sent photos. The Man I Love and I Skyped or chatted almost every day. Others sent messages or electronic mail in ways that were still warm despite the frigidity of the devices that conveyed those messages. So crucial was my portal to communication back home that I named my computer "Wilson" after the character in *Cast Away*.

Among those who kept in touch with me was a very dear friend from childhood, Alfredo. He and I had spent summers together when we were kids at a camp in California's Sequoia National Forest. That was my family's annual vacation: overloading the Dodge station wagon, having it overheat half-way up the mountains while my dad fired off a fantastic fusillade of F-Bombs until we eventually arrived at the Shangri-La of my youth.

Alfredo and I share memories rowing across Lake Sequoia, my left hang lingering in the mossy water tracing infinity signs in the gentle wake. During evening campfires, he and I would play the guitar and sing. There was a whole pack of us, a band of brothers and sisters, treasuring each moment of each day as it came, grateful for each breath of clean, fresh air. These memories are very precious, these memories of just being happy to be alive, not yet knowing the specific pain life had in store for each of us.

One afternoon when I checked my e-mails after the days had turned into weeks, and the weeks had turned into months, I opened an e-mail from Alfredo. He had one question for me. He asked what a typical day for me was like in Bukoba.

Alfredo's question was lovely in its simplicity. It was also fitting that it came from him because my days in Bukoba reminded me a lot of our life at camp. I was in the mountains. A forest surrounded me. Time seemed suspended. Days were slow and communal. Alfredo's question also pulled me back to the outside world as I reflected on his question, realizing that I had adapted quickly to my new habitat. By the time I got Alfredo's e-mail, I had been in Bukoba for nearly six months, each day barely distinguishable from the last. This is what I told Alfredo:

Each morning I wake to a crescendo of morning songbirds, my eyes practically blinking open with each sweet chirp. Inevitably one or two birds rap on my window like my neighbor Brian did when we were children. Sometimes I hear the call to prayer or the cathedral bells or the horn of HMV Victoria as she pulls into port, but mostly it is the orchestra of birds. I wake up slowly and peacefully and rested. During the rainy season, *masika*, the water falls from the sky like daggers. The birds frolic in it, and the combination of their calls and taps along with the insistence of the downpour pulls me out of bed.

One of the most salient differences between my days here and my days back home in California is my position to the sun.

Back home I mostly notice the sun when I am saying good-bye to it, as my world spins away from the solar embrace, and I watch the sun set into the ocean's depths. In California, I often feel a tiny pang of nostalgia and loss under the canvas of purples, pinks, oranges and indigos. Another day is gone. In Bukoba, I am up before the sun and am consistently surprised when I remember that I get to watch the sun *rise*. Here I am facing eastward where I can see the sun slowly peek up out of Lake Victoria as Earth rotates. The same purple, pink, orange and indigo trails splash the sky, but here the sun greets me with a wink of an eye announcing optimistically that another day begins!

From 7:30 to 8:30 we eat breakfast. This is a fluid community with visiting professors, nuns and priests who come and go according to their schedules. With few exceptions, there will always be me and the four Fathers at the table lingering amiably over warm teas and coffee that were grown and cultivated just down the road. We eat cassava or eggs or *andazi* (frittery bread) or chapatti or oatmeal or seasonal fruit, depending on what is available.

At 8:30 we are out the door on our way to the college. The drive, like most activities here, is communal. Father Joseph and I sometimes get a ride with Father Charles. Driving with Monsignor is my favorite though because he says this little prayer before he starts the engine, and every time he recites it, I wish someone had said it before my brother-in-law and aunt had started the journeys that would end their lives in separate motorcycle accidents:

> *"Protect us today in all our travels*
> *Along the road's way*
> *Give your warning signs*
> *If danger is near so*
> *I may stop until the path is clear*

Be at my window and direct me through
When objects appear from out of the blue
Defend this vehicle and everyone inside
Keep me focused and be my watchful guide
Carry us safely to our destined place
And bless this journey with your love and grace"

He recites these lines every single time before he starts the car. Every. Single. Time.

The route is always the same. Along the two-and-one-half-mile road, we wind through banana plantations and tropical forests, stopping to pick up any students, faculty or employees of the university we might see on foot along the way until the car is full.

Along the main road to the university, a sloping, lush valley stretches out to the east, and my eyes follow it all the way to the shores of Lake Victoria just out my left window. Every possible shade of green imaginable is visible from pale lime to deepest emerald. Children in uniforms line up outside a primary school classroom. People of all ages and sizes walk along the road, sometimes alongside a herd of goats or cattle. Small, corrugated tin homes as well as large brick houses dot the landscape. Sometimes a few cows are at a watering hole. Sometimes a giant bird swoops past. If we are lucky, a monkey will run across our path or jump mischievously from a branch above. Some mornings the car is filled with the chatter of enthusiasm or even singing. Some mornings we are silent.

The mood is consistently joyful.

When I first arrive at my office, I answer my e-mails, but not before greeting every student, administrator or professor I should encounter on the short walk. By the time I have greeted others appropriately, answered my e-mails and done some paperwork, it is time for tea break with Ocham. We talk about language, teaching, literature, poetry, movies, T.V., our families. I love these conversations, and they remind me of some of the precious, long talks Alfredo and I shared when we were kids and had the luxury of time that eludes so many of us in the adult, "real" world.

During one tea break, a visiting professor named Dr. Kerry from England, remarked that the campus reminds him of a rehab clinic with its peaceful, slow pace and tranquil flora and fauna. Out the window of the canteen where we drink our tea, I can see a menagerie of trees dripping with bananas, guava, mangoes, avocados or papaya depending on the season. The calls of the birds have become so familiar that they have simply become background music that I take for granted. Sometimes as I walk across campus, I will stop simply to observe a hunting lizard, an army of unimaginably large ants or the flight of a bird I had previously only seen in pictures.

I work at a leisurely pace, and it doesn't even feel like I am working at all. During the second week of classes I was frustrated at the lack of professional urgency of my students and colleagues. Schedules are more like the sequence of events for the day rather than the exact times of those events.

"Calm down," Father Joseph told me several times. So, I did. I calmed *way* down. I have only lost my temper twice in these six months, an unimaginable personal best. My work is quiet. I teach. I read. I see what needs to be done on campus. I write. I plan a teaching activity or workshop with Ocham, and then I read some more.

Each day the entire faculty and staff eat lunch together, laughing and teasing. Every day the food is the same: beans, rice, cooked bananas, fish. Afternoons pass in the blink of an eye. I am always surprised at how quickly 4:30 comes, and it is time to go home.

At home I enjoy yet another tea break, and afternoon tea is always with Father Charles. Of all the men here, he feels most like a brother to me. These afternoons remind me of times with my brothers after school when we sat around the table for a few moments to talk about our day and have an after-school snack. If the rains have stopped (they usually have by mid-day), I take my afternoon walk in the forest after tea.

How can I describe these walks?! I do not just walk a few miles down a dirt road. I walk thousands of years back in time, and these few geographical miles seem to cover the entire universe. Anyone who watches me pass would see a woman walking alone, but I feel that everyone I know and have ever loved has accompanied me on at least one of these walks.

I walk along a red dirt road that bisects a part of the forest. The trees are covered with ancient vines whose slender tentacles have probably spent decades embracing the trunks and branches of these pine and eucalyptus trees. Gargantuan palm trees that would fetch tens of thousands of dollars in Southern California are everywhere. At any given time, I see no less than 20 creatures in the panorama of my vision: frogs, lizards, white or exotically patterned butterflies, birds of all possible plumage and silhouettes, rascally monkeys who don't hesitate to throw a piece of fruit at me if I get too close. The sun sneaks through the forest canopy wherever possible and dances along the ground and in the clean air around us.

But it isn't just the life that I can see here in the forest that beguiles, it is all the life and love that I can *feel* here. Genetic analysts for the National Geographic Genographic Project have traced the DNA of all modern humans back to a single common ancestral source (shouldn't that actually be TWO?) from this area less than 100,000 years ago, and I don't know how else to say this, but I can just *feel* those ancestors here. Somewhere near this forest, these long-forgotten family members lived, laughed, loved and played before their multitudes of progeny left the ancestral home to cross deserts, mountains and oceans until we eventually populated the rest of the planet. And I have seen more prehistoric skeletons and cave paintings since I have been here than I have in my entire life. These are the original ancestral burial grounds. There is something very sacred about this place.

I also feel the presence of others. My memories and love for friends and family back home float around like the butterflies of the forest, and occasionally they land safely for a moment in my heart and linger long enough for me to appreciate them. Those who have loved me and whom I have loved are all here with me, and the children hanging from the trees laughing and waving as I pass are waving at all of us. The old women with their brightly covered dresses and head-dresses who pay their respects to me as they pass are also paying respect to my entire family.

I'm sure the fact that I am usually listening to George Harrison on my iPod enhances these sensations. When I first started these walks, I would listen to other music, but the juxtaposition was often too unpleasant: the whining of the Buzzcocks, the melodrama of Puccini, the sensuality of Sade, the ostentation of Debussy and the breeziness of The Beach Boys all seemed wrong. Harrison just seemed to fit, so his songs combined with the magic of the forest cast a perfect spell.

As the silent echoes of ancient ancestors happily greet me in the breeze and remind me that not all of the wonders of the world can be seen, I listen:

> "What I feel I can't say...
> I can feel you here...
> There comes a time when most of us return here
> Brought back by our desire to be more perfect entities
> And living through a million years of trying"

As regret and melancholy start to insinuate themselves into my thoughts:

"Beware of sadness...
That is not what you are here for"

As I watch a Great White Egret rejoice in the miracle of flight:

"Give me love
Give me life
Give me peace on earth"

As an old man and a little girl walk ahead of me hand in hand:

"Love's our true concern"

As each day passes and I lose myself in each moment in the forest:

"What is life?
I Dig Love."

I never get lost in the forest, except transcendentally.

My walk usually ends with a swim at the Waalkgard Hotel. I quietly swim laps in a beloved pool surrounded by a lovely garden that overlooks Lake Victoria.

I inevitably trace my way back home, usually around the time the sun is setting.

Weekends are slightly different, of course, especially when Sister Charlotte comes to Bukoba.

When she is in Bukoba, Sister Charlotte is a wonderful friend and colleague to me. She often accompanies me shopping downtown on Saturdays. We must be quite a sight to see. She is calm and composure personified while I look like I just crawled out of the jungle with my wild hair and dusty boots.

Lee Anne McIlroy

On most Saturdays, I search for comfort food at the local luxury market called Fido Dido. Trying to satiate my cravings from home like a greedy, modern-day gatherer I scour the shelves for peanut butter and Nutella while Sister Charlotte seems to levitate in the corner with a halo, courtesy of the front window's reflection.

After mass on Sundays and after the Fathers all leave for their various Sunday obligations, Charlotte and I wrap ourselves in our *Kanga*, turn the volume up on some of her favorite traditional Congo hymns and join Irene and Asimwe in the chores of the day, washing our clothes and hanging them in the sun to dry, sweeping the porches and singing. Some Sundays, kids from the neighborhood come over, and we give them candy. Those are the rare days when DESIRE is a woman's domain.

Each evening I quickly shower and go to dinner at our dining hall. Like all of our meals, this is an engaging time. We talk about religion and politics without giving each other indigestion. Sometimes the fathers sing for me after dinner.

After dinner I retreat to my little "cottage" as Ocham calls it. My home here is a round building with two bedrooms, two bathrooms and granite floors. It is perfect! My bedroom has a desk and a very comfortable bed with a mosquito net and faux leopard blanket.

Before going in for the night, I take a few moments to appreciate the moon, and it is impossible to ignore the night sky. It looks as if Zeus had thrown goliath handfuls of diamonds into the air and they had frozen up there in the stratospheric lapis. In the background, I can hear the choir practice at the Rugambwa School down the road.

I always think of my dad, an astronomy aficionado, in these moments, of the many nights we have spent staring up at the sky while he explained that the stars are as innumerable as grains of sand on the beach and that we are mere particles in this vast, expansive cosmos with neither a beginning nor an end.

Each night's sky offers new wonders. A shooting star crosses a crescent moon. A pale pink coral reef of clouds encircles a full moon. A mysterious and silent presence—perhaps a satellite—flickers from out of the darkness of a gibbous moon.

After these brief observations of mere slivers of the cosmos, I go inside to talk or Skype with loved ones from home. Around 10:00 I climb into bed with a book, and I tuck the mosquito netting around my mattress with great care. Cricket lullabies drift through my curtains. Invariably I drop my book, barely able to keep my eyes open. As I drift off to sleep, I often imagine that I am carried up into the dark sky where from a distance I follow the sun moving slowly towards home, across this continent and then across the Atlantic Ocean towards the Americas and finally up over the Sierra Nevada Mountains to the Pacific Ocean where my childhood heart plays. The last thoughts of each day are of those I love. I imagine the sun sneaking in playfully to optimistically surprise and warm the faces of my daughters on the other side of the world. As another day ends for me, I surrender to sleep and know that for them, it is just beginning.

SEEING IN THE DARK

During the rainy seasons, time seemed to stop, and I sat alone in my obscurity. Literally. During the rainy seasons, there was often no electricity, and the rainstorms kept us all hostage. On days of heavy rain, the electric company either turned off the power or Mother Nature took it out herself with a bolt of lightning that would humble Thor. The two rainy seasons in Bukoba are unpredictably torrential, and many mornings I was awoken by rain pounding so loudly on my windows that it sounded like the birds were throwing rocks. I often peeked out the window thinking that I would see a bird only to see nothing but abstract images of mottled color mutating with the transparent molten water rolling down the glass. On many days, clouds came racing from Lake Victoria like darkened angels unleashing seemingly endless rivers. Often it was so extreme that the roads were closed, making it impossible to go to work. These days were long and lonely and dark.

I typically love the rain, but I also came to realize how much I love electricity. We were lucky in Bukoba with a relatively reliable source of power from TENESCO, a company that brings in electricity from Uganda. Only about 20% of Tanzanians have access to regular electricity, so I realized that my temporary lack of power was a ridiculous complaint.

On such days and nights, I was left to occupy myself. Typically, I would work on Wilson and read on my iPad, but once the charges had been drained, I was really left to my own devices.[8]

Monsignor had lent me a massive flashlight, or torch, as he called it. Between the torch and the votive candles I had purchased at the church bookstore, I had enough light to cast enough illumination to draw, play my ukulele or, more than anything, read.

Thanks to the fully stocked university library, I was able to check out an unlimited supply of books. During those rainstorms, I read books from the library on Swahili and Haya culture, Tanzanian history, various textbooks, poetry and literature. I also read the books that Rebecca had lent me. Still most alluring of all was the book that outlined an aquatic theory of human evolution.

I would read, then contemplate while staring out the windows. Read, contemplate, stare. Read. Contemplate. Stare. Then quite often I would fall into a trance-like nap, careful that the candles were blown out first.

My dreams during such naps were fantastical.

In one dream I was floating above the Bukoba Waterfalls in the body of a butterfly. In another, I was an ancient scribe studying constellation maps by candlelight. In yet another, I was a primitive human ancestor like the ones described in one of the books Rebecca had given me. In the dream, I am in the ocean shallows at night. My offspring is cradled in the nook of my left arm, and my right cheek rests on a nest of kelp. Beneath a full moon we are sleeping, with massive felines of prey pacing back and forth along the shore hoping to feast on us. In my dream, I open my left eye to make sure those

---

[8] Get it?!

potential predators are at a safe distance, unable to swim out to where we are. I close my left eye, embrace the baby and then fall back to sleep until I am awoken again, this time in my present physical form and by the girls at the Rugambwa School singing their evening hymns, signaling me that I am late for dinner.

It is quiet, except for the distant harmonies of the schoolgirls and the voice of the water. Besides mine, the only other heartbeats in the house are those of the lizards scaling the walls, their tiny stegosaurus bodies so weightless that I can't even hear the pitter patter of their little feet.

WHEN YOU BELIEVE
IN THINGS THAT YOU
DON'T UNDERSTAND

Ever since I arrived at DESIRE, and especially after the excruciating loneliness of Charlotte's absences and the long rainy season, I had been asking the fathers, begging really, for a pet.

"Can we get a cat, please?"

No.

"How about a chicken or two for eggs?"

No.

One day while Father Mgeni and I were driving home, I spotted a stray dog.

"Can we have that dog, *please*?" I pleaded.

"Sure," he said. "We can have him for dinner."

Father Mgeni comes from Iringe, an area reputed for eating just about any animal under the sun. The night I asked everyone what their favorite animal was, he had responded: "meat."

I was relentless about wanting a pet, and one day after begging for an animal, Father Joseph finally responded:

"If you get an animal then people will *really* think you are a witch!"

"What do you mean that they will *really* think I am a *witch*? What are you even talking about?" I asked.

Silence. And then The Look.

This was not the first time, nor even the second time in my life, I had been called a witch. And I don't even include the times when my ex-husband called me one by curiously mispronouncing the first sound by using a voiced bilabial stop.

Even my brothers think I am a witch. I blame my paternal grandmother for this reputation in the family. She was one of the most superstitious people I have ever met anywhere in the world. Not only did she claim to be a witch, when I was eight-years old, she declared that I was one too. She had an uncanny ability to read my thoughts and always carried a tiny ball made out of Wonder Bread much like the ancestor stones used in West Africa to speak to long-dead relatives. My Nana called her ancestor stone "pookie."

My Nana also loved animals and believed in animal spirits. She was convinced that the one-legged sparrow that showed up in her backyard one day shortly after my grandpa passed away carried his soul. Toward the end of her life, my dad discovered a bowl of food outside of her front door. She fibbed when she said she was feeding a cat; we later found out that it was a skunk. She often told me to never turn away an animal.

"If an animal shows up at your door, take care of it. You never know who it might be."

Her beliefs were so strong that even now when my brothers and I dream about her, we talk about her "visits." We never say that we dream about her; we really feel that she has been there with us. Sometimes my brother Neal even gets a little jealous if she "visits" me more than him. I tell him that it's not my fault that she likes me best.

One of the many superstitions I inherited from my Nana was that you should always be careful about who cuts your hair and what happens to that hair once it is cut. Nana explained that curses could be placed by just using a strand of hair. Although I rationally knew this wasn't true, the advice stuck and has manifested into one of my many bizarre idiosyncrasies: I kept every strand of hair that was ever cut off my daughters' heads well into their teen-aged years just in case. Instead of having the hairdresser sweep those precious locks of DNA away to do who knows what with, I would ask for it back, carrying it home in a special bag to bury in a safe place.

Maybe this is why my daughters wear their hair long. You can imagine how traumatizing this must have been for them.

I have also kept all of their lost baby teeth and excised wisdom molars. They rest safely in a special ceramic vessel. You never can be too careful.

After Father Joseph's concern about my reputation in the community I told him about these strange rituals. He responded, "That's not so strange. And let's not forget about fingernail clippings!"

As in every culture, Tanzania has a variety of super-stitions: Hooting owls are bad omens, as are snakes. In conversations along coastal regions, water *djinnis* and spirits surface like sprites. In Dar es Salaam there is a spirit pur-ported to be under the main bridge leading to Kipopera Beach, and cemeteries are often the sacred places for rituals. Traditional healers abound in Bukoba, and the Kagera region is renowned for medicinal plants and herbs.

Almost ashamedly, Ocham didn't seem to like to talk about superstitions. "I am embarrassed by it, actually," he told me one day at tea.

He didn't seem to believe me when I told him about American superstitions, how there are no thirteenth floors in American buildings, how a studio in Hollywood is not used because it is believed to be haunted, about breaking mirrors, splitting wishbones, knocking on wood and avoiding opening umbrellas indoors or walking under ladders. It takes hours of conversation and companionship before Ocham accepts that I hold beliefs about ancestors and ghosts. He, like most people close to me, is utterly repulsed by my confession about collecting my children's teeth and hair.

When I asked Ocham what Father Joseph might have meant about me being a witch, he shrugged his shoulders but also uncharacteristically avoided looking me straight in the eye.

So, I asked Father Joseph again and pressed him about his comment about people thinking I might be a witch if I got a pet:

"What do you mean, they will *really* think I am a witch?"

He eventually answered in one of his catch phrases.

"Think about it."

So, I did.

Usually, it is my intuition that inspires people to think I have supernatural skills: my brother David calls me the human lie detector, and The Man I Love thinks I can read his mind. However, there are other philosophies and cultures that value intuition as a legitimate source of knowledge, so I needed to think beyond that.

After careful thought and reflection, I eventually compiled a list of several possible signs that might associate me with witchcraft not only in Tanzania but back home as well. I came to see why Father Joseph didn't want me to add to that list and why my incessant requests for an animal had gone ignored, at least by humans.

Here is my list of the Top Ten reasons why I might be perceived as a witch in East Africa and elsewhere:

10.) My level of independence: Historically, those accused of being witches are single women, often of a certain age, and I just recently fell into that category. Financially independent and successful women who live on their own are often accused of sorcery to explain their success. How else could a woman possibly survive without a male benefactor? In Tanzania, it is not uncommon or even considered rude for Tanzanians to ask a woman about her marital status.

"Are you married?"

"No."

"Why not?"

I responded in several ways, from the truth to the fabricated. I sometimes said that my husband was dead, but stopped using that most socially acceptable reply here because of the bad energy I was invoking.

9.) My appreciation for witches and traditional healers: I have been known to concoct herbal remedies and teas and to consult homeopaths in addition to medical scientists. Because the area around Bukoba is renowned for its medicinal herbs, I visited some of the local herbal shops.

8.) My sunscreen: I am an extremely fair-skinned woman living one degree south of the Equator, so I need strong sunscreen. Throughout my life, the best sunscreen has been zinc oxide, and although the tubes I have brought with me from California claim to be "clear" and "invisible," the precious substance still leaves delicate trails of white across my face.

7) My hair color: As a child I had been an olive-skinned, raven-haired elf. By my teens, my skin was fair and freckled, and my hair was auburn. While my best friend's hair turned to golden blonde in the summer sun and ocean, mine turned orange. I started dying it black, and then dark brown until I finally gave up because I loved spending time in the ocean, and the sun and the salt water washed that dye away faster than you can

say Raggedy Ann. Resistance was futile. But I still wished I looked different, not just so that I might have beautiful hair, but because redheads—in just about every culture—get a bad rap. Recessive traits like red hair often come in pairs, and redheads are more likely than other people to be left-handed, which leads me to the next reason I might be considered a witch.

6. My left hand: My preference for using my left hand for writing was a consistent source of questioning and commentary in Tanzania.

"What is the logic of that?" or "Why are you doing that?" were the most common questions. Even the logical and refined Felix remarked:

"Be careful, people here will think you are bewitched."

Left-handedness is another remarkable abnormality in Tanzania. Hardly anyone uses their left hand here. During possibly the most boring experience of my entire life, "invigilating" (moderating) exams (an excruciatingly tedious task to which Ocham assigned me), I walked around a lecture hall for three hours with nothing to do but observe the students. During quite possibly the slowest one hundred and eighty minutes ever recorded, I counted all the students. Then I counted all the left-handed students. Out of over four hundred students, only six were left-handed even though lefties naturally make up 10% of the population. What had happened to the other thirty four students in that room who should have been writing with their left hand?

After the exam I asked the left-handed students about this. They explained that teachers had tried everything to get them to stop, and that some of their fellow left-handers had been able to transition. When I asked this particularly obstinate group how they had been able to retain this ability in a school system that does not tolerate it, they all said that they "just couldn't help it."

Although there are practical reasons for preferred handedness in Arabic culture so prominent on the coast, the main explanation I received in Bukoba as to why left-handedness was so discouraged in Tanzania was due to its association with "being bewitched." And once again, this association is not unique to Tanzania.

As I explained to Felix, writing with my left hand was not a matter of logic, it was just my genetic predisposition. In Tanzania more than anywhere else I have ever lived, what I see as an asset (my left-hand produces some very elegant writing and decent artistic renderings thanks to the lateralization with the right hemisphere of my brain) is often seen as a curse, a source of suspicion that something is not quite, well, not quite "right."[9]

5.) <u>My teeth</u>: My dominant recurring stress dream is, I'm told, not that uncommon. In this nightmare, my teeth start crumbling one by one. In the dream I panic, and as I try to hold my teeth in place, they turn into calcified dust. It is horrifying. I wake up and make sure that my teeth are intact. I have over-analyzed the symbolism of the dream and deciphered that the teeth represent permanence (for it is my permanent teeth that are crumbling in my dream), and my horror at losing them represents my fear of change, more specifically of growing old, even more specifically of death.

Because of this dream, which I recall having as a child even as my permanent teeth had just come in, I am a little (well, quite frankly more than a little) obsessed with teeth.

Because of my fixation with oral hygiene, I apparently have the teeth of a much younger woman, even by obsessive American standards. In Tanzania, the quality of my teeth and

---

[9] Get it?

the fact that I have all of them is even more prominent.

One day when Ocham was complaining of a toothache, he told me he would just go have it pulled. I almost fainted at the idea, once again my squeamishness a luxury most cannot afford.

Even some of my students who were half my age had fewer teeth than I do, so when a few people in Tanzania learned my age or that I had grown children they often responded, "But those *teeth!*"

So, this age-defying dental phenomenon, the result of thousands of dollars of childhood orthodontia and a lifetime of bi-annual exams, may be yet another cause for thinking I am a witch.

4.) My amulets: Because of my nostalgic and nesting tendencies, I had several small totems while I was in Tanzania. The trove of my daughters' teeth back home was just the tip of the iceberg. I left those precious calcium pearls at home, but I had brought some talismans from home that, although meaningful to me, may have seemed suspicious to others.

The week before I left for Tanzania I met with my friend Hue, a Buddhist nun. She gave me several tiny jade Buddhas on red string and a lovely black silk fan that says, in Vietnamese, "In One Hundred Years Your Hair Will Be Gray, But Your Soul Will Live Forever." Although misleading—because I will do everything in my power to fight the gray hair—the message is very special. The black fan is not only a thoughtful, but a practical gift: in the sweltering heat of the Swahili coast I carried it everywhere and used it to cool myself. The strange script on the fan caused some suspicion, but the main problem was that it looked an awful lot like a mythical, vengeful creature from Zanzibar called *Popobawa*, which means "bat wing."

Another amulet was a necklace, a gold crab (for Cancer,

my sun sign) dangling from a chain, once given to my mom by my dad. The day before I left for Tanzania, my mom placed it around my neck and said not to take it off until I came back safely, so I always wore it. There are two problems with this amulet: 1.) it seems peculiar to be wearing a crab and 2.) the crab, a dangling critter around my neck, looks an awful lot like a spider.

A week before I came to Tanzania, a group of fellow moms met me at a memorial playground we had established years before for a beloved teacher who had passed away too young. At this farewell, I thanked the women for all of the love and support they had offered during the challenging years of being a single mother. I wanted to honor the years we had spent together as a new chapter began for me. They all brought gifts, many of them little stones with words of encouragement engraved on them as well as tiny *milagros*.

When Father Joseph said that if I got a pet, people would *really* think I was a witch, I think the "people" he was referring to most were Asimwe and Doreen. Asimwe and Doreen had each been in my cottage and seen this assortment of trinkets. I arranged these little treasures in varying configurations throughout my time in Tanzania for good luck. Sometimes I placed them all in a circle around my bed. Sometimes I placed them inside the window sills around the house. I once placed them all underneath my pillow along with the jade Buddhas. After following Father Joseph's advice to "think about it," I could see how this might also seem a little suspicious.

3.) <u>My love of water</u>: In Tanzania there are plenty of stories about sea *djinnis* and bewitched underwater towns. My absolute love for swimming wherever and whenever I could is "unusual" as one Tanzanian friend politely put it.

Ocham was more direct, by calling me, yet again "weird" (although later he asked me to teach him and his kids). My

near daily swims at the Waalkgard pool bordered on com-
pulsive. This activity combined with the myriad beliefs about
water being a supernatural realm may have contributed to
what I was beginning to see was a practical certainty that I
was a witch.

2.) Yoga: One Sunday, someone who worked at DESIRE asked
me if I was a Muslim. When I told her that I was not, she asked
me about my prayer rug. I realized that a view of me in
extended child's pose would look much like a morning prayer
to Mecca. I explained to her that it was actually a yoga mat.
When I told her about yoga and meditation, she asked me
what kind of religion that was. When I described the poses and
their animal names, it sounded like the practice of shapeshifting. The more I tried in vain to explain it articulately, the more
suspiciously she looked at me. As it turns out, she was not the
only one concerned about what I was doing on that spongy
prayer rug, another going-away gift from my mom.

Some of the neighborhood children had the sometimes
adorable, sometimes intrusive habit of spying on me by
peeking over the fence and looking in through my open front
door. Sometimes this happened as I was shapeshifting into a
lizard, a tree, a dolphin, a cat, a dog, a happy baby. If they were
able to hear the strange breathing from the back of my throat,
I'm sure those kids were doubly intrigued. I can only imagine
what those strange contorted poses of me while sweating and
breathing strangely looked like.

1.) My interactions with other animals: Historically and cross-
culturally, witches are often associated with animal "familiars."
I realized that it was not simply my request to keep animals as
pets nor my avoidance of eating them that contributed to my
possible reputation as a witch in pursuit of animal familiars.
More than any other characteristic associated with witchcraft,

the interactions that I had with animals—particularly my tendency to talk to them—had at times also seemed a little suspicious.

The first instance I could recall occurred one Saturday morning in the dining area. We ate and kept the food in a separate bungalow, a cottage like the rest of the houses with windows all along the octagonal perimeter. On one particular morning I went in for my tea and found that a bird had inadvertently flown in and could not escape. I opened all the windows so that the bird could fly free. It kept flitting about elsewhere, unable to navigate out. I said in Swahili, "*kuruka bure.*"

Fly free.

I approached the bird, and to my surprise it stood still and let me pick it up. I walked outside and un-cupped my hand, but the bird stayed there for a moment, just long enough for me to compliment its beautiful markings. It was also long enough for someone to see me talking to a bird who was sitting tamely in my hand before flying safely off.

Another afternoon while at work, I opened up my office door to find a massive black bull with Texas-sized longhorns standing right at my door. Having apparently gotten lost, he just stood there and stared at me. I laughed and then, just to be polite, asked him where he'd come from and what he was doing here. I offered him a few words of welcome, then asked politely if he would step aside a bit so that I could pass. I started to move forward. He kindly stepped aside to let me pass, and I headed down to the administration block where I saw Charles standing near the flagpole. He had been watching the entire interaction. As I walked towards him a few moments later he said, "Ah, Lee. I see you've made a new friend."

"Yes!" I answered and smiled.

"You must be careful," Charles warned.

"Oh, I know—I won't get too close," I tried to reassure him.

"That's not what I'm talking about," he said.

"Oh, you mean I have to be careful about how it looks if I'm talking to a giant black cow that just happens to be hanging out in front of my office?" I joked.

He chuckled and shook his head.

Another instance happened while I was away from Bukoba and teaching a group of high school students at a beachfront summer camp for teenagers just outside of Dar es Salaam.

The students and I were all walking along the beach when we came upon a group of fishermen and their impressive haul. Thousands of fish thrashed and flickered about in the sand, still entrapped in the giant nets. As the fishermen sorted through the catch, they discarded all matter of unwanted collateral damage—seaweed, trash, and even a puffer fish that had expanded into a perfect globe with tiny spikes—onto the sand. A few local children had taken the pufferfish and were using it as a soccer ball. I stopped them and told them the fish was still alive. They balked. I could see its tiny mouth, also a perfect circle, pursed in tiny gasping kisses.

I bent down and picked up the pufferfish, looking directly into its eyes. "You're safe now," I said and waded up to my waist in the water. I placed the fish delicately in, or rather on, the ocean. Because of all the air, the poor fish rolled over onto its back, staying there for eternal seconds upside down bobbing along the water. The kids on the beach laughed. And then...within about one minute, the fish ever so slowly deflated, turned right side up and quietly submerged into the water then swam gracefully away.

"*Uchawi*," whispered one child.

Magic.

There were recurring examples of me treating animals like humans, like consorts. The parrot at the Waalkgard, Kusiku, would stick his head out of the cage whenever I was in the lobby. He craned his neck out for me to scratch and pet him like a kitten. Father Mgeni shuddered when I did not scare over snakes. The nuns in Mwanza were flummoxed when I challenged them about throwing rocks at the mischievous monkeys in their yard. Those who laughed so hard at me the night of the Bishop's party were laughing partly, I later found out, because I had been *speaking* to the goat in my effort to calm her.

But there was one incident, one wonderful interaction that would absolutely seal my identity as, if not a sorceress, at least a conjurer.

From time to time over the summer break, I would have to leave Bukoba to work in other parts of the country. During one such absence, and after my barrage of requests for a pet, the fathers woke up one morning to find a magnificent black and speckled dog sleeping on my porch. The guards chased the dog away, but each night—for three nights—the dog returned and curled up at my front door. They tried to chase him away with an intensified interest the day I returned, but it was pointless. I had just arrived and made myself a cup of tea when I saw the flash of a black tail across the courtyard.

"Is that a dog?!!" I asked as I jumped up like a child on Christmas morning. Everyone looked at me with a slight look of defeat.

I ran into the courtyard.

The dog ran straight into my arms.

And the simple arrival of this animal who would offer me unwavering companionship and protection throughout the rest of my time in Bukoba reminded me why I, too, believe in magic.

A DOG WITH NO NAME

"Can I keep him?" I asked Father Charles because Father Mgeni was away in Mwanza.

"I have no choice, Lee," he said, breaking my heart.

"Please?" I begged like a child just as I had been begging for a pet practically since the day I arrived. I had misunderstood Father Charles' answer.

"It is out of my hands, Lee. God has spoken. He is yours."

Father Charles explained that during the last three nights of my absence, this dog who looked like a cross between a hyena and a German Shepherd, had just appeared one day and went straight to my front porch. The security guards chased him away every morning, but he returned late each night.

The dog, as magnificent as I think he is, needed a little (actually a lot) of TLC. He was so emaciated that his ribs were visible, even through his thick coat. He had slashes across his face and such a colony of juicy ticks that I didn't have any idea how he could be so seemingly happy. He wagged his tail generously and made eye contact with no ambitions of being the Alpha Dog. He let me clean him up, even allowing me to treat his wounds.

The fathers gave me very specific rules about the dog. Only

Father Joseph seemed to be happy about the new arrival, having several times told me where I could go to buy a puppy if I wanted.

"It must be chained up when you're not here."

"It can't go inside the house."

"It's your responsibility."

"Eh hem, you mean 'he,'" I corrected.

When they asked me what I wanted to name him, I offered, unoriginally:

"How about 'Simba'?"

Lion.

"Why do you want to give him such a ferocious name? He might live up to it. No, that is not a good name."

I decided to call him "Twiga" because Monsignor admired the politeness of giraffes and also because this dog was so skinny and knock-kneed. And he more than lived up to this second name.

But after about a week, I noticed that everyone was calling him "Simba" after all.

"You can't call a dog 'Twiga,'" said Father Mgeni. "He needs a strong name."

I have never known a gentler, more loyal dog. I was able to negotiate one rule, and we did not keep him chained up. Simba followed me wherever I went. If I walked to the corner store, he came along. If I was in the dining room, he waited on the porch. When I was home, he was resting outside the window of whatever room I was in. At sunset I would sit next to him on the front porch looking out over Lake Victoria with my arm draped around his neck and his head resting on my shoulder. The children who spied on us or passed by on their way home from school laughed and called out, "*Mzungu na umbwa.*"

White person and dog.

During the first rainstorm after Simba's arrival, I woke up

in the middle of the night, worried about him. I found him sopping wet outside my bedroom window and then quickly put together a makeshift doghouse out of an old table I had salvaged from the Waalkgaard and some old blankets. I looked across the courtyard to see Father Joseph standing on his porch, watching over us through the sheets of rain. I think that he had also been worried about Simba.

The night of the second rainstorm (and every rainstorm after that) I snuck Simba into my cottage where I had placed some blankets next to my bed for him. Awoken often by thunder and lightning, I would look over at him. His eyes often looked worried, and his ears were back. I rubbed his thick fur as I told him there was nothing to worry about, talking to myself as much as to him. Eventually we both fell back asleep, often with my hand still resting on his head.

Among my circle in Bukoba, only I seemed to marvel that this animal had arrived so mysteriously and auspiciously, a perfect response to my request for a pet. For everyone else, this just seemed like the most natural thing in the world.

When I told Ocham about my new friend and his fortuitous arrival, he shrugged and smiled. "Ah, a gift from the ancestors!"

And every evening on the front porch and every stormy night with Simba snuggled up next to me, that is exactly what he felt like.

HERE COMES THE FLOOD

One afternoon, a fellow classmate of Pauline's walked into my office and asked if he could discuss his research project with me. Honored, I put down my book and gave him my full attention.

"It's a little...sensitive," Patrick worried.

I assured him that there was no need to be embarrassed around me, so he continued:

"I want to write about the lack of health and counseling services for teen-age female students in Tanzania and the impact this has on their education."

I told him that sounded good but recommended that he might want to be a little more specific.

"Well, that's exactly why I wanted to talk to you," he stated.

Patrick wanted to do research on institutional responses to "possession of evil spirits" among female teen-aged students in Tanzanian public schools. Suddenly I understood Patrick's discomfort around me. Although I knew it was an awkward cross- gender topic of conversation, I said:

"Patrick, I just want to be sure that we both know what we are talking about here. We are talking about menstruation, right?"

He looked down, but bravely said, "Yes. That's what I was thinking."

The history of female "possession" by "his Satanic Majesty" has a long history in Tanzania. One young female inhabitant of Zanzibar in the late 19th century wrote:

"Adults...are frequently possessed, although far oftenest the women. The outer signs are cramps, loss of appetite, listlessness, a partiality for dark rooms, and like morbid symptoms."

I had heard about this phenomenon that very first week in Kilwa. The teachers there told me that often (actually about once a month) some girls would suddenly become "possessed" during class. This possession manifested in all variations of histrionics: crying, running out of the classroom, screaming, and rolling on the floor.

"The way we deal with this," one teacher told me "is to throw light stones at the girl. Sometimes that takes care of it."

Um, not with my daughters it wouldn't. Unless those light stones were made out of chocolate, and I was throwing them into their mouths.

It is hard being the parent of a teen-aged girl. Even harder than that is being the parent of two teen-aged girls. Even harder still, is being a teenaged girl anywhere in the world and especially in places like Tanzania where access to feminine hygiene products and open discussion about the borderline schizophrenic psychobiology of puberty is limited.

When Patrick asked me, with a true desire to help his students, what we do in my country, I told him about some of the resources my daughters had. They had attended one of the best public-school districts in California, and again I was reminded of how fortunate we have been, and I realized that this was not a representative American experience.

In fifth grade, my daughters began their formal Health Education and preparation for the impending changes in their bodies with a sweet little film called "Just Around The Corner" which was a huge improvement to the campy "It's Wonderful Being a Girl" from my childhood days.

Parents like me had to sign a permission slip to allow our children to watch the movie, and we even had the opportunity to view it beforehand. I did. It was hilariously straightforward with an accompanying and catchy song that haunted me for days.

When the day came for my daughters to watch the film, the female students were separated from the boys, and the whole affair was supervised by the school nurse. For reasons I couldn't understand, some of the other parents (none of whom watched the movie with me during the parental screening) refused to sign the permission forms. There wasn't anything in that movie or the accompanying literature that my daughters had not also heard already from me. My daughters didn't seem affected much at all by the film. We talked about it and sang the "Just Around The Corner" song sarcastically. My daughters even joked around. My daughter Alex's April Fool's antics that year included her putting drops of red food coloring in the toilet and telling me she had "turned the corner."

Ha. Ha.

Middle school is where it got more intense, and karma paid Alex back for her little joke. As part of the health curriculum, topics extended beyond the physical and emotional changes associated with the developing reproductive system. A very pregnant and direct teacher discussed the reproductive organs, all the places they could go, all the diseases they could transmit, and all the ways to avoid pregnancy. Poor Alex, she came home every day with a headache.

"All I keep thinking, Mom, is that my teacher has probably done all those things. Ew."

But middle school was also where some of the really outstanding resources became available to my daughters, resources that are not available in Bukoba nor in many American schools for that matter. The school counselors organized "Girls Night Out," events that continued throughout high school: self-defense workshops, authors' visits, rap sessions, sporting events, movie nights, pool parties. These events encouraged female solidarity and mutual support. The counselors were also available for one-on-one appointments to all students as they transitioned through the challenges of rapidly changing bodies and lives.

My daughters' middle school also had a peer mentorship program in which my daughters participated, negotiating disagreements, lending a compassionate ear, challenging bullies. The best part about this was that the problems of fellow students put my daughters' own personal problems into context and perspective.

I also told Patrick that in the school districts where I live and work in California, women of all ages have access to a whole possibility of taxable feminine hygiene products. Entire aisles at the grocery store are stockpiled with such a variety that on more than one occasion I have had to assist a husband, boyfriend or father sent out on the unenviable errand of buying supplies for his partner, wife, girlfriend or daughter who was probably at home dealing with "cramps...and like morbid symptoms." Knowing the dreadful consequences of coming home with the wrong product, they often stare terrified at the rows of tampons and pads in different sizes, shapes, colors and specialties. Other customers and I offer advice. Usually I also suggest that they bring home some ice cream or a heating pack for that extra special touch.

After I told Patrick about all of these resources, I agreed with him about the merits of his research proposal to improve access to resources for young girls in Tanzania. He was teaching nearby in a local school where he watched helplessly as his students showed "signs of possession," and he wanted to help. I offered him some suggestions in terms of research and welcomed him back anytime. As he left, I realized I had not told him an important truth: All of the support and resources in the world may still be unable to stop a young woman from feeling "possessed."

Despite all of the resources available to my daughters, there were times when I received a desperate phone call or a text message announcing their periods ("BLOOOOD IN THE DUNGEON!") and pleading for strange combinations: a Snickers and a Midol, a burrito and an ice compress, a taco and a tampon. These requests (more like demands from a deranged super villain) are invariably accompanied by a very urgent need for aggressive snuggling. I gave up many, many hours to gather the requested items and then spend long afternoons napping in teen-aged embraces that seemed more like mauling. My daughters' red manes barely covered their wild eyes, their fingernails almost perforating my flesh at times. Even the stockpile of supplies and the cuddling was sometimes just barely enough to keep them calm.

And at those moments, I may have wanted to throw not just tiny, but possibly large and sharp, rocks at my daughters.

But I didn't because I was one of the few mothers who was lucky enough to have the luxury of time for such patience. Also, because I had a multi-generational herd of related females who helped me in the raising of the offspring. And, also, because I remembered exactly how it feels.

When I was about thirteen, one afternoon I was just rolling around demonically on the floor of our living room crying hysterically. My poor, sweet mother looked down at me with the exact expression with which she would look at me years later when I went through childbirth, a look of absolute and vicarious pain.

"What's wrong, sweetheart?" she plaintively cried.

"I DON'T KNOW!" I screamed.

And, honestly, I didn't.

Nothing was really wrong, except *everything* felt wrong. I looked gangly and awkward. A sleeping dragon had awoken inside me unleashing an army of hormones through its fiery breath. My face was full of pimples. I had to say good-bye forever to a childhood that I loved. And most dominatingly overwhelming, some "force" seemed to be hijacking my body.

And really, when you feel like this, what you really need to do is yell and scream and cry and run around or roll on the floor instead of having to sit quietly in a classroom. And people will look at you like you are possessed. And you yourself may feel that you are.

And this is why, along with my luxury of time and support of the herd, I was able to be so attentive to my own daughters during what to outsiders (usually men) seemed like atrocious and unacceptable behavior.

Because of this, in addition to looking at research and quantitative factors to improve the conditions of young women in Tanzania, I also shared with Patrick my two go-to panaceas for qualitative, albeit temporary, improvement of a young woman's life during those challenging days: chocolate and hoodies.

In cases where I didn't have the time or the patience for the best response to my daughters' monthly meltdowns, access to chocolate, even if just one piece, has proven an excellent quick fix. Also, a soft sweatshirt with a hood, preferably slightly worn-out and hideous-looking (to repel males) will provide the best wardrobe choice. Something about putting that hood on and hiding inside the warm cocoon of fleecy cotton comfort is very soothing, especially if coupled with chocolate.

Of course, there are many traditional approaches to

guiding a pubescent female student through life, and throwing rocks at young girls is not *de riguer* in Tanzania. There are effective traditional approaches to dealing with the challenges of guiding girls into womanhood in Tanzania, and they seem to be shared privately.

Just as in California, there is great socioeconomic disparity among schools in this part of the world. I saw this inequity as I visited schools throughout Tanzania, and it looked a lot like the inequity among schools I visit back home. Of course, the public schools my daughters attended are not the same as public schools in other areas of California. Sending children to private schools in California is mostly an option for the wealthy or the religious. In Tanzania, many parents, regardless of socio-economic status or religion, try to get enough money together to send their children to private schools. This is why Ocham and Pauline's children are away at boarding school. Even the best public schools in Tanzania cannot compare to the private schools.

This difference between the public and private school system, particularly as it pertains to females, was most evident one very special and stormy Sunday when Father Charles was asked to fill in for the local parish priest to hold Mass at two local girls' schools. He graciously invited me to accompany him.

The first Mass was held in the grand hall of Cardinal Rugambwa Secondary School, the school just around the corner from us, a public girls' school with an excellent reputation. As Father Charles and I pulled up in his blue RAV4, the students surrounded the car. Father Charles was already in his Roman Collar and robe, and I was wearing my pink dress (which was looking even shabbier by then). I went into the giant hall which was transformed each Sunday into a church while Father Charles went into another area that served as a vestibule. He had a little traveling priest's sacristy from Italy—a small suitcase with Holy Water, communion wafers, and other priestly accessories.

The hall was absolutely filled with young female students of various ages and sizes. Known as one of the few public schools to welcome students with physical challenges, there were also quite a few students in wheelchairs and on crutches at The Rugambwa School. All of the students wore their uniforms, which had been cleaned for Sunday, but even still many of the garments, like my tattered and faded dress, were not in the best condition.

There was a relentless downpour that day, but as I watched the girls file into the hall, I noticed that very few had umbrellas or even coats. Instead, many of them held giant banana leaves above their heads to keep as dry as possible.

I sat towards the back, so that I could take in the congregation. As the Mass began, I was stunned to see the arrival of an altar boy in a room full of females. He and Father Charles were the only males in a room of hundreds, and they were both at the front leading us all. Hmpf.

And just when I could feel my brows furrow in frustration, the entire congregation erupted into a beautiful and pure song, a song I had heard from the distance at night when the school choir was practicing. A girl of about twelve dressed in a skirt that was losing its hem led us all in a song for the angels, and my heart melted. Father Charles started speaking, and the wind suddenly blew open the shutters letting in the deluge. The rain beat down in buckets until a few girls scrambled from their seats to bolt the shutters in place. The rain was so strong that it often drowned out Father Charles' homily, which was about education and love. The candles flickered in the draft. A final hymn emanated from the mouths of hundreds of young girls, heralding the end of Mass.

Father Charles and I stayed for a few minutes afterward to visit with the congregation. Some of the girls showed me their dormitories. These girls didn't have a lot. For sure, they weren't texting their mothers for comfort food, feminine products or aggressive snuggling although some of them told me it was their "time" and asked if I had any supplies. I was so ill-prepared that I didn't even have a single piece of chocolate.

I saw these girls almost every day as I walked past the school, but the image of them on that Sunday with their lovely voices drowning out the rain as it poured down is the one I will always cherish and remember.

As soon as we got in the car, my brow may have started to furrow again. The first thing Father Charles said was, "I have to see what I can do about getting one of the girls to serve at the altar next time." This was another moment when he seemed to read my mind.

The next stop was a private and expensive all-girls' boarding school just about a half a mile down a dirt (now mud) road situated on the top of the hill. This school had one of the most magnificent views of Bukoba, even rivaling that of the Waalkgard. Though less than a mile away from each other, the two schools Father Charles and I visited that day were worlds apart.

There were no broken windows or drafts in the room of the second school where Father Charles held Mass. With less than thirty students, the service was the modicum of organization: one student had organized the room and altar, another was responsible for collecting and distributing the generous offering, and another helped with communion. I sat in the back, observing all of this. The room was immaculate. The view was awe-inspiring. It was warm and dry. These young girls, like my daughters, were the lucky ones. As the rain raged outside, I began to observe the clothing of these students and was thunderstruck by the casualness and perfection of their attire: instead of scratchy and uncomfortable uniforms, all but three of the girls were wearing some type of hoodie.

Throughout my time in Tanzania, I shared some of these observations with Patrick. He did some great research, and I am hopeful that some enhanced support for young women will come to the school where he teaches. I appreciated that he thought that I could offer some insight into his research, and I realized that it was my age and life experience more than anything that led him to me.

In California, my waning youth is a disadvantage. In Tanzania, it is an advantage. With my age and life experience come valuable life lessons. And on one day early in August, I was able to successfully apply that knowledge to a child who was not my own.

During the break from classes in Bukoba, Rebecca sent me to work at an English summer camp for high school students. As part of the camp, I was helping to teach students how to swim. I knew it would be a challenge on one particular day because when I walked into the room where all the girls were staying, it looked like an under-aged harem: they were all lying around, aggressively snuggling, holding their stomachs and showing a "partiality for dark rooms."

Luckily, I had brought a lot of chocolate and Midol.

I convinced most of the girls to get in the pool, assuring them that the water always makes me feel better. I gave some tired lecture about how the ocean tides and ours are controlled by the moon. Somehow it worked, and before I knew it, most of them were, albeit begrudgingly, in the water.

They were making excellent progress, submerging their heads and practicing their breathing. Things were going great. Until. Until one of the girls accidentally swallowed water, struggling with when to hold her breath and when to breathe. She thrashed in the water, gasping heavily like a fish on land.

She couldn't catch her breath. She started to hyperventilate. And everyone around her in the pool, recognizing the fomenting "possession," immediately dispersed.

All of my maternal training and personal experience had prepared me for this one moment in time, when for once, I said and did exactly the right thing.

While everyone cleared away, I moved closer, demonstrating exaggerated and deep breaths. "Breathe," I said as I modeled deep inhales and exhales.

I understood. She was scared. The water that she inhaled or swallowed had disrupted an already tenuous physical equilibrium, and at that moment it all was spinning out of control. And she was probably embarrassed. Like me at that age (possibly even now) she was a little awkward. She hadn't blossomed as gracefully as some of the other girls, and sometimes they didn't include her in their songs and secrets. I really did understand although I didn't know the specific challenges that she was facing in her own life.

Following my breathing technique, her breath became a little more controlled, but then she started trembling. I hugged her. She clutched me so tightly that I could feel that familiar sensation of fingernails digging into my sides and threatening to perforate my flesh. Her tears fell so hard that they rolled down my shoulders and back, mixing with the drops of pool water dripping from my hair. I held her as tightly as she held me, hoping to "cast out the evil demons" of self-hatred and doubt, and I whispered these incantations:

> "Everything is going to be all right. I love you. You are beautiful."
>
> "Everything is going to be all right. I love you. You are beautiful."
>
> "Everything is going to be all right. I love you. You are beautiful."

"Everything is going to be all right. I love you. You are
    beautiful."
"Everything is going to be all right."

Then finally:

"It won't always feel like this."

The spell eventually worked. Slowly, her tears stopped,
and her breathing calmed. The vice-like grip loosened. Sensing
that the "demons" had dispersed, some of the other girls came
back, coaxing her sweetly back into the water, calling out a
final incantation of their own for good measure.
"Don't give up."
Calmed and reassured, she reluctantly returned to the
water still holding my hand. Slowly she re-immersed herself.
Eventually, she let go of my hand and shimmied away
awkwardly like a tadpole, completely powerless over the
inescapable and irreversible transformations that awaited.

KINDRED SPIRITS

There weren't a lot of Westerners around Bukoba, so when one day I saw a white woman walking alone on the road, miles away from anywhere, I was intrigued.

That first time I saw her I was driving with the fathers out towards the hospital near Kemondo, and there she was. In the middle of nowhere, walking alone.

The next time I saw her a few weeks later, it was during a downpour. Again, I was in a car with Father Charles. She was getting on the back of a motorbike, unfazed by the deluge. She was soaking.

The third time I saw her, I was coming back from a walk, and spotted her near the corner store where I buy my water. I did what I normally do in this type of circumstance: I introduced myself.

Anna was from London, and despite her lovely glow of hip bohemia—a delicate nose piercing, vintage clothes, long brown hair, an open warmth and approachability—she speaks the anachronistic and prestigious version of English so respected around here. She sounds like a very happy and kind queen of England to me.

After a quick introduction, I gave her an open invitation to come for tea, pointing to my little cottage just down the road.

"How's this afternoon?" she asked.

"Perfect."

A few hours later, Anna and I were sitting on my porch sipping tea, Simba sitting happily at our feet. I learned that she was a volunteer coordinator for Volunteer Service Overseas (VSO), the largest international Non-Governmental Organization (NGO) in the world. She and her Tanzanian counterpart, Eve, supervised young volunteers from both England and Tanzania who worked in schools to help develop teaching aids and after-school clubs.

Like me, Anna had experienced some pretty wonderful things in Tanzania.

At twenty-eight, Anna had already worked for VSO in Kenya and England. Her blue eyes alighted no matter what the topic, and I have never met, and I mean this as a supreme compliment to her, such an unreserved Brit. She absolutely effused enthusiasm, energy and passion. She lived in a relatively remote village in Tanzania but explained that she came into Bukoba on the weekends for workshops or provisions. She often stays, conveniently as it turns out, at the Waalkgard Hotel.

Before we knew it, the sun had set, and I invited Anna (after checking with the fathers and the cooking staff) to stay for dinner. After dinner and exchanging phone numbers, I walked Anna to the gate of DESIRE where she hailed a motorcycle. I watched as she swung onto the back, like a cowgirl on a horse, and I could see her waving until the red brake lights of the motorcycle disappeared down the hill.

Over the weeks and months that followed, Anna called whenever she was in town. She left messages like "Do you fancy a lunch at the Waalkgard?" or "Would you care to join me and Eve for dinner?" Sometimes she spent the night in the cottage with me, sleeping in Sister Charlotte's room when she was not here.

Our friendship was sealed quickly through our shared experience as foreigners, temporary immigrants who would never be able to fully share this experience with our families and friends back home. We both knew that no matter how many pictures we shared or how many stories we told, most of our loved ones back home would never fully understand how truly lovely Tanzania is nor how truly loving Tanzanians had been to us. We knew that the skewed and distorted negative single narrative of Africa perpetuated by other, more influential, foreigners would remain ingrained.

During some of our conversations, we lambasted some of the movies (cue the wealthy white woman with a farm in Africa who will be the salvation to the unfortunate locals), the books ("the cannibal natives would boil us in a pot and eat us"), the endless commercials to raise money for the needy (have you ever seen one without an emaciated African child, often swarming with flies?) and even songs ("And there won't be snow in Africa...where nothing ever grows. No rain nor rivers flow...spare a thought for the deprived"). It's all too much.

One of our main frustrations is that such depictions present such an ultimately dehumanizing and incomplete image of an apparently homogeneous "Africa," and this was all entirely, well, inaccurate. Africa is a huge continent with fifty four very different countries each with different languages, religions, cultures and histories. Many of our conversations not only included how people in our countries had been influenced by such depictions; we also noticed how much our Tanzanian friends had been as well.

Anna and I bonded quickly and thoroughly over these shared experiences and the shared perspective that there was indeed a lot to learn from our counterparts. Most likely what we learned would not be fully accepted back home because it contradicts what most people from our home countries see in movies and on television, much like Plato's Allegory of the Cave.

Whenever Anna came to town, we would stroll the streets of Bukoba or eat lunch in the garden of the Waalkgard or the Kolping Hotel just across the street where we spent one entire afternoon just sitting there and watching the birds.

"Do you think you've changed since you've been here?" Anna asked as we admired the creature we called Dracula, a black bird with a massive crimson underwing.

"Yes!" I did not hesitate in my answer.

"Me, too," she said, and then paused. "But I'm not exactly sure how."

"Me neither."

Then we sat there silently for about a half an hour.

Whenever we were apart, people often confused us for one another although we don't look anything alike except for our skin color, and we are almost a generation apart in age.

Sometimes when we were together people thought Anna was my sister; others thought she was my daughter.

"Well, we are both free spirits," she said one day, as we remarked at the confusion, neither of our egos caring whether or not we could be easily distinguished from one another.

Anna also loved to swim, and we often swam together. Some afternoons we drifted on the surface of the pool on round lifesavers, the water so glassy that our reflections made it look like four sets of hands instead of two. We floated endlessly in the pool at the Waalkgard, our cloaks of self melting away like ice cream in August. The edges of our reflections rippled outward in concentric circles, blending together, then finally disappearing along with the miniscule atoms of pool water that eventually and invisibly evaporated into the magnitude of the sky.

COLONIES

Knowing my sensitivity toward animals, Monsignor asked me one day if I ever killed mosquitoes.

"Not if I can help it," I told him.

But I *did* admit to my childhood insect massacre and collection. As he did so often during those months, Monsignor just shook his head and offered an amused laugh.

Before my interest in insects resulted in my killing, labeling and putting them on display during my peculiar tween years, I was one of those kids who rescued bugs drowning in the swimming pool, who moved snails out of footpaths on rainy mornings so they wouldn't get stepped on, who carried spiders outside to spare them the wrath of some arachnophobe.

And now I am the kind of woman who does the same. Such acts are not so much a testament to any kind-heartedness as they are to the depths of belief in *jiva*: you never know who those insects and spiders might be.

Besides I actually like these tiny creatures, and it is a good thing too because there are a lot of them in Bukoba.

In fact, insects outnumber humans all over the world, and they have existed long before we were even a species and will probably outlive us all. Often when we try to obliterate them from our lives, we hurt ourselves more than we hurt them (to wit: pesticides). As we futilely try to annihilate them, I imagine that they are, especially the unstoppable cockroach, laughing at us in their tiny 78-rpm voices: hahaheeheehoho.

The most notorious insect in Bukoba, and probably around the world, is the mosquito. Monsignor is right to kill any that fly across his path (and I probably would be wise to as well): They kill. They have killed loved ones of so many people I met in Bukoba, prompting many of them who were children when parents or siblings died of malaria to imagine that the insect was a giant animal, bigger than a lion, because it was able to kill so easily and quickly. Mosquitoes are definitely the most insidious insects here, but they are not without competition for peskiness or fascination.

Probably the most visibly ubiquitous insects in Bukoba are the irritating Lake Flies. They make you bow down before them because the only way to penetrate a Lake Fly wall is to duck and walk through. If you take HMV Victoria across the Lake from Mwanza, you will definitely encounter the power of the Lake Fly. They cover the walls of the ship. When you enter the harbor, even just to buy a ticket, you will inevitably either walk into or observe a low-lying cloud of Lake Flies. If you are walking along the lake, or even at the bottom of the hill, be forewarned that you may inadvertently find yourself suddenly caught in a swarm, and you will bend at the waist and possibly kneel down to avoid them in an unintentional (but I am sure, much appreciated) curtsy to the Lake Flies. They may interfere with your lakeside candlelight dinner. They may interrupt a relaxing stroll. They abound. They rule this place. And you will, at some point or another, bow down before them.

One day at work I was waiting for Ocham outside, and I looked down at the ground. For a second I thought the ground was moving until I looked closely to see hundreds of ants busily working and crisscrossing paths. They were each about an inch long. Ocham came along, thoughtlessly stomping out entire teams. When I groaned, he said:

"Do you know what those monsters did to me yesterday?"

He then told me how some fire ants had silently crawled on him and climbed up his legs while he was standing near the banana trees in order to make a cell phone call. By the time he returned to his office he was in so much pain that he had to lock the door, tear off of his "trousers," jumping around like a flea. That's how much power those tiny insects have: they can strip a high-level administrator down to his birthday suit in his own office faster than a femme fatale.

I respect insects like ants because they have an excellent work ethic. They move things, they build things, and they help with the decomposition process, but there are just some insects I do not appreciate, and at the top of that list are tiny hellions called "jiggers." I am terrified of them. Jiggers (or sand fleas) are a serious threat to my arguably best physical asset: my feet. While some women are bestowed with long legs, voluptuous chests or symmetrical faces, Mother Nature granted me almost perfect feet. They are a dainty size 6 1/2 with high arches and delicate toes. Sand fleas like to burrow themselves into human flesh, usually feet, then lay pea-sized eggs that then hatch causing serious infection, swelling, ulceration, even gangrene or tetanus. Feet that have been jiggerized look painful and doomed. If sand fleas get into your feet, they can only be removed with a knife or a scalpel. I am terrified of them. Such is my terror of sand fleas that every night before bed, I slather my feet with Vaseline because that repels them and prevents them from burrowing in. Then I cover those feet with knee-high socks. Every week I scrub and soak my feet in rubbing alcohol just to make sure. One day when I did not recoil from a snake in our path, Father Mgeni asked me if there was any animal I was afraid of. The only one

I could think of was the sand flea.

Next on my list of insects that I do not appreciate are ordinary fleas and ticks for obvious reasons. Once Simba came into my life, I felt obligated to tell Monsignor of my policy change on manual insecticide. I washed hundreds of fleas off of him. If I saw or felt a tick on my beloved Simba—bloated and bulbous from gorging on his canine blood—I would pluck it off AND curse it. Karma be damned!

Perhaps the most well-known insect in Bukoba is the termite, or *tsenene*, which is roasted and eaten as a delicacy. *Tsenene* were the only snack sold at the Bukoba airport, and they can also be purchased from local vendors at the market. On a dare from Father Mgeni, I ate *tsenene* and found that they tasted a lot like nuts. One afternoon during the termite season a man and his son came to my door to ask if they could eat my *tsenene*. When I explained that I didn't have any, the man pointed to a termite nest out of which flew hundreds of flying termites. Of course, they could have my termites. The father and son spent the next hour collecting the emerging insects in mid-flight, with huge smiles across their faces.

Rebecca knew about the impact that insects would have on my life here. During my final Skype interview with her before she offered me this job, she asked me some unorthodox questions:

"Can you handle centipedes the size of Cuban cigars?"

"Are you afraid of rain spiders whose webs are as big as tents?"

"What do you think about snails as big as Tonka Trucks?"

One afternoon at the Waalkgard, Anna and I talked about the insects of Bukoba. We lamented the Lake Flies and celebrated the butterflies. No matter how hard the ants work or how much delicious honey the bees make, they will never gain the adoration of humans the way butterflies do. Even Monsignor, swift to squash a flying pest, would not kill a butterfly. Butterflies are the supermodels of the insect kingdom, but Anna tells me that there is even a more beautiful insect here in Bukoba.

She tells me of "glowing spiders" that locals call "stars." She tells me how one night she went to the outhouse in the middle of a banana plantation, thick with wide leaves that block out the light of the moon. She told me how she saw tiny lights, like embers on the grass and the ground.

"It was just lovely," she cooed.

I was jealous. How is it that I had never seen these insects? Perhaps it was because I didn't have to use an outhouse. Perhaps it was because I was home every night before dark. In any case, I listened as Anna described the insects, and how her host family laughed at her when she marveled at them. Days later when I asked Father Charles why he hadn't told me about the glowing spiders, he replied:

"What was I supposed to tell you? They are everywhere. You can see them with your own eyes!"

I realized that no matter how long I stayed here or how closely I looked, I would never see all there is to see.

One Sunday, Anna and I enjoyed the pool and the gardens of the Waalkgard as afternoon turned to evening. It was one of the rare times that I walked home in the dark. Anna and I walked up the hill towards DESIRE as the Lake Flies settled down and the crickets came out to fill the air with their lullabies. On the left side of the road I thought I saw the ember of a cigarette in the grass, and for a split second I thought that someone was sitting there. And then I smiled.

The light was the first of hundreds of "stars" lining the hill, a lone sentinel announcing a miniature kingdom, lights twinkling all the way up the slope until they met the stars in the sky. I stopped to stare, an inconsequential observer to a powerfully infinitesimal, and possibly eternal, empire. And I could almost hear their celebrations as I felt the joy of finding wonder in every tiny, little thing.

FAMILY TREES

During tea one morning, Ocham showed me a picture from the local paper. It showed a woman riding on a bicycle carrying several children. One child was sitting on the handlebars, another on the back of the bicycle. The child on the back had a baby strapped on his back. The mother had a small toddler strapped to hers. The mother was also balancing a basket full of food on her head while peddling the bike, and somehow it was moving. One woman, one bicycle, four children and food for them all.

"*That,*" Ocham said, "says everything you need to know about an African woman."

Throughout my time in Tanzania, I observed women of all ages, particularly mothers, conduct themselves with a distinctively nonchalant and gentle élan: the mother working in the field, in an office or in the market with her baby or small child strapped to her back with a *kanga*.

One of the women who worked at the photocopy kiosk on campus brought her son, Vincent, with her everyday where he either rested on her back or at her breast. The women who cleaned on campus brought their babies with them to work. As the babies grew and became more mobile, they were released from the confines of the *kanga,* and sometimes caring for the toddler became a campus community endeavor. One day, Pauline even brought young Dylan while she took an exam, and I had the joyful honor of carrying him around campus.

In the case of young Vincent, his mother let people like me come by and take him for a while. All I had to do was walk into the office, and she would ask me if I wanted to hold him.

"You know I would!" was always my response.

She would let me take him to my office or around campus, laughing at me whenever I would come by to let her know where we would be in case she got worried. It never occurred to her not to trust me or any of the other women with whom Vincent spent time.

"Don't worry. I'll find you if I need you," his mom would always say.

When I asked Pauline about this generosity of sharing one's baby, she explained that first of all, it would not really occur to a mother to worry about someone running off with her baby. Communities are very close-knit and people recognize each other's children, so where would someone go? Secondly, she explained, "people just don't do that here." She also continued to explain the extended relationships and sharing of maternal responsibilities. Here, one's mother's sister is not called "aunt" but "little mother."

"We have to know that our children could survive without us," she reminded me.

Such attitudes contrast sharply with mine when I was a mother of little ones. I felt a little embarrassed and ashamed when I told Pauline about some of my behavior which can only be described as totally neurotic.

When my first-born Alexandra was a babe in arms, I had to use a cramped public bathroom stall at a county fair. A kind-looking older woman near the sinks politely offered to hold my baby for me as I struggled with the lock with my only free hand. You would have thought that she had threatened to give my baby to Rumpelstiltskin the way I recoiled and responded.

"No," I practically yelled, snatching my precious baby even closer and then waiting in the stall until long after the woman left. I wouldn't be surprised if I had made that poor woman cry. This reaction says a lot about both my ego and the culture I raised my children in.

Attitudes about motherhood seem more natural and generally healthier here. Tanzanian children have a freedom that most American children no longer have. One of the striking observations about life here is that it is perfectly normal to see little children, toddlers even, running around in a field or walking along a road without any adult supervision whatsoever, sometimes even carrying buckets or small machetes. And kidnapping and abuse are almost unheard of. There are no "mommy blogs" or support groups of women complaining about the challenges of motherhood and how much they deserve a break or glass of wine. Instead, women help each other out and accept motherhood as a perfectly normal experience that is not unique to them: the child is the focus, not the mother.

Besides Pauline, the woman I talked to most about motherhood was Beatrice. Each afternoon when I went to swim at the Waalkgard was pretty much the same. I walked through the lobby to greet Beatrice, and if she was not too busy, we sat down for a soda or tea. Once we had told each other the stories of our lives, we spent almost all of our time talking about our children. Our children were still our main focus, and we shared their photos and achievements. Even though we were both physically separated from our children (like mine, hers were away at school), our "precious babies" as we called them were on our minds and in our hearts every day, in fact, probably every waking hour of every day. Beatrice worked and lived at the hotel, spending every shilling she could on her children and their education.

Sometimes we watched television in the lobby together. Between the Brazilian or Philippine soap operas or Bruce Lee movies, there were a lot of National Geographic shows on. On those wildlife shows, narrating across the footage of various mammals, a male voice said things like, "There is no stronger bond than that between the mother (insert name of mammal) and her cub/calves/whelp." Shows about the breeding habits of lions, elephants, monkeys and dolphins all demonstrated how vulnerable infant mammals are. One show about dolphins showed the soul-crushing grief of a mother whose three-week old calf had died, yet she continued to gently push her baby to the water's surface and nudge that child into life. Beatrice and I both ended up in tears after that show.

After visiting with Beatrice, I would greet Kasuku, who always stuck her neck out of the cage for me to scratch. Often I wanted to let her out of the cage. I think Beatrice did too because sometimes she placed the cage outside for Kasuku to get some sun and fresh air.

"I wonder if she remembers how to fly?" we wondered and laughed.

One afternoon, Beatrice told me that one of the monkeys living around the gardens had given birth to a baby. "Maybe you will see them after all!" When she told me this, her eyes smiled as much as her mouth did. She and I were both so excited and happy that you would have thought one of our own relatives had given birth.

It was at this moment that it occurred to me that Beatrice and I suffered from a biological Stockholm Syndrome: our lives had been hijacked by an overwhelming genetic force, the same force that had overwhelmed me so much during those pubescent years. Granted, I had more access to family planning than Beatrice had, but at that moment I really doubted my own free will. Here we were—two women who spent every waking hour thinking of two other people, spending all of our money on them and actually *missing* the demands of young children. We missed babies so much that we were truly excited, truly longing, to see the monkey baby.

I realized that I had about as much control as a salmon who is called to swim upstream to safe spawning grounds. It reminded me of something in one of the many books I had read in Tanzania, the words of Haruki Murakami:

"Human beings are ultimately nothing but carriers—passageways—for genes. They ride us into the ground like racehorses from generation to generation...They don't care whether we are happy or unhappy. We're just a means to an end for them. The only thing they think about is what is most efficient for them."

While it did seem that genes had once kidnapped my autonomy and spirit to the point that I actually liked it, I hope that humanity, and life by extension, is much more than that. Still, what drew me most to the monkey that day was her baby, for during my time in Tanzania I had seen many Vervet monkeys. It was the baby that inspired and awed me.

Beatrice had to get back to work, and she had already seen the mother and her baby, so I said good-bye to her and Kasuku and headed up to the gardens and pool.

The pool area was completely empty. Not even Egbert was there as he usually was. I quietly entered the water, not wanting to disturb the peace and near silence of the afternoon. After swimming several laps with my head out of the water, I heard the sound of something moving around in the branches. I stopped and held onto the side of the pool, looking out into the gardens.

Again, silence.

After a few moments I fully submerged myself and swam back the other way, this time completely under water. When I emerged, there they were. Mother and baby. They seemed to have appeared by magic—suddenly, quietly, and preternaturally close.

At that moment, I could feel neither time nor gravity.

Suspended in water, I floated weightlessly as the monkeys sat at the side of the pool, no more than three feet away. They were both staring at their reflections and then me. And I stared back. Although I had seen many Vervet monkeys, I had never been so close. At such close proximity, the hands, so similar to mine, looked familiar even down to the fingernails. I became lost in the mother's hazel eyes as we stared at each other in silence across the narrowest of genetic divides, a shared curiosity passing between us. Or perhaps a shared recognition of mystery. She broke our gaze as she looked again at her reflection in the pool then at the reflection of my head floating between us.

As she contemplated her reflection, I looked more closely at her fur, grey tufts of feathery hair flowing along her body. I admired the delicate features of the baby and its ability to hold on so independently to the mother. They looked like all of us primates do, and our genetic connection was undeniable, but there was something else I noticed in this encounter. Whatever was behind her eyes, and behind mine, transcended our taxonomy. It transcended our genetic responsibility. It seemed to be something sacred, divine, infinite.

And then a mango fell from a tree, breaking the silence and the magic.

Time and gravity returned as the mother embraced her baby, then leapt into the trees, slowly disappearing into the sky above. I let my body sink to the bottom of the pool, and, just as I had when I was a baby in that Los Angeles pool, I looked up to see the sun glistening through the surface of the water. I rested for a moment at the bottom of the pool then slowly floated back up toward the light.

PART 3
Ghosts

Ya kale hayapo, zingatia uliyonayo

The past does not exist.

Reflect on what you have now.

– Tanzanian *kanga*

SOUTHERN CROSS

Just across the lake from Bukoba lies the second largest city in Tanzania. Mwanza is called the Rock City and for good reason: it looks as if the gods had played a marathon game of geological Jenga and didn't bother to clean up afterwards.

Massive boulders abound with some stacked several stories high, some strewn across gargantuan hillsides of granite. Located at the southern-most shores of Lake Victoria, Mwanza is home to nearly one million humans and innumerous other creatures including troops of mongoose living under the rocks and lizards with bright pink torsos and deep purple tails who scurry frantically then stop every few yards to do tiny push-ups.

The giant boulders of Mwanza were hewn from the furnace of the Earth's core so long ago that even the insect kingdom seems like a flash in the pan by comparison. The goliath stones stand proudly and abruptly, having experienced all of Earth's phases. These elements have been there since time immemorial, and their humble silence reveals a confidence that they shall remain there forever. And I hope they will. The rocks simply exist. It seems—impossibly—that the past and future exist simultaneously within them.

Travel from Bukoba to Mwanza is challenging, especially during the rainy season. Travel by road can be unpredictable. The route has not been completely paved, and it is not uncommon for buses to become stuck in the red mud for hours or even days. This mode of travel usually takes eight hours, but it can be up to fourteen depending on the road conditions.

Travel by air is faster but painfully expensive and at times equally unpredictable depending on the rains. The half-hour, one-way trip costs about $200, and flight times are fluid depending on the weather conditions making connections at the Mwanza airport almost challenging. Because the runway was also unpaved, take-off was impossible during the rain. I once made the flight across Lake Victoria sitting in the co-pilot's seat of a tiny aircraft on the last plane out of Bukoba before all other flights that day were cancelled due to the downpour, grown men praying for their lives and bordering on tears in the seats behind me. The pilot, a rugged American in a worn leather jacket like a Harrison Ford character, was as calm as Mahavira while I gaped out of the rain-pounded window thinking, well, if I have to die, this is the way to go.

In my opinion, the best way to travel from Bukoba to Mwanza is, without a doubt, aboard the steamship HMV Victoria.

HMV Victoria looks like something out of an Agatha Christie novel, her faded elegance, however dilapidated and unnecessary still evident in the craftsmanship of the wooden decks. Originally built in Glasgow in 1960, HMV Victoria was then "knocked down" and sent to East Africa in over one hundred crates and reassembled at Kisumu on the shores of Lake Victoria. To my eyes she is beautiful, not least of all because one of my daughter's names is emblazoned on her bow.

The trip from Bukoba to Mwanza aboard the Victoria takes

all night, and for an additional price sleeping compartments are available. First-class compartments sleep two to a room; second-class compartments sleep six to a room with two rows of bunk beds stacked three beds high. But the majority of passengers stay on the third-class level with open seating for the duration of the nearly twelve-hour trip across the lake.

On the evenings when the Victoria makes her crossing (she departs from Bukoba every other night), the port is a frenzy of human activity: passengers push through the gates, immigration officers check visas, porters carry all sorts of wares and luggage on their heads as they walk gracefully up and down the gangplanks. Cranes load ton after ton of bananas into the center hold of the ship.

With a capacity for 230 passengers and 200 tons of freight, it is clear that most nights, HMV Victoria is overladen and above capacity, but that doesn't stop the latecomers who sometimes jump across the watery gap between the dock and the ship as she pulls away, leaping onto the ship as stealthily as cats to the cheer of the passengers who encourage the mavericks. No one should be left behind. As HMV Victoria lumbers and trudges away from Bukoba Harbor, the crowd of landlubbers wave and cry and blow kisses as the horn bids a final baritone farewell.

The sleeping compartments are equipped with a small sink, a tiny desk and life jackets. The first-class deck has a restaurant and a small but perfect observation deck where passengers gather around to eat, drink and look out over the glassy lake. There is nothing but starry sky above and star-filled water below. When the moon is out, it seems as if you could reach out and grab it.

The first night I crossed Lake Victoria on HMV Victoria, there was a full moon that followed us until sunrise. Sleep for most of us in the sleeping cabins arrives quickly. Whether sharing a room with one other person or six (including once with a snuggling baby), I routinely fell fast asleep underneath the ship-supplied sheets and blankets. The songs and carousing from below deck along with the roll of the water lulled me to sleep until the first sunlight scurried across the room of the tiny cabins.

Arriving into Mwanza from Bukoba is arriving into a different world: whereas Bukoba is wet and rainy, Mwanza is dry and dusty.

And those giant rock formations echo another planet.

The port of Mwanza also bustles. A modern skyline emerges. In the middle of town looms a hill upon which sits a deteriorating German mansion that is now inhabited by some Maasai. Temple Street in central Mwanza is lined with Hindu and Sikh temples and old Indian trading houses. *Shagala-bagala* markets offer fish, fruits, vegetables, housewares created from scrap metal, traditional medicines and beads, and of course—the very embodiment of business and commerce in their old-timey suits—crowds of Marabou Storks.

Despite the high visibility of Maasai here, Mwanza is the homeland to the Sukuma, the largest tribe in Tanzania. Known for dances with animals, including—to Ocham and Father Mgeni's chagrin—the *bazwilili bayeye* aka "The Snake Dance."

All the activity in Mwanza—shopping, eating, driving, building, demolishing, loading, unloading, working, walking, running, dancing with animals—is a human hive of frenetic movement upon the ever-silent, ever-still, ever-permanent boulderous landscape. The steadfast focus and concentration of the rocks is mystical, never deterred or distracted by our human Sisyphean hustle.

Whenever I went to Mwanza, I stayed at a convent hostel just down the road from the main campus of the university. The sisters who run it know what they are doing. My small room was always spotlessly clean. If the power went out, there were always candles at the ready, illuminating the hallways and staircases with an incongruous yet supreme sense of romance. There was always plenty of water—and plenty of warm water at that—thanks to a system that includes an elephant-sized hot water tank in the hallway. The food was outstanding and takes the term locally grown to new heights: all of the food is planted, cultivated, raised and prepared on the convent grounds.

During my first stay there, I walked around the compound marveling at the self-sufficiency and organization. On one end of the property was the henhouse where eggs were collected. Those that were not eaten here were sold at the little store across the road. On the other end of the property were the cocks whose social habits needed some major refining, if you ask me. They were brutish and bullish, pecking the smaller members and pulling out their tail feathers for no apparent reason other than that they could. Next to them was a large pen for goats and sheep who were allowed to walk around freely. Smack dab in the middle of the grounds was a fish hatchery where small herds of Nile Perch grazed on marine grasses. Next to the fishpond was a small gazebo with chairs where guests would relax during twilight.

My curiosity guided me to some of the other buildings: a chapel, a small warehouse, and a curious bungalow with nothing inside except tile, a hose and a floor drain. Inside the chapel I lit a candle for loved ones back home in California. In the repository I inspected the bags of rice flour and armies of bananas. In the curiously-tiled building, I looked around for a moment before the horrifying function of the room became clear to me. I could almost hear the shower scene music from *Psycho* shrieking as I realized that this was actually the abattoir: Not only were the animals born and raised on the premises, they also died here. *Here.* In this very room, throats were slashed, tiny bodies eviscerated and quartered, all at the smooth, clean, benevolent hands of those gentle nuns. Suddenly overwhelmed by the reality, I ran out of that building.

The main campus of the university was up a hill even steeper than the one in Bukoba. Just outside the convent gates, buses and vans full of students passed by every ten minutes or so. No matter how crowded they seemed to be, it was a very rare occasion that a driver passed by unable to make room for a new passenger. Usually the vehicle pulled up, the doors opened and passengers scooted around, sometimes moving onto laps or squeezing into impossible contortions to make room for the new passenger.

Sprawling across acres, the main campus of the university boasts gargantuan lecture halls, dusty footpaths, dormitories, faculty and guest housing, small restaurants including a burger joint, and several monumental, multi-storied buildings including a massive library. In the center of campus is Dr. Steven Kerry's house, a single-storied bungalow with chickens and a mango tree in the yard and a front door that is literally always open.

Dr. Kerry is the professor who visited Bukoba from time to time to supervise the students in the Master's program and the one who told me that the Bukoba campus reminded him of a rehab facility. Originally from Liverpool, Dr. Kerry simultaneously looked like a football hooligan and spoke like a pirate. But in his approach to the students, he was as virtuous and dedicated as a saint.

In between workshops or meetings, I would stop by his home for a cup of tea and a visit. Dr. Kerry's wife is an elegant woman from Zanzibar. She had tingling bells attached to her ankles with elegant chains and jewels adorning the side of her nose and her earlobes. Steven served us tea and biscuits on the floor of their living room, and in between his passionate discussions with the students who would come in and out to discuss their dissertations or papers or exams, we would try to hold a conversation. He was almost obsessively devoted to his students without any sense of their intrusion into his personal life.

Invariably, the patter of a monkey crossing his roof was followed by the sound of rocks thrown by the nuns across the way trying to chase away the little rascals who attempted to sneak into larders and baskets to steal food. Dr. Kerry would call out words of encouragement to the nuns:

"Nice shot."

"You need to aim higher."

"Aha, you got him right in the kiester that time, Sister!"

In addition to eating meals at the convent or taking tea with Dr. Kerry, I also often ate at the guesthouse dining room with its long table and bustle of visiting scholars, students and speakers. Each meal was an impressive buffet of Tanzanian dishes, each guest an enjoyable, albeit transient, dining companion. One afternoon when I arrived for a late lunch, the room was mostly empty except for a group of young and enthusiastic students speaking German, a language I had once loved but now avoided because of its association with my German ex-husband and his equally German mistress. For the first time in nearly twenty years, I bravely dared to return to this language and greeted the group in their mother tongue.

I learned that these students were all from the University of Vechta, completing their practica in social work. Through the partnership between their university and St. Augustine University, they were all working with Tanzanian project coordinators to gain practical experience that they could take home with them. Some of the students worked with street children, some with the elderly, some with other students. Like me, they loved Tanzania.

We spent over an hour talking at the table and then met up again later. They told me about how much they had learned from Tanzanians and about how they had camped out in the Serengeti when hyenas entered their camp. I told them about the pool at the Tilapia Hotel I had read about, and we agreed to meet there the next day. I told them all about Bukoba. I described the boat ride and the return to Bukoba to them. I described the slow silence of HMV Victoria as she pulled back into Bukoba Harbor, how the green hills rise up from the lake and how the birds swoop and circle all around as if they were actually calling out "*karibu*."

"I don't want to even think about the last time I get to see that," I told them as I shared the details of my plans for my last weeks in Tanzania, my eyes already tearing up at the thought of saying good-bye to Bukoba.

This group was extremely generous with what little spare time they had, and after hours of listening to their experiences, dreams, goals and ideals I started to realize how narrow-minded I had been with my post-divorce aversion to anything German.

After meals, work resumed quickly. The work at the main campus in Mwanza was more harried and official than in Bukoba: Classes sometimes exceed 1,000 students; meetings are break-neck fast. We often worked right through morning tea. As much as I appreciated the change of scenery and pace that Mwanza provided, I always looked forward to my return to Bukoba. I knew what awaited me. I would arrive early in the morning, one of the fathers would be waiting for me at the port and after the short ride back to DESIRE, I would see Simba prancing around the yard in excitement at my return. Then I would walk into the dining room where the rest of the family would be waiting for me to have breakfast.

Buying my return ticket to Bukoba often tested the patience Cesi was teaching me. Traveling to and from Mwanza on HMV Victoria requires a trip ahead of time to the docks to purchase a ticket in person. Sometimes the ticket office was open; sometimes it wasn't. Sometimes a sleeping cabin was available; sometimes it wasn't. Sometimes you could depart when you wanted to; sometimes you couldn't. But every time I finally boarded HMV Victoria, any inconvenience was forgotten as I watched the giant rocks of Mwanza slowly drifting away, the massive boulders slowly shrinking into molars, tauntingly conveying that undeniable sense of permanence that my own teeth yearned for.

It is here at this very spot, about thirty miles from Mwanza, that HMV Bukoba, the sister ship of HMV Victoria, sank on the morning of May 21, 1996, killing over 700 people, many of whom are still interred twenty-five meters below the water's surface. Reportedly overladen with passengers and cargo, the ship capsized just thirty minutes before arriving into Mwanza port from an overnight trek from Bukoba. Rescue workers found the bodies of passengers in the third-class compartment particularly hard to retrieve because many of them had linked arms in solidarity as the water filled their lungs. A few people survived by holding on to the flotillas of bananas from Bukoba. As the details emerged (there weren't enough lifejackets, few knew how to swim), the country held three national days of mourning. So powerful is this memory that when I finally convinced Ocham to take HMV Victoria to Mwanza instead of the bus, he insisted on sleeping with his life vest on.

So powerful is this memory that each time we passed over this spot, a moment of silence seemed to fall upon the passengers of HMV Victoria to pay respect to the souls still resting in the watery grave below.

This sacred spot during the crossing back to Bukoba always sang a silent yet reliable refrain, the dimming lights of Mwanza still visible from here flickering like prayer candles on a memorial altar. Just as they faded from sight, I usually stood near the starboard bow, looking out into darkness as we moved ahead, toward an invisible horizon.

GHOST STORIES OF
ZANZIBAR

In most cultures, respect for the dead plays a significant role in rituals. Many, like me, believe that the spirits of the dead still linger around us and influence us in one way or another. In Bantu culture, the spirits of those who have died live on only as long as those who can remember them live. Once forgotten, they disappear from this realm forever.

Nowhere in Tanzania is respect and awareness of the dead more pronounced than in Zanzibar, a "fertile haunting ground of the supernatural." Not only is Zanzibar a culturally-rich archipelago with an eclectic and sordid history of Shirazi explorers, Omani sultans and European traders of all sorts, this is also a world of ancestral specters: *djinni*, sea spirits, ghostly seductresses, shapeshifters and even an iron-legged monster.

Zanzibar is the setting of some of the best ghost stories I have ever heard.

There is the legend of a young, veiled female spirit named Baibui who strolls the narrow, winding streets of Stone Town alone at night, lamenting a lover who jilted her and sometimes carrying a disappearing baby. Stories abound of moonlight trysts at places like the Forodhani Gardens that end with lovers vanishing mysteriously or even more peculiarly, turning into animals. Silent and inexplicable midnight funeral processions pass along the road near the Majestic Cinema and then suddenly disappear. Sea spirits inhabit underwater towns. Witches turn into birds. Tree creatures steal the voices of children. Broken-hearted women haunt the Palace Museum.

As much as Zanzibar is a land of the supernatural, it is also a land of earthly, sensual delights. At least for the tourists. Every imaginable type of spice, oil and exotic fruit is available in the marketplaces to satisfy every imaginable appetite. The fragrance of flowers and cloves permeates the air. Music pours out of clubs and hotels. Even the conservative Muslim locals who must take offense at the ostentation of bare skin revealed by the throngs of tourists pouring in from the ferries reveal their own physical allure from the jingling anklets to the toned muscles underneath fine textiles. Young Europeans languish half-naked along the beaches as ancient dhows float above the sea-ghost towns.

I had come to Zanzibar for a weekend after finishing an intensive English camp for a group of high school students near Dar es Salaam. With a few days off before flying back to Bukoba, I was exhausted after spending eight days and nights teaching and supervising 30 students, and Rebecca suggested that Zanzibar would be the perfect place to relax and escape. I would spend a night in Stone Town and then head out to Mangapwani Beach to snorkel and explore the caves.

Father Mgeni had warned me about the ferry ride across the Zanzibar Channel from Dar es Salaam into the port of ancient Stone Town on the island of Mnemba. He told me he had never been so sick or terrified in his life. The ride was indeed choppy and rough, and combined with the collective memory of HMV Bukoba, the reaction of some passengers bordered on mass hysteria. Used to a similar ride from Long

Beach to Catalina Island in California, I stood at the bow with some other passengers and we watched a mother whale and her calf breeching throughout much of the journey.

The massive rope of tourists uncoiled into the city, yet even as we intruded on its anachronistic allure and elegant façades, quintessential Zanzibar proudly displayed its distinctive architecture—ornate verandas and courtyards, massive wooden doors with carvings of fish, lotus and trees. One's first impression of Zanzibar is striking. Within Stone Town itself many of the geographic landmarks of this area's history are condensed and venerated, perhaps explaining the willingness of so many spirits to remain here.

When I arrived, many *papasi* (unauthorized tour guides) prepared for the infestation of tourists, and a clash of crowds ensued upon initially stepping foot on Zanzabari soil. I chose to explore on my own, wandering through the spice markets, the somber Anglican cathedral built upon the Old Slave Market, the wondrously named *Beit el-Ajaib* or House of Wonders, the Palace Museum, the waterside Forodhani Gardens, the labyrinthine alleyways whereupon perch mosques and coffeehouses and homes and stores.

The sensuality of the island is undeniable for anyone, but it was particularly magnified for me as it was such a striking difference from the pious and abstinent life I had been leading during my time in Tanzania. At the compound of DESIRE and the campus of the college I had found a spiritual tranquility unlike anything I had experienced before. Living with the priests and Sister Charlotte I had adopted many of their customs, including celibacy. I had not really thought much about the pleasures of the flesh until I came to Zanzibar. In Zanzibar, I felt suddenly and absolutely lascivious.

It wasn't for lack of opportunities that I had remained chaste for all that time. There was nothing ambiguous whatsoever about the courting rituals that I experienced in and around Bukoba: twice, they involved a male staring me up and down, then approaching me with the simple statement, "I would like to sleep with you." Perhaps other nuanced overtures had been made that I did not recognize. There was also the French oil executive at my apartment complex in Dar es Salaam who liked to watch me swim at night, the electrical engineer from South Africa, a Marine from the embassy, and an immigration officer from Mwanza. There was even a European couple who asked me to be their "unicorn" or *troisième*. I refused them all. And not just because I had been living among priests and nuns. I refused them all because my heart was still haunted by a love I did not want to forget.

Although we were a half a world apart, and he had moved on to a new chapter in his life without me, I was still in love. I had not moved on. Strangely, all this time away from him made me actually feel closer to him. I probably wouldn't have come to Tanzania if he had stayed with me, so in a strange way I felt grateful for the break. We both needed a change. Still the decision and the distance hadn't estranged us: We stayed in close, almost daily, contact the entire time I was in Tanzania via Skype, phone calls, text messages and e-mails. I often felt as if he were right there beside me. When those men tried to seduce me (if that is what you can call some of those efforts), my own respect for a metaphysical love was far stronger than any physical temptation.

My self-imposed celibacy was also the result of acculturation into life at the rectory. I had begun to emulate the life of austerity, asceticism and discipline of the fathers and Sister Charlotte. Daily prayers, gentle exercise, a simple diet, a quiet and monastic daily routine had their way with me, but when I arrived in Zanzibar, I was like an Amish teen-ager on Rumspringa.

At Rebecca's recommendation, I had chosen to stay in possibly the most luxurious accommodations in Zanzibar. The price for a single night stay was more than I had spent altogether in my months in Bukoba. Overlooking the Indian Ocean, the hotel is opulent and antique, looking like something out of an E.M Forster novel, if he had ever written one set in East Africa.

Walking through elegant corridors to my room, I started to feel the secure knots of self-restraint loosen as I welcomed the effects of the tropical drink that one of the regal receptionists offered me from a brass tray during check-in. Suddenly, my hands, for much of the last few months folded demurely in my lap, wanted to touch everything: the indoor palms, the carved doors, the white-washed walls, even the red, plush carpet under my feet. By the time I had thusly explored my room, I was on the verge of wantonness.

The room and its balcony were so extraordinarily arousing that I seemed to lose my mind as I found my senses once again. Fit for an Omani queen, the massive hand-carved bed was piled high with pillows and fine linens. I wanted to jump naked into that bed with The Man I Love. Resplendent in hand-painted tiles, the bathroom had a shower big enough for two. I wanted to jump naked into that shower with The Man I Love. The *coup de grâce* was my discovery of two white robes hanging in the closet side by side. I quickly stripped down to my birthday suit and placed one robe around my shoulders and hugged the other one while pretending that it was The Man I Love as I danced on tiptoe out the double doors onto the veranda.

Overlooking the beach, the balcony offered an incredible view of the sunset, with *dhows* crossing the kaleidoscope screen like shadow puppets, just as Rebecca had promised. Hoisted upon a hammock built for two, I swung back and forth in the soft breeze with a robe laid out next to me. Holding onto the sleeve's cuff as if I were holding his hand, I imagined that he was there with me. I dozed off to his hands caressing my lips. I awoke to the sounds of music rising up from the beach. It was dark.

I went inside the room and turned on a light that cast the glow of a candle. I looked around the room again. High up on the wall, just underneath ancient-looking wooden beams, loomed a magnificent and massive painting of a windy Stone Town alleyway with just the faintest outline of a female draped in a white veil floating inches above the cobblestone road.

How wonderful and fitting, I thought, to have a painting of a ghost, especially one who resembled Baibui, in Zanzibar.

An assortment of fresh fruit seduced me from a basket on the desk. A tiny bouquet of plumeria romanced me from atop a pillow. Yearning for The Man I Love and having been abstinent for so long, I felt the powerful urges of adolescence sending a rush of blood to my seventh chakra and was drawn to the fruit basket. I started to have impure thoughts about the banana. After living among all of those thousands of Bukoba bananas for the last few months I wondered what it was about *this* particular one that made it so special, so practically and phallically irresistible. I controlled myself, knowing that nothing satisfying could ever come from this interspecies, non-consensual tryst. Instead, I gripped it tenderly, pressed my lips to its thick skin, then placed it unrequitedly back into the basket.

Next, I plucked a mango and sliced it open. As I ate the soft flesh, sweet juice rolled down my fingers and down my décolletage with a delicate caress. I closed my eyes and remembered the same sensation when the Man I Love placed the gold necklace he once bought for me around my neck, the delicate chain dangling on my breasts. I retrieved the plumerias from the pillow and placed them to my nose. I closed my eyes and remembered the similar fragrance of a gardenia he had bought me on that same trip to San Francisco when I thought he was going to ask me to marry him.

Preparing for dinner, I went to the shower and closed my eyes again, remembering the pleasures of our showers together. I could no longer bear the idea of being separated from him. I missed him more than I ever had. Tears rolled down my cheeks and down through the drains into the sea where the water *djinnis* could use them for casting bad-luck spells. After drying my body and my eyes, I put on my black strapless jumpsuit and placed a plumeria in my hair before going down to the poolside for dinner.

I should have stopped with the single drink I had upon arrival, but I decided to let go of all self-control for my night in Zanzibar. I ordered a glass of white wine and then a man seated at the bar sent me a drink, then toasted me from afar with a wink when the server pointed him out to me. The buffet had a display of every possible type of food imaginable, including roasted meats of all kinds, pasta and some very pretentious *vitumbua* hanging out on a silver tray instead of in some newspaper like they do when Father Joseph brings them to me. I think I may have actually had a conversation with those little coconut cakes about the virtues of humility after my third drink, but I'm not sure.

What I am sure of is that I fully enjoyed the Michael Jackson cover band that provided the evening's entertainment so much so that I couldn't resist dancing, imagining that The Man I Love was there, laughing and tripping the light fantastic with me as we had done so often in his living room. The man who had sent me the drink tried to join in, but The Man I Loved shooed him away as the band played "Butterflies."

After the band's finale ("...don't blame it on the sunlight, don't blame it on the moonlight"), I staggered back to my room alone where I stripped off my clothes and fell asleep while singing to The Man I Love, the image of his face resting on the pillow next to me.

I just want to touch and kiss
And I wish that I could be
With you
Tonight.

I reached out to him and air slipped through my fingers.

I don't know exactly what happened in that room the rest of the night while I was sleeping. I don't know what was dream and what was reality. When I awoke, I reached for the Man I Loved and was surprised not to find him there.

I looked around the room and saw all of the covers strewn about, a trail of my clothes from the door to the bed and my body covered with delicate yet obvious scratches. I must have tossed and turned all night, and my erotic dreams may have been accompanied by my own attempts to reenact some of the carnal pleasures I had been missing for so long. The basket of fruit had been toppled over, and the banana was fortunately intact. A chair near the desk lay on its side.

It looked like a wild animal had been trapped in that room with me all night long.

After taking a shower, careful with the scratches on my chest and legs, I dressed in my increasingly faded looking pink dress. Tidying up the room and packing my miniscule travel bag, I scanned the room for any lingering evidence of my presence.

Surveying the room one last time I looked up at that magnificent painting high on the wall and was shocked to see that it was nothing at all like I remembered it. It was just a simple townscape. The woman in the picture was gone.

PRIDE AND JOY

Often my friends and colleagues in both Tanzania and in California ask me "Why Africa?" meaning, "Of all the places in the world you could be drawn to, what is it about this part of the world that appeals to you?"

My response varies from time to time, but the underlying allure of East Africa for me has deep roots in my childhood and my love for animals. "Born Free," a story about Elsa the lion and her two brothers who were raised by a British couple in Kenya, was the first movie I ever saw. I would daydream about the lion cubs and the plains of Africa during school, singing the theme song over and over in my head.[10] Those lyrics were a powerful mantra of my inner childhood monologue. I would visualize the reunion of Elsa and her human parents when I should have been paying attention to my elementary school lessons.

---

[10] "Born free, as free as the wind blows, as free as the grass grows, born free to follow your heart. Live free, and beauty surrounds you. The world still astounds you each time you look at a star. Stay free, where no walls divide you. You're free as the roaring tide, so there's no need to hide. Born free and life is worth living, but only worth living 'cause you're born free."

I was obsessed. I often spent long hours after school curled up on my beanbag chair with my nose buried in the "A" encyclopedia. With its pictures and descriptions, this volume made it very clear that one of the best places to see animals was in Africa. And the *only* place to see lions in the wild was in Africa.

My parents were of modest means, so a trip to Africa was out of the question. The only vacations we could afford were our annual week-long camping trips to the Sequoia National Forest where my Dad would spend hours looking up at the night sky teaching me the names of the constellations, explaining the immensity of the universe and his contemplation of our place within it. As serene and precious as these trips were, they did not completely satisfy my childhood longing for adventure. Though modest in means, my parents were (and still are) richly ostentatious in love for their children, so they took me to the one place that seemed to satisfy childhood dreams on a universal scale: Disneyland.

Just a few miles away from our home, the admittedly culturally and geographically problematic "Jungle Cruise" transfixed my young imagination. The rustic riverboats and the Audio-Animatronic animals seemed real to me. When I got a little older and realized the animals were fake, my parents took me to the zoo, which I hated. Seeing the animals in enclosures and cages made me cry. Luckily for my parents, a free-range zoo called Lion Country Safari opened its gates just a few miles from my home when I was six years old.

Lion Country Safari was basically a drive-thru zoo, offering a safari experience for families like mine who would not otherwise be able to have such an actuality. In our forest-green Dodge station wagon, we drove through open fields and observed "wild" animals—elephants, giraffes, monkeys and my beloved lions—who sometimes even approached and climbed across our car. The faux "African Village" even had canned cicada sounds piped in through speakers. During one visit, my parents bought me a small stuffed lion cub to add to the menagerie that dominated my bed, and I slept for months cuddled up with it.

The most famous resident of the park was Frazier, an elderly circus lion from Mexico who was donated to the park and who went on to sire over thirty lion cubs, earning him the nickname "Frazier the Sensuous Lion." I loved Lion Country Safari until the inevitable catastrophes. In 1978 Bubbles the hippopotamus, pregnant with her second calf, burrowed under a fence, snuck out of the barricade and hid in a muddy drainage ditch leading to a nearly three-week-long standoff with park rangers. She was finally tranquilized and then given another "potent calming drug" after which she promptly died. I was devastated watching the T.V. coverage. Even the park rangers cried. Years later, Misty the elephant broke free and crushed the skull of the head game warden, killing him instantly. Misty ran off the property, causing evacuations and traffic jams on the 405 freeway. Misty was recaptured and promptly "absorbed" into the circus industry.

In addition to these tragedies, several lions were quarantined in a fenced section of the park as punishment for hunting and killing some of their natural prey in the park. Monkeys stripped rubber bumpers off of automobiles and jumped rowdily on car hoods. Insurance claims soared; attendance of once-enthusiastic customers like me dropped. The park eventually closed. I always wondered what happened to all those animals.

By this time in my young life, I was so completely disillusioned by observing animals in captivity that I refused to even go to the highly respected San Diego Wild Animal Park, which has the world's largest veterinary hospital and is responsible for valuable conservation efforts. Although I lost interest in seeing non-indigenous animals, especially lions, in

California I never gave up my desire to one day see them in their natural habitat. Over the years, my interest in Africa expanded into ideas about language, people and culture. Although I had come to East Africa to work and to learn more about language, people and culture, my childhood dreams were also answered during my year in Tanzania, especially when I was able to travel across the country during breaks. The wildlife and wilderness I was able to see in Tanzania put my childhood dreams to shame.

In Dar es Salaam's South Beach, I was able to see turtle nesting sites and watch tiny hatchlings make their way into the sea.

Crossing the Indian Ocean from Dar es Salaam to Zanzibar on a ferry I saw humpback whales breaching so close to us that the giant fountains of water spouting from their blowholes splashed on me.

After meandering the ancient Stone Town of Zanzibar with its markets of spectacularly colored spices, I snorkeled among equally spectacularly colored marine life. Several times I beheld Mount Kilimanjaro in wonder: When Africa's highest mountain is visible from the clouds that often obfuscate it, its superior domination is clear, and I had no longing to attempt the climb it even though there are serval cats up there.

What I did long for was to see even more of the quintessential animals of Africa, and thanks to Tanzania's National Parks (and possibly another gift from the ancestors) my childhood dreams were realized. Rubondo Island National Park is just a two-hour drive from Bukoba with a short boat ride across Lake Victoria to the isolated animal sanctuary, which is the only national park on the lake. Animals like giraffes, elephants and chimpanzees were initially brought here to keep them safe from poachers, and they now co-exist with the native animals which include hippos, a multitude of birds and curious amphibian antelope called *sitatanga*—a fascinating breed of animal that escapes giant feline predators by seeking shelter in the shallows along the shoreline. Although the beaches here are enticing, human swimming is prohibited because of the crocodiles.

In the southeast, the Gombe Stream National Park, the smallest (but due to its connection with Jane Goodall, one of the most renowned) of Tanzania's national parks, is home to over one hundred habituated chimps with whom I share about 98% of my genes. Looking into their eyes, I felt the same flicker of understanding as I had with the mother monkey at the Waalkgard pool. I thought about that woman I had seen so long ago now on the afternoon talk show with the baby chimp in her lap, forced to play the role of surrogate child, and I wondered where that baby chimp came from, whose maternal arms she had been wrested from.

In addition to the chimpanzees at Gombe, there are also other primates and over two hundred species of birds in the park. After sunset, lanterns on wooden boats illuminate the lake, hovering mysteriously on the surface like tiny UFOs. As wondrous as all of these experiences were, nothing compared to the astounding, you've-got-to-see-it-to-believe-it, there's-a-reason-it's-so-famous, natural wonder of the world: the Serengeti Desert.

Usually I traveled alone throughout Tanzania with the exception of my safari in the Serengeti, and thank goodness for that because if I didn't have a witness, nobody would ever believe what happened there.

Anna had introduced me to Janet, a lovely British woman who had just come to Bukoba to work for the same volunteer organization as Anna. Like me, Janet was a single mother who now has grown children. Like me, she missed and adored hers terribly. Soft-spoken, well-read and polite with long, wavy gray hair and spectacles, Janet proved to be an excellent travel companion. I had arranged a safari to the Serengeti National

Park with a guide and a driver from the university, the same guides who had taken the Germans when the hyenas came into their camp.

It might have appeared improper for me to travel alone with any of my male Tanzanian friends, and none of the Tanzanian women had any interest in camping out. When I asked Janet if she wanted to join me, she gave an excited "yes!" When I explained that we would be sharing a tent inside the Serengeti she seemed a little nervous and asked, "Are you sure it's safe?" to which I waved my hand and dismissively said, "Of course."

We took HMV Victoria from Bukoba to Mwanza, and then drove from Mwanza to the Ndabaka Gate with our driver, Ben. Just outside the Serengeti we picked up our tour guide, Richard. Before we even drove through the gates, flanked by pillars atop which rested massive water buffalo skulls as if to say, "Beware All Ye Who Enter," baboons meandered along the side of the Landcruiser, and the stripes of zebra flirted just across the plain. Crossing the portal into the Serengeti is a juncture like no other.

To say the Serengeti is otherworldly is an understatement. Stretching over 5,700 square miles, this is a world where non-human animals are sovereign. What is most striking is the sheer expanse of space. In the early fall, the plains and hills spread out in fields of gold. After the heavy rains they turn to blankets of green, dotted with wildflowers.

Adorned with the bouquets of some of the most unusual-looking trees, the Serengeti offers a habitat that I only wish animals like Frazier could have occupied. Miles separate herds of antelope, zebras and gazelles. The long, graceful, spotted necks of giraffes protrude from the horizon. Herds of buffalo with their handlebar mustache horns meander in sprawling multitudes. A massive male elephant passes, staring authoritatively with the grace and gigantic eye of a whale. Massive crocodiles and hippos languish in pools of equally massive watering holes. Even the warthogs have their allure.

"They are so sweet," I said to Richard.

"Oh, yes they are!" he enthused. "When did you have the occasion to eat one?"

He laughed hysterically when I explained that I didn't mean that they *tasted* sweet.

Richard's knowledge of the plants and animals of his country surpassed anything I could ever read in any book. With a natural and impromptu depth of detail, he offered perfect narration of each living thing we encountered.

While coming across a herd of giraffes, Richard explained that mature males leave the herd and generally spend their lives alone except during mating seasons. An alpha male may mate with all of the females within a single herd, a "socialization habit" that he says is very common in animal groups where the males are dominant. Typically, males and females keep their distance from one another with the females grouping together with the children and the males usually off on their own. We observed herd after herd of female giraffes with infants or adolescents staying close to their mothers, grannies or aunties. We also saw several massive adult males, each one standing alone.

Richard also directed Ben to drive us to several watering holes to see hippos. Like the giraffe, Richard explained, male and female hippos tend to segregate themselves. Offspring stay close to their mothers, and the males create "bachelor areas" for themselves. There is usually a dominant alpha male who controls the females. We were able to see several pairs of eyes and ears on the sludgy surface of the water. One lone and gigantic male languished on the other end of a watering hole, his back toward us.

Richard went on to tell us that the magnificent elephants also grouped into herds of females and their offspring. Grown male elephants spend up to 95% of their lives alone, while packs of elephants are matriarchal with generations of related females living together and working to take care of the youngsters.

We saw a leopard resting underneath a tree, and Richard recounted how dedicated leopard mothers are, only leaving their cubs to go hunting and occasionally bringing something back alive so that their babies can practice their skills.

The water buffalo impressed and humbled me in many ways. Like many of the other animals, the core of the herd consists of females and their offspring; however, these herds are then surrounded by sub-herds of dominant males and females as well as elders. During the dry seasons, Richard explained, the males split from the herd and form "bachelor" groups. Adult males will spar as a form of play, to establish dominance or to actually fight. Adult females rarely fight with one another; instead they exhibit a type of democracy and altruism. Through a series of shuffles and movements, females instinctively and collectively "decide" which direction to travel. When chased by predators, a herd will remain close together with the calves in the middle. An entire herd will respond to a distress call, especially a distress call from a calf.

As we became engulfed by one herd of the apparently gentle and elegant gazelle passing across the trail we were on, Richard reminded us to be careful of all animals out here.

"All females are extremely aggressive when it comes to protecting their young."

Janet and I chuckled, and I said, "You don't need to tell us!"

Richard replied: "I am happy that this is fun for you, but for us this is *very* serious, *very* dangerous."

That seemed like an appropriate time to ask Richard about the possibility of seeing lions. He sighed to me as if to say (like so many others have before) "Did you even hear what I *just* said?" then continued with his excellent explication of lions.

Perhaps the most famous of all cats, the lion is also the least typical. While other cats live alone, lions live together in prides. While other cats hunt alone, lions hunt in groups. One of the most intriguing aspects of lions is that the females are the foundation of lion society. They do it all: hunt, rear cubs, "own" property, and defend. While females can survive on their own, they really thrive as members of a kin group. Few creatures are as communal as the female lion. The essential part of lion prides is that the females are all related. Males fight amongst themselves over what the females catch.

The most common socialization behaviors of lions are head rubbing and nuzzling. This rubbing, or snuggling one's face, forehead and neck against another serves as a form of greeting, and is often demonstrated after a physical or emotional separation.

We drove through the desert looking for more animals, specifically lions or rhinos, until the sun began to fade and we needed to set up camp. By the time we pulled into camp, many of the other campers had already set up their tents and were eating in the impressive dining tent.

Because the campsite was already practically full, Janet and I found a spot at the perimeter of the grounds on the fringes of the campground and put up our two-man tent in minutes. Ben and Richard set up their tents further away, near the parking lot next to the Landcruiser. After eating an unexpectedly delicious dinner of rice and vegetables, we lingered for a while sharing the experiences of the day with other tourists from China, Germany and Boston—everyone's eyes shining brightly, emblazoned by the soft light of lanterns and the thrill of the day's sights.

As we lay in our sleeping bags that night, Janet and I talked until the sky was black, a heavy moon floating impossibly close over the village of tents. Janet too has had many adventures in her life, having traveled and lived in South America, Israel and the Middle East. Despite all of our adventures and accomplishments, Janet and I spent most of our time talking about our children, more specifically about how overpowering maternal intuition is.

Eventually we both drifted off to sleep with the memories of the day and of our love for our offspring tucked warmly in with us as the cool plainsong of the Serengeti hummed outside. The temperature had dropped substantially, but I thought that it was too early in our relationship to ask Janet if she wanted to snuggle. Eventually, the warmth of my body heated up the sleeping bag, and we both drifted peacefully off to sleep.

Sometime in the middle of the night, a shout punched through the peaceful night.

"Nobody get out of your tents," a voice quivered and then: "THERE ARE LIONS IN THE CAMP. NOBODY MOVE!"

Deeply hibernating, I barely absorbed the warning, momentarily opening my eyes and then resuming my dreams until I heard Janet stir as if she were preparing to head off to the loo.

"Hey..." I said with a nonchalant slur, "Don't go outside because someone just yelled that there are lions in the camp."

I could hear her sit up and gasp: "Oh, my!"

At that point I realized that maybe this was not the kind of moment that one should be sleeping through, and perhaps there was something to Janet's concerns after all. Again, a voice called out, this time more urgently.

"EVERYBODY STAY VERY STILL AND REMAIN IN YOUR TENTS. THERE ARE LIONS IN THE CAMP!"

And then suddenly, I felt as if we were moving through water and that time had frozen.

While Janet sat straight up, I remained horizontal in my sleeping position.

Beams of flashlights darted across the canvas of our tent.

I heard what sounded like low-throttle motorcycle rumbles that came increasingly closer.

Then quadruped footsteps in the sand and then...

Suddenly across the side of our tent passed the shadow of the first lion.

Then... there...was...a...second.

And... then... a...third.

They looked huge.

And close.

Just as the shadow of a fourth lion began to pass, I felt the warm and furry brush of one of the giant cats as it passed with nothing between us except the thin tent canvas.

And immediately the shadow and the warm body both stopped.

And then the other three shadows returned.

I stayed perfectly still. Before I knew it, I could feel the heads of the giant beasts pressing against me. Two of the animals were on my left side, and one was at the top of my head. I could not only hear but also actually *feel* the purrs of a thousand kittens, and I inhaled the musk of wild animals. They were trying to head rub.

As soon as I saw a claw cut through the top corner of the tent where my head rested and then slice all the way down to the ground, I sat straight up, curling up as closely to Janet as possible. We looked at one another, strangely communicating without uttering a single sound. It was automatic, almost telepathic:

Let's move to the center of the tent.

Don't panic!

Don't make a sudden movement.

Don't scream!

Let's shine our flashlights at them.

Stay calm!

Remember, be silent.

And shockingly, this is exactly what we did in perfect and

silent unanimity. We could see flashlight beams swirling across the side of our tent from the outside like desperate and frantic searchlights. I wondered what was going on outside and why it had suddenly become so quiet. Nobody was yelling out to remain in our tents anymore. Nobody was saying anything. I heard human footsteps running away from our tent.

Away!

Through the massive tear in the tent entered first one, then two magnificent lion faces, one atop the other, with tufts of shaggy, camel-colored fur and sweet amber eyes that seemed happy to see us. They were right at the spot where my head had been just seconds before. We were face to face with two wild lions.

I had two thoughts: 1.) Those lion heads didn't look as big as their shadows, and more pressing 2.) WAS ANYONE OUT THERE GOING TO HELP US?!

No sooner had I thought this than the loud sound of a car engine approached quickly and closely, its headlights filling the entire tent with a brightness so white that for a split second I couldn't see anything. I contemplated that maybe this was "the light" that people report after near-death experiences, and I thought "Well, I'm not ready to leave this life, but if this is how I go what a great way to die!"

Alas, it was the headlights from Ben's Landcruiser.

Before I knew it, the lion heads had disappeared and I could hear the big cats running away, the sound of their purrs and their steps retreating in a bittersweet decrescendo.

Then I heard Ben's booming call, "Are you okay?"

Janet ran out of the tent faster than a cheetah, and I flung myself back down on my sleeping bag. To everyone's surprise, I just lay there and started to laugh. I couldn't stop. I couldn't believe what had happened. It was as if my six-year-old self had re-inhabited my body and taken over all of my senses, shrieking with joy and exhilaration.

When I finally came out of the tent there was a huge crowd around us. I looked in vain for Ben.

"Where is he?" I asked Richard.

"He is throwing up," he replied.

When Ben emerged from the bushes, I threw my arms around him as if we were teammates who had just won a championship. When he told me his side of the story, I not only understood why he threw up but also why I was so strangely elated. Like us, Ben had been awoken by the warning from the cooks who had first seen the lions while preparing breakfast. Following the advice to stay in our tents, Ben did so...until one of the cooks came to his tent to tell him that the lions were surrounding his patrons. He ran out of his tent towards ours to see a large female in repose about five yards from our tent admiring her four cubs, two of whose heads were inside our tent by the time he arrived on the scene.

Ben said it looked like they were ransacking the tent, and our silence from within convinced him that those cubs were feasting on us.

"How can you be laughing?" so many people asked me.

Maybe it was the adrenaline, but the feeling can only be described as sheer joy. As some of the other campers expressed their refusal to camp out there one more night, their furrowed brows extinguishing the luster in their eyes from earlier, others just stared silently at the massive tear in our tent with their mouths agape.

Convinced that those lions wanted to eat us, Janet could have been furious with me, especially after my cavalier answers to her questions about safety, but she remained gracious and lovely. Although I later found out that hundreds of people are killed each year by lions, I never believed that Janet nor I would be among them that night.

If they had wanted to eat us, they would have eaten us.

"I have never seen such a thing," Richard almost whispered. "You are *very* lucky."

While most of the other campers, feeling rattled and uneasy, decided that this event marked the end of their safari, Janet and I begged to continue on. As we drove through the park the next morning, instead of narrating the majestic biodiversity before us, Ben and Richard questioned us about the night before:

"How did you know not to scream? That would have been the worst thing to do."

"How did you know to remain calm?"

"How did you know to shine light into their eyes? That was very wise."

"How were you both able to communicate with each other without speaking?"

"How did you know?"

"How did you *know?*"

These same questions had perplexed me. How indeed *did* we know exactly what to do? How could we so clearly know what we had never actually been taught? How had we been able to synchronize our response so automatically and precisely? And the answer was clear, somewhere deeply latent within us, Janet and I each had an instinct for such a scenario.

After the barrage of questions and recollections from the last night's events subsided, we all settled into silence.

The adrenaline rush subsided.

The Landcruiser rolled across the plains, its motor drowning out the calls of the cicadas.

The wind whipped through my hair as the top half of my body emerged from the top of the vehicle. I closed my eyes for a moment, took a deep breath of the warm desert air, and I thought about how grateful I was to be able to appreciate what it means to not only see, but to be, an animal.

A DOMINANCE RITUAL

One Friday afternoon after my trip to the Serengeti, Beatrice told me that during the upcoming weekend the hotel would be more crowded than usual because a cadre of mining executives would be staying there.

She seemed sheepish, almost embarrassingly apologetic about this fact. Only when I arrived that weekend for my usual swim did I fully understand what she was trying to prepare me for and why she seemed embarrassed.

The pool area was crowded indeed, just as Beatrice had told me it would be. Seated at tables that had been set up around the pool were dozens of men, mostly foreign, staring ahead expressionless, like generals with their sunglasses, the tabletops lined with beer bottles standing at attention like child soldiers. Lingering on the edge of the pool, their lovely legs languishing in the water, were eight stunningly beautiful adolescents in full make-up and each with exquisitely coiffed hair.

At first, I was clueless. As I prepared to dive in, I greeted the girls and asked them their names and what school they went to. They giggled and told me that they didn't go to school.

I was a bit confused because clearly these girls had money with their extravagant fashions, and my experience here in Tanzania was that girls with money went to great schools.

Only when a very large male made disapproving eye contact with me and approached us with all the proverbial bull-in-a-china shop elegance did I put the pieces together. The girls were here for the mining executives, and this was what Beatrice was trying to prepare me for.

As I looked again around the pool deck, I laughed at my naïveté. Maybe Beatrice had even been trying to delicately ask me not to come that weekend because it soon became clear that my presence at the pool was not welcomed. When the alpha male approached, he placed himself directly between me and the bevy of beauties who he seemed to treat as his property.

The men seated around the tables shifted uncomfortably.

Even the ever-effusive Egbert seemed elusive.

Only the young women extended the traditional Tanzanian greetings to me:

Karibu.

"How is your work?"

"Do you have children, Mom?"

"Where are you from?"

When they heard that I was from Los Angeles, the young women drew even closer to me, sitting side by side on the lip of the pool with me treading water at their pedicured feet.

"You mean Hollywood?" one of them asked.

When I explained that where I come from is indeed very close to Hollywood there seemed to be a collective gasp of awe followed by a barrage of questions.

"What is it like? It must be incredible!?"

"Ooh! Have you ever met Will Smith?"

"Why would you leave such a wonderful place to come *here*?"

I tried to give some general answers and descriptions that wouldn't be too cynical until several of them started to share their Hollywood aspirations:

"It is my dream to go to Hollywood and become a famous actress."

"Do you think I am beautiful enough to be in the movies?"

"Could you introduce me to any famous people?"

"I would give *anything* to go to Hollywood."

I tried to tell them the truth as I had tried to tell Ocham so many times. Having gone to college on Sunset Boulevard, not far from Hollywood, I saw how it can be a wretched place that has enticed beautiful young people from all over the world with false promises of fame and glamour, practically swallowing young beauties alive. I have seen too many of them living on the streets in the shadows of derelict hotels, addicted to drugs, often turning to sex work. The place is sprinkled with greasy grime that is marketed as stardust.

During my college years, it only took a few times going out there to realize that my Saturday nights were better spent in the Powell Library.

"It's not actually as nice and glamorous there as the movies make it seem," I told them.

I realized I might have taken my descriptions a little too far when I noticed that the girls began regarding me with the sad and familiar "I-can't-believe-Santa-isn't-real" look. When I stopped talking, one just said:

"You speak very fast, Mom."

There was so much I would have liked to say to them, but the alpha male was giving me the evil eye, and besides I wasn't sure what I could really say. Could I really say to them, "You're better off here?" I didn't know their reality. I could only fathom what they would be paid to do that night behind the doors of the Waalkgard. I didn't know what their lives were like before they fell in with the alpha male. I didn't know what the future held for any of them. I don't even know what the future holds for me.

I felt terrible about my tirade about the filth of Hollywood. Who am I to disenchant? I felt particularly rotten once I made another delayed observation that made me realize that Hollywood—particularly West Hollywood—would actually be an idyllic haven for a least one of these women. For a moment I was quiet, and then I said, careful to speak more slowly this time.

"Do you know what a leading lady is?"

"She is the star," replied one girl who told me her name was Beyoncé.

"Yes. And you know what? I think each and every one of you could be a leading lady. You are all so beautiful."

And the smiles and giggles returned.

"I'm going to swim now," I announced because I needed to disguise the tears that were announcing a visit.

With each stroke I fought back the tears and tried to get rid of a massive lump building in my throat. I was thinking of the girl at the side of the pool who called herself Jade and the lump in *her* throat—the enlarged Adam's apple revealing the complexities of her life and identity.

As much as I had come to love Tanzania, there were a few aspects of life that, just like in my home country, troubled me. Perhaps the most widespread, blatant and troubling human rights violations in Tanzania were the widespread and systematic condemnation of anything that did not conform to strict heterosexual and gender role norms. I did not know Jade's exact sexual preferences nor anything about her except what she was paid to do; however, what was clear was that she was willing to pay a higher price than any of the rest of us at that pool to be a woman.

A 2013 U.S. State Department Human Rights Report found allegations of torture and abuse of lesbian, gay, bisexual and transgender individuals while in police custody in Tanzania. Homosexuality is illegal and socially taboo here.

Wasenge like Jade are probably the most stigmatized, and victimized, of all.

After swimming two laps, I saw one of the life preservers splashing down in front of me, blocking my lane and practically hitting me in the head. I stuck my head out of the water to hear more giggling, and one of the girls said to me:

"I want to learn how to swim."

"Me too, me too!!" the others joined in.

"Can you teach us how to swim?"

OK, I thought. I can do that.

Throughout my time in Tanzania, teaching others how to swim had turned into one of my unexpected and unofficial duties. I had helped teach dozens of students to swim during the summer camp in Dar es Salaam; I had taught school-children how to swim here at the Waalkgard after school; I had even tried to teach Ocham and his kids how to swim.

Before I could respond, the alpha male approached and admonished:

"No! You can't learn how to swim. Don't be stupid."

I was dumbstruck. But just for a moment.

"Oh, it's no problem, sir," I told him. "I would be honored."

Ignoring me, and looking austerely at the girls he scoffed: "Women can't swim."

I was heartened when one of the girls said, pointing at me "But *she's* a woman, and she can swim...really well."

"That's different," he said. "She's *mzungu* and *mzungu* women are like half woman and half man. They aren't women like you."

This was not the first time that I had heard a Tanzanian comment about gender ambiguity of *mzungu* women. For example, Janet—with her long and uncoiffed gray hair and complete lack of jewelry or make-up combined with a powerful independence—had been asked by some of the children in the village if she was a man or a woman. Some even went so far as to grab her crotch to check.

My own unabashed candor and freedom inspired observers on more than one occasion to say, almost stunned, "You look like a woman, but you act just like a man!"

Yet there was something in this particular proclamation that insulted not only me, but also the other females sitting around the pool that day. I resented being called "half" a woman. In general, I also resent any statement that begins with "women can't," but it was his final insult that was the *coup de grâce*:

"And she can't even swim that well anyway."

I saw red. I discovered the threshold of my integrity: I now know that I will kowtow to a pimp...unless he insults my swimming ability.

"Is that so?" I asked, using one of Father Joseph's catch-phrases. I stared directly into the man's eyes with my own bloodshot ones.

A hush fell across the pool deck as we faced off like a couple of gunslingers at a high-noon shoot-out.

"Then I would like to challenge you to a race, sir," I affronted with all the maturity of a toddler. It was all I could do not to triple dog dare him, but I knew that I had already gone far enough by challenging him publicly. When he dismissively guffawed, I upped the ante:

"Are you afraid I'll win?" I asked, loud enough for the silent generals to hear.

The girls around the pool were unrestrained in their enthusiasm.

"Yesyesyesyesyes!!"

There was nothing for him to do but to name his poison.

He first chose to race just two lengths of the pool freestyle. I won.

Next, he suggested four lengths. I won that one, too.

I then suggested a race of ten lengths of the pool, and he ungraciously declined with a wave of his hand and a look of disgust.

By now, the bevy of beauties was also drenched in water, having so enthusiastically remained at the side of the pool only to be doused with the splashes from our ambitious kicks. I looked over at my opponent who hoisted himself out of the water as several of the young girls jumped into the shallow end, cheering and clapping.

First using the life preservers lingering around the pool, I showed some of them how to float and then to propel themselves by kicking. The most adventurous two came with me into the deep end and even held their breath under water. Only Tiger Lily dared to let go of the life preservers and learned a basic breaststroke, and by sunset she could tread water and swim a lap with me.

Before I knew it, it was dark. Candles had been placed on the tables around the pool. Most of the mining executives had gone.

I glanced around and was stunned to see that the girls I had been swimming with had completely transformed. It looked as if the water had dissolved mannequins to reveal the human children underneath.

Mascara had smeared around the girls' eyes; a fake eyelash sailed in front of me; pressed and ironed hair returned to its natural curl; a wig sat on a chaise lounge like a cat; hairpieces floated on the ripped surface of the water like canoes.

This tableau along with the empty chairs around the pool suddenly made me realize that I had seriously interfered with my swimming opponent's "business," and I became worried about the consequences that my competitive and feminist hubris would have for these women.

I got out of the pool, wrapped a towel around myself and

approached the alpha male.

"May I buy you all a drink?" I asked.

He agreed and asked me to sit down. As Egbert took orders of soft drinks and tea from the girls in the pool, I apologized to the man for chasing so many of the men away, explaining that this was a common theme in my life. He laughed.

There were so many awkward questions that I wanted to ask, but I didn't. Instead we just sat there quietly for a few minutes while he drank a beer, and I had a tonic water. When Egbert came with the bill, I paid. I then placed all of the cash I had on me under the beer bottle in front of the alpha male.

"This is for the girls," I said. "I really appreciate the time with them."

He took the money and just nodded. I then cannonballed back into the water, joining the girls who were still perched on the side, their legs dangling in the pool. As I was talking to them, I heard a giant splash, and the entire pool suddenly churned with concentric waves of miniature tsunamis. The girls squealed.

Up from the surface emerged my opponent, laughing at the effect of his far superior cannonball.

"Now, I challenge YOU," he said.

And for the next fifteen minutes or so, we had a diving contest, and the girls decided who won. True, I couldn't compete with the power of his cannonballs, but I could win a round or two by doing a cartwheel or a back flip.

In the end, no one really kept track of who won the diving contest.

Once Egbert starting closing down the pool for the night, I went to the changing room and was joined by Jade and Beyoncé, each of us undressing uninhibitedly.

"Can I do anything for you?" I asked them.

"Can you bring us with you back to Hollywood?"

I couldn't do that. Instead, we just exchanged phone

numbers, and in the end, I never did anything at all for them, and I never heard from them ever again.

Walking back toward the pool after we'd changed, I noticed that the alpha male was still in the water calmly and patiently showing two of the girls how to swim.

As I stood under a canopy of wild flowers, he looked up and saw me. And he smiled. And in a reflexive gesture that still disturbs me, I conveyed either a deep-rooted betrayal against or a true revelation of my core self: I genuinely, and almost conspiratorially, smiled back.

Walking home that evening, a lot of thoughts flooded my mind.

I thought about all of the animal species in which alpha males vie for access to females.

I thought about how much I took my own gender expression for granted.

I thought about how little I appreciated the sovereignty of my own sexuality.

Mostly, I tried to reconcile what I had done (or more importantly, what I had not done) that afternoon at the pool, and as I turned up the hill, I wondered just how much of a woman I actually am after all.

PART 4

Ancestors

Utakwenda, utarudi.

You will go. You will return.

– Tanzanian *kanga*

CAVE OF FORGOTTEN LANGUAGES

South of the Oldupai Gorge near Ngorongoro Crater is a trail of hominid footprints from 3.6 million years ago. These ancient footprints have been preserved by a combination of volcanic ash and light prehistoric rain that worked like cement to preserve this evidence of ancient bipedalism and wandering. These footprints look shockingly similar to those of modern humans like me and are much different from those of chimpanzees or other primate relatives of mine. The smaller of the clearest sets of footprints suggest that whoever left them was weighed down on one side, most likely a female carrying a baby on her hip.

The Laetoli Footprints represent just one reason that Tanzania is considered one of the great archaeological and anthropological sites in the world. Mary Leakey (credited with the discovery of the Laetoli Footprints) spent most of her professional life here in Tanzania digging up ancient skulls, tools and fossils. Professional and amateur anthropologists alike still abound here, exploring excavation sites, Iron-Age ruins and an abundance of ancient cave paintings.

One of the geography lecturers at the college in Bukoba

was born and raised near Nyakijoga—a village here in the Bukoba District known for several ancient cave paintings. One day, he suggested to Ocham that we should arrange an outing to see them. When they approached me with the idea, I jumped at the chance.

I arranged a driver through Beatrice at the Waalkgard and invited as many of the university faculty and students who could fit into the van. After several miles driving on the tarmac road, we merged onto a flat dirt road that became increasingly bumpy until we eventually reached a very rocky road that simulated the effects of a tactful rollercoaster.

Suddenly, the *shagalabagala* ended, and stretched out several miles in front of us was a perfectly straight and clear road that led directly through an enchanting valley and into the hills. This stretch of road is lined on both sides with a narrow and shallow moat filled with wild waterlilies.

At the bottom of the hills the line of the road bends distinctly upwards, tracing its way along the green terrain. Just to the right of where the black line of the road cuts across the lush green of the hillside, a massive oval-shaped stone opening stares out from aloft like the eye of a Cyclops.

This is the cave of Nyangoma.

When I asked the geography professor to describe the cave, he demurred and embarrassingly admitted that he had never actually been inside the cave although he had grown up just down the road from it. Explaining that the site was reputedly haunted according to the village elders of his boyhood, he revealed how nobody, not even the locals, ventured near the cave. It was a sacred spot to be respected and appreciated from afar.

As we drove along the road bordered by floating water lilies, our rowdy conversation dissipated as we all focused on the view sprawling out in front of us. As our van staggered up the hill, only an occasional compliment or quiet exclamation of appreciation could be heard. By the time we parked atop the hill, there was a mist of rain and nothing but reverential silence.

Peterson helped me out of the van while the geography professor approached a white-haired man who was herding a small flock of goats. Before long, the antique shepherd waved his care-worn hands, shook his white head and swiftly led his tiny herd away from the slope of the hill...and from us. As we approached, he explained that he had asked the man about the cave, but the man—looking himself as old as these hills—said that he had also never been to the cave although he too had lived here all his life.

"You don't want to go there," the man had warned, "It is bewitched."

Undeterred, we slowly descended the face of the hill into a narrow crag, and as soon as we entered the cave, we all realized the power and efficacy of such traditional approaches to cultural preservation: the cave walls remained perfectly intact after generations.

Hundreds of years of warnings about entering the cave had prevented the destruction of this magnificent site. Dozens of glyphs, painted in an unknown and apparently indelible reddish substance, adorn nearly every nook of the cavern: horizontal and vertical rows of dots that seem to connect one figure to another, arrow-like structures, pronged and fork-like shapes, perhaps a silhouette of a bull, something that looks like a leopard, indecipherable patterns.

Although there were twelve of us in this small space, it was as quiet as the library. The wind reverberated and whistled up from the valley. All of us, trained to decipher and analyze the abstract symbols of human language, were at a loss for comprehension. We exchanged glances. We whispered.

"What do you think *that* means?"

We shrugged or shook our heads. We were tempted to

touch the paintings, reaching our hands out just centimeters away, mindful not to disturb these masterpieces, but longing to somehow touch the past. We lingered for over an hour.

As the others hiked back toward the van, Petersen and I stopped near the mouth of the cave, contemplating the scene.

"Can you feel it?" he asked.

"Yes," I whispered.

We both rolled up our sleeves to reveal goosebumps. With sighs we wondered: "Had the ancestors been trying to leave a message for future generations?"

"Were they documenting the past?"

"Were they trying to capture their present?"

"What did all those signs mean?"

What exactly was that "it" that we both felt?

Reluctantly we tore ourselves away from the paintings and turned our backs to the cave's massive hollow orb staring out over the valley. The mists had turned to rain.

Our feet sank into the mud as we made a small trail of footprints toward the car. I stopped to look back, noticing how small my tracks were compared to Petersen's and how evenly my weight was distributed between my two feet. I watched as the rain splashed upon the trail, a tiny deluge slowly eroding the meager walls of each footprint, washing away any trace that any of us had ever been there.

DISARMING

European vintage maps identify the land that is now Tanzania as "German East Africa." After the World War I defeat of Germany, this part of the world was "reorganized" under The Treaty of Versailles, "taken" from Germany and placed under British control.

Though paling in comparison to the British influence, the German effect can also still be felt here, most notably in the languages: The German word for "school" (*Schule*) is also the Swahili word for school (*shule*).

These designations of Tanzania as "German" bothered me for several reasons, particularly due to my animus related to my ex-husband. However, I did not always have such animosity toward Germany. In fact, I once had felt a very solid affinity. Once enthralled with the language and words of Schiller and Goethe, I studied German until I was fluent. Well, actually, this all may have been inspired less by a particular interest in German philosophy and more by my interest in that certain German exchange student I met during my junior year of high school.

One day in the library he saw me studying Spanish and

then spoke the first sentence of what would eventually become too many:

"Vy don't you study a real langwich like Gehman?"

The next semester I enrolled in German classes.

My father and girlfriends tried to hinder our dating, pointing out the parade of red flags that spelled bad news. By the summer after high school graduation I ignored them all, setting myself up to be the headline of that bad news.

I sure showed them all. Not too long after I had married him, moved to Germany and had our two daughters, I received that eight-page fax in German from his mistress outlining the history of their three-year affair. Not long after that, I was divorced, emotionally broken and financially devastated.

After that, I hated anything German, and actually never spoke a word of German again.

That is until the day I met the students from the University of Vechta in Mwanza, and they unknowingly reminded me of the pitfalls of overgeneralization.

As much as my time in Tanzania had given me a much-needed fresh outlook about my future, it also gave me a new perspective about the past.

During the last few months of my time in Bukoba, I had stayed in touch with the Germans, mostly via text messages or occasional visits to Mwanza. On my final visit to Mwanza, after finishing up some work at the main campus and preparing to purchase my final ticket for HMV Victoria, I called Christian, one of the German students, to make arrangements to say good-bye.

"It's not time to say good-bye yet," he told me.

I tried to remind him that I would be leaving Tanzania soon, and that this would be my last visit in Mwanza. He said:

"I know! That's why we are all going with you!"

Having remembered me telling them how beautiful Bukoba was and how I was dreading my last trip into the harbor alone, some of the students I had met that day in the guest dining room had made arrangements well in advance to accompany me on the last trip across Lake Victoria. They had remembered all the details.

At that moment, I felt that whatever was left of the shell of loathing I still bore shatter and fall away. I had never been so appreciative of Germanic organization and planning as I was at that moment. I was profoundly touched.

"We'll just stay with you for the day," Christian clarified, explaining that they didn't want to impose upon me.

I then also realized how much I had missed their cultural values regarding respect for personal space and time.

"We just didn't want you to have to go alone."

This gesture made it a little more bearable saying good-bye to the sisters at the convent hostel and to all of my colleagues in Mwanza. Nothing could make saying good-bye to Father Mgeni bearable.

Father Mgeni had been promoted to a very high-level administrative position in Mwanza a few weeks earlier, and it was tough enough for all of us in Bukoba to watch him leave, but having to say farewell to him for good was the worst.

He had treated me like a true sister, and I will never forget the feeling of homecoming he gave me that afternoon when he picked me up from the lonely house and brought me to DESIRE. We shook hands collegially and professionally in his grand office, and I momentarily detested the protocol here that prevented me from having the type of high-level, emotional good-bye I prefer.

Near sunset, I met up with everyone at the port just as the sun was beginning to set. Our group included the German students, Stephanie, Christian, Catherine and Gjey as well as a Dutch student. Also, our group included two Tanzanians—Shadrack, an artist with whom Catherine worked, and Francis, a young employee of the university who was being transferred from the main campus to the Bukoba campus.

We ascended the gangplank with an energized euphoria, all the while reassuring Francis and Shadrack who, remembering and respecting the tragic history of HMV Bukoba, were more than a little apprehensive about traveling by ship.

"You know, hundreds of people drowned here," they reminded us solemnly as Mwanza slowly drifted away.

A silent memorial ensued.

We were all shown our sleeping cabins, and I was surprised when the porter showed me to a single cabin.

"For your last journey, ma'am," he bowed.

Awkward at the embarrassment of luxury and privilege, I tried in vain to refuse. He didn't believe that I actually preferred the geniality and sense of community of sharing these small rooms for the journey. He insisted. I accepted, giving him an obsequious tip. He bowed again, and we both laughed when I bowed back.

I met up with everyone on the front deck where we sat in a semi-circle on top of overturned buckets and shared stories with other passengers until midnight. The moon was full, just like it was on my first voyage, and once again it seemed to be flying alongside the ship, a silent but conspicuous companion.

When I returned to my quiet cabin, I climbed into the miniscule bed and tried to stay awake for as long as possible in order to enjoy these final moments in these quarters, but again my efforts were in vain: the purr of the engine and the gentle sway of the water had the effects of a lullaby and cradle.

Before I knew it, the bellowing baritone of the ship's horn announcing morning and our arrival vibrated through the hulk of the ship. I jumped up and quickly found the rest of the group on deck. We gathered along the railings with blankets around our shoulders.

"It's just like you described," Gjey said as she draped an arm around my shoulder.

And it was: The unabashedly proud horn of HMV Victoria as she pulled back into Bukoba Harbor, the emerald hills rising up from the Lake, the birds swooping and circling all around in a flying ballet of welcome song. It was spectac-ular.

Hesitantly, I retrieved my bags from the small cabin. I ran my hand along the neglected and deteriorating woodwork before locking the door behind me. As we waited for all of the docking procedures to be completed with the other passengers, Stephanie noticed all of the bananas waiting to be loaded.

"Is this banana season?" she asked.

We all disembarked together, and I pointed out some distinguishing features and warned everyone about the Lake Flies, suggesting that they bow down before them according to custom, assuming an air of such intimate acquaintance as if I owned the place.

I had called the Waalkgard Hotel the day before to arrange a van for the day, and the driver was waiting for us just outside the harbor gate, a genuine smile on his face.

Karibu Bukoba.

Welcome to Bukoba.

"Where would you like to go?" he asked.

"Everywhere!" we said, only half-joking.

First, we went to the Waalkgard for breakfast where Beatrice had prepared a table laden with local coffee, tea and fruits alongside eggs and toasted bread. We discussed plans for the day, deciding to see as many of the local sites as possible.

Our next stop was DESIRE where Simba dutifully expressed his devotion by prancing around us all and nestling in my lap. The fathers had already left for work, so we decided to pay our respects to them at the college campus.

I showed everyone around the campus and made proper introductions. I had invited several of my colleagues from Bukoba to join us. With the euphoric sense that the whole world was ours, we left the campus for our explorations. We hiked to the Bukoba Falls. We visited the tea plantation down the road from DESIRE. We made another excursion to the caves with the ancient wall art. We went to the German graveyard, where I thought the visiting students might want to clear away the cobwebs and trash that adorned the tombstones. Only our Tanzanian friends and colleagues took the time to enter the building adjacent to the graveyard to ask for permission to enter and try to explain to the grounds-keepers what in the world the rest of us were doing there.

As we stood in front of a littered crypt I asked: "Do you think we should clean this place up a little?"

Catherine, who seemed to take every opportunity to touch anything, surprised me by declining.

"Let's just leave this alone. This has nothing to do with any of us."

And as we all walked silently away, I wished it really was that easy to just leave the past behind.

THE ALLEGORY OF DESIRE

On one of my last nights in Bukoba, the power went out.

Again.

Not wanting to sit alone in the dark, I took the giant "torch" that Monsignor had lent me for such occasions and sat out on the steps of the front porch with my loyal Simba for one of the last times.

The courtyard was dark, except for a few lightning bugs. The moon was waning. The stars filled the sky. As I sat on the porch steps where Sister Charlotte so often did, I started humming one of her favorite songs. Simba rested his head against my shoulder.

I turned on the industrial-size flashlight. As the light cut through the darkness, it cast stark shadows across small sections of DESIRE. Nothing looked familiar to me. All the buildings had disappeared into the darkness. The torch projected a spotlight on an impromptu-and-heretofore-invisible pageantry in the foreground.

An army of ants marched before me as if I were their sovereign protectorate, demonstrating their flawless teamwork and strength by carrying muskets of leaves and the corpse of a grasshopper.

The white roses swayed gracefully in the wind darting in and out of shadow, their thorns just visible enough to give a gentle warning on the perils of beauty.

A lizard demonstrated his limitless patience and skill as an expert hunter.

Small rocks sat silently and unmoving except for the sparkles shimmering from deep within their surfaces, whispering a promise of permanence.

Simba's fur seemed to glow at the tips.

A fleet of moths demonstrated their endless and hopeless optimism, always seeking the light and charging devotedly towards it no matter what. Within seconds, they danced and darted in the glare of the flashlight, inches from my grasp.

As I moved the light, I noticed how the magic of the shadows revealed the weightless complexity of this dimension.

The line of ants cast shadows hearkening the synchronized treks of the Great Migrations of Ngorongoro.

The lizard cast the shadow of a crocodile then, with a slight adjustment of the light beam, that of a massive dinosaur.

The bushes and small trees cast shadows that looked like the forest, the giant shadows of the moths resembling the massive butterflies of the Minziro Forest.

The silhouettes of the small rocks extended into tiny mountains stretched out on the ground, then suddenly disappeared with the movement of the light.

The shadow of Simba (who had left his place next to me) prancing around looked like the shadows I had seen along the side of my tent that night in the Serengeti.

Across the courtyard Father Joseph slowly opened his door and quietly pointed his flashlight in my direction just as I was making a shadow puppet with my hands—an elongated and intangible bird waving its wings in unison with my outstretched fingers. As my light and Father Joseph's mixed, the ephemeral and ethereal shadows shifted once again.

In his final act of concern for me, Father Joseph called out, "Is everything alright?"

A delicate mist had started to fall, infinitesimal particles of hydrogen and oxygen returning to earth after the rapture of evaporation. The tiny kingdom before me glistened with aquatic gems.

I took a deep breath and one last silent look before calling back to him, breaking the spell:

"Yes. Everything is just perfect."

GOOD-BYES

My last week in Bukoba was devoted to saying good-bye. As it turns out, farewells in Tanzania are just as elaborate and important as greetings are. There were, despite a request from Father Joseph, a lot of tears.

"Go ahead, Lee," Father Charles said, repeating one of my mantras, "feel your feelings."

And I did.

I made sure to go to the Waalkgard every day to visit with Beatrice and Egbert. As far as I am concerned, it has the finest pool in the world.

Anna left Bukoba the week before I did. A group of us women treated Anna to dinner at the Waalkgard before she boarded HMV Victoria, which would take her to Mwanza where she would take a flight back home to England. After dinner, we accompanied her down to the port where there was an immigration check. Luckily, all of our papers were in order—mine thanks to Cesi.

We stayed there, long after the final horn announcing HMV Victoria's departure sounded. As the ship lifted anchor, we all stood there waving like women in older times who waved their handkerchiefs to loved ones setting sail on long voyages. We watched as the boat drifted across Lake Victoria, disappearing into nothing more than a small dot in the dark.

During that last week I made sure to go around to everyone on campus to properly say good-bye. The librarians hugged me, and I responded with the words from that book we processed almost a year ago that was now sitting on a library shelf:

"I love you to pieces!"

And they answered, one last time, "I love you three pieces!"

I walked (quietly, according to protocol) around that little library, admiring the rows and rows of shelves now filled with books.

Felix was, as usual, formal and exuded kindness. He bent at the waist and shook my hand. Petersen was, as usual, cool and exuded kind-hearted bravado. He hugged me and smiled. We all promised to stay in touch.

Some of the students invited me for tea or lunch, and I spent a lot of time sitting in the canteen or under the trees on campus just chatting with them. I was even invited to an all-male coffee break on my very last day on campus.

On the last day, the university hosted a lunch in my honor, and the entire faculty and staff came. There were speeches and gifts. There was a lot of food. And a few more tears. Kind words were shared. Despite my love of words and language, I am sure I did not accurately express my gratitude, respect and above all, my love.

I don't think the faculty and staff of that small teaching college on the Western shores of Lake Victoria will ever know how much I learned from them nor how profoundly and thoroughly they have impacted me professionally and personally.

Ocham and I were unusually sad the last day. Morning tea

was melancholy. We could hardly look at each other at lunch. When he left campus before me, we both just shook our heads. Rebecca had assured me that the projects that Ocham and I had worked on would continue and that this was not the end of our partnership, but he and I had seen enough well-intentioned but broken promises by governments and well-meaning organizations to be skeptical about working together again any time in the near future. We made arrangements for him to meet me at the airport the next day.

Pauline lingered after he left and helped me finish cleaning out my office.

"Do not forget us," she commanded as she clasped my hand. I promised her that I never would.

My last hour on campus was spent walking and taking in the scenery and breathing in the fresh air. I grabbed a machete from the ground and collected a final handful of wildflowers. I returned to my office where I spent the last minutes there, standing in front of my window admiring the rolling hills. I closed the windows, grabbed the last of my items and locked the door behind me.

Having been bequeathed a trove of gifts worthy of a queen, I walked to Father Charles' car. With Maasai necklaces dripping off my neck and a handful of fabric, books, flowers, cards and hand-woven baskets, I climbed in. We pulled up the dirt road toward the main highway, and I waved to the guards one last time. I only looked back for a moment then looked ahead as the road opened up, cutting a clear path home.

That last day in Bukoba passed at an accelerated pace. Wanting to take both a final walk in the "forest" and a final swim at the Waalkgard, I spent the morning packing and cleaning. I retrieved all of my talismans from their places around the house from nooks, shelves and windowsills. The shell given to me by that boy on New Year's Day, the very first tangible thing anyone in Bukoba gave me, was added to the trove.

Sick and tired of most of the clothes that I had been wearing in monotonous rotation for the last year, I gave almost all of them (except all the clothes Cesi had sewn for me, my pink dress, my boots and hat) to Asimwe and Doreen.

I returned my post-mortem insect collection to the earth, placing all of the tiny bodies in a circle underneath a rosebush. In the evening, a gust spread through the courtyard, scattering pieces of wings and antennae with the dust in the wind.

My final afternoon walk in the forest was too short, more an affirmation than an activity. I took in deep breaths and vivid eyefuls. The light shone and flickered through the tree canopy as wonderfully as always.

Also too short was my final swim at the Waalkgard, but mainly because I wanted to spend the last lingering moments of sunshine visiting with Egbert and Beatrice instead of swimming. What sanctuary they had both provided me, each in their own way! Beatrice had been the first friend I had made on my own in Bukoba, and she had given me a home here when I needed one the most. Egbert too had given me another home here in Bukoba. He had not only built this pool but also took great care to maintain it and to make sure that nobody ever had to swim alone.

I had offered to provide dinner that last night at DESIRE, wanting Doreen and Asimwe to have a break but also wanting the fathers to have something special for the last night. I ordered all kinds of food from the kitchen at the Waalkgard, including some of the fathers' favorites: beef, butter chicken, pilau, rice. Janet met me there while I waited, longer than I had anticipated, for the food to be prepared. Beatrice and I watched one last beautiful sunset in Bukoba from the exact vantage point from which I had looked that first afternoon. Again, like then, Beatrice was right by my side, holding my hand.

By the time the food was ready, it was dark and well past

our usual dinnertime. Hightailing it through the dark banana plantations with Janet, I felt like I did when I was a child who didn't make it home by the time the streetlights came on. By the time I did get home, I was overheated and the food was cold. And the fathers were all there waiting patiently for me, a pile of presents stacked at my place at the table.

It was all I could do not to cry when I read the card with precious words from each man, each one having always made me feel as if they not only understood but also appreciated who I really am. I felt loved unconditionally by them. They never judged me on how I looked but on what I could do. And because of this, they each—in their own way—inspired me to become even more of who I really want to be. They allowed me to live lovingly and peacefully alongside them. And *that* is really all I have ever wanted from *any*body, regardless of gender.

Opening the presents, I bit my lip, blinked and breathed deeply. I was indeed "feeling my feelings," which ranged from intense affection, pain at the idea of leaving this wonderful family, a yearning to return home and a sense that the woman returning to that home was not the same one who had left. It was wonderfully bittersweet, but I somehow managed not to cry, only because I didn't want to disappoint Father Joseph.

The only thing Father Joseph ever asked of me was not to cry, especially upon my departure. He is not the only man to ask that of me, and I have never been able to control myself with, as my dad calls it, the waterworks. My friend Monica likes to recall how I cried when we turned ten years old because, as I lamented, "Our ages will never ever be a single number again as long as we live." When we left our grammar school for the last day, I cried and asked her how she could be so happy as we crossed through the doorway of our class for the very last time. Upon crossing that threshold of childhood with her I was already mourning those early days even as they were happening, knowing that "everything will change now."

In fact, most of my life's tears flow because of my life-long nemeses: The Last Time, Never Again and Change. Even as a very young child, I have always wanted to hold on to every moment, but in Bukoba I learned—thanks mostly to Father Joseph—that I can do this without crying. I learned so much from him, not just about how to live in this culture, but how to live.

As I read the card and opened the presents, I realized that I had truly learned one of the most valuable lessons he taught me: Don't cry because it's over, smile because it happened.

The presents were lovely and thoughtful. They were all the things I had looked at and admired the day we drove to the Tanzanian-Uganda border in the spring: Yards and yards of beautiful fabric, a zebra print shawl, a locally-made clutch purse. I knew that Father Charles had selected them all, and that was where he had been the day he couldn't come to the caves with us.

We all gave short speeches. Again, I fought back tears of joy. Father Charles declared that my departure did not mark "the end" of our connection to one another, resonating with the new philosophy I was trying to adopt. Monsignor, however, consistent with the philosophers and the faith he loves so much, countered with the fact that with each parting there is, indeed, a tiny death. His speech so eloquently expressed the reason for so many of my life's tears: these tiny deaths need to be mourned. But, he counseled, they should be lamented with a joyful mourning combined with faith and hope in the new beginning.

After the effusive and fantastic formal expressions of honor, I offered an inadequate speech of my own—how could I ever sufficiently express my deep love for these priests? We reminisced on the year, remembering the goat the night at the Bishop's dinner, the time I cried when the bird flew into

Monsignor's window and died. Then eventually, we fell into our usual flow of conversation, discussing politics, religion, weather, work and books. At one point I sat back quietly, "This is the last time we will all be together like this," I thought.

And I smiled.

We lingered just a little bit longer than usual over dinner until we all got up to return to our respective cottages. One last time, the fathers sang for me and our communion was concluded with our traditional finale: Father Joseph's deep velvet voice acknowledging, "As it was in the beginning, is now and ever shall be. World without end."

And as sad as I was to say good-bye to these men and this world that I shared with them, I was comforted, as I will be for the rest of my life, by these words that I have heard so often that they are engrained into my consciousness.

Walking out of the dining hall and crossing the courtyard, we called out our final *lalasalams*. I stood at the door on my front porch, looking down at the light of Bukobatown, Lake Victoria sparkling in the moonlight. Simba sat at my feet, and I whispered not so much a prayer but a wish:

"Is now and ever shall be."

I would be leaving the next morning just after breakfast. As much as I didn't want this last evening to end, I had to get back to my cottage and finish packing. Besides, I still had one very important thing to take care of before I left.

A DOG'S LIFE

Probably the biggest challenge, both emotionally and pragmatically, about leaving was what to do with my beloved Simba. Rebecca and I had already discussed the possibility of bringing him home with me or even bringing him to come live with her, Chris and Addie in Dar. Logistically and compassionately, I could not bring him home to California.

For one, there were no veterinarians in the region to verify his provenance or health let alone immunize him. I'm not sure that anyone could guarantee that he was "a 100% domesticated" animal, so strikingly "wild" were some of his physical features. Most importantly, the journey would either have killed or traumatized him in the most tortuous way. He was so terrified of getting into a car that I couldn't even convince him to take a fifteen-minute taxi ride to get his ticks professionally removed. The ride to Mwanza alone would have been cruel, let alone a trip all the way to Dar or (even more unimaginable) to California via Nairobi and Zurich.

Whenever I left Bukoba to work or travel somewhere else in Tanzania, Father Charles looked after Simba, giving him table scraps and the occasional pat on the head. Father Charles often described Simba as very "pragmatic" because during my absences, Simba was Father Charles' loyal companion, but whenever I returned, the practical pooch acted as if I were the only person he noticed. So, initially, it seemed like Father Charles would look after Simba when I returned to California, but then Father Charles found out that he might be sent elsewhere for further studies in chemistry.

Although Father Joseph was supportive of having a dog at DESIRE, his unpredictable and busy schedule precluded him from having full custody. It would have been completely out of the question to ask Monsignor who kindly, but just barely, tolerated the canine presence. I did not know Father Mlengula, who was Father Mgeni's replacement, well enough to ask or impose. During my last weeks in Bukoba, I asked Father Charles if I needed to find another home for Simba. "I think that is a good idea," he suggested.

Because my dad had not only taught me to have a Plan B in life, but to also have a Plan C, I had been preparing back-up plans since Simba first came into my life. Because I so often asked people what their favorite animal was, I knew the dog lovers. I had mentally kept a list of them as possible candidates.

Addie, the woman who worked in the gift shop at the Waalkgard Hotel, made the short list not only because dogs are her favorite animals but also because she was incredibly reliable and kind. One of the security guards, Aristide, was also a contender because he was Simba's favorite. When Aristide was on the graveyard shift, I could hear the two of them playing or walking around the grounds together. Looking out the window late one night, I found them sitting together like dual sentries just outside my door. Despite his tentative offer to take Simba, I worried about the financial burden for Aristide and his family.

The best candidate was Francis, one of the young

Tanzanians who had come over on HMV Victoria with the Germans and me and who had just been transferred to Bukoba for work at the college. Friendly and fun, he was the best candidate because he had a yard, disposable income and, most importantly he not only loved dogs, he loved *this* particular dog. Francis happily agreed to take Simba, and I promised I would coordinate the transfer before I left.

During my last week in Bukoba, I presented the arrangement to the fathers, hoping that someone would say, "Oh, no. He must stay here with us." Instead they simply suggested that Francis not take Simba on the day I left. "That would be too much stress for the poor dog all at once."

"At least have Francis wait until the weekend," (I would be leaving on a Tuesday) they counseled.

They were worried that Simba might escape and run back to DESIRE if Francis was away at work. Francis and I agreed to wait until after I left for him to take Simba, but I still wanted to meet with Francis the night before I left to make sure that everything was in order.

On my final night in Bukoba, Simba and I were sitting on the steps of the front porch as we had so many nights before when Francis pulled up on a motorcycle. Immediately Simba got up and walked towards Francis wagging his tail. The three of us sat there for a while. I sat back a little to make sure that Francis and Simba bonded. They did.

I showed Francis where Simba's leash, bowl and bed were. Francis told me about his ample yard. We exchanged e-mail addresses and phone numbers, and he agreed to contact me if anything went wrong.

"Do you promise me you will take good care of him?" I implored, a silly and obvious rhetorical question.

"I promise."

"Will you be happy with Francis?" I asked Simba.

He wagged his tail and opened his mouth revealing his dolphin grin.

Francis and I laughed.

After some farewell conversation interrupted by quiet moments, just the three of us looking out over the lake, Francis said good-bye.

"Okay, then. I hope to see you again, my friend," Francis called out to me from the motorcycle.

Me, too.

Then once again, silence returned to DESIRE. Simba and I sat there on the porch steps, side by side, my arm draped casually across his shoulder, my hand gently scratching the scruff of his neck. We just sat there, as usual, looking out toward the lights of Bukoba for the last time.

THE LAST DAY

That last morning started just like any other morning. I awoke to the usual sounds: Father Joseph and Monsignor greeting one another on their way to early morning mass, a bird pounding on my window. I got dressed and ready while everyone was at mass and snuck Simba out of the cottage. When I heard the cars return, I emerged onto the front porch and went to breakfast.

Over tea and fresh fruit, the mood was light and convivial. We talked as if it were any other morning. Father Charles was going to drive me to the airport where Ocham would be waiting for me. Once everyone stood up and Father Joseph said the last prayer, everyone gave me a quick hug and wishes for a safe trip. I watched as Monsignor and Father Joseph drove away, Father Joseph giving me the thumbs up for not crying.

I dreaded saying good-bye to Simba, fearing that his canine instincts would cause him to howl or whine, especially when we loaded my suitcase in the car. I crouched down and wrapped my arms around him giving him a bear hug. Like a child who is suddenly embarrassed by a parent's affections, he pulled away and gave me a look like, "Stop smothering me." As I prepared to get in the car, he gave me one sweet, knowing last look with his ears back against his head. He had gained almost twenty pounds since arriving here (I know because I weighed him occasionally on the scale I had in my bathroom), and all of his wounds were healed. As I climbed in the car to leave, Simba stood next to Aristide with his tail wagging and his dolphin grin.

Father Charles and I passed through the gates and proscenium of DESIRE then turned right onto the hilly Kanazi Road. Directly in front of us, a monkey adroitly swung from branch to branch in the arcade of trees above us and looked almost like she was flying. We laughed, and I said I thought that was a good omen. Because the Bukoba airport is so close, we arrived in a matter of minutes. After unloading my suitcase, Father Charles extended his hand, saying:

"Okay, Lee. We shall miss you. Please let us know when you arrive safely."

We had already exchanged all forms of virtual and physical addresses. I hugged him, declaring, "I love you! Thank you so much for everything. I'm going to miss you so much!"

Politely, he responded, "Yes, Lee. It was most excellent."

Ocham, already at the airport, walked over to get my suitcase. Father Charles got in his car, headed back up the hill towards the university presumably to the quadrant of everyday activities. As I watched his car shrink away, he too gave me the thumbs up.

Ocham and I said good-bye in exactly the same spot where we had said hello. We exchanged some last-minute ideas and hopes for future collaborative projects. "Okay, buddy. I guess this is it," he finally said.

"Alright, pal," I answered.

On this very spot almost a year ago wearing the same pink dress, I had been right when I recognized the beginning of a beautiful friendship. Months ago, we had given up calling each other by formal, let alone actual, names. He was my "pal." I was his "buddy."

Ocham offered to stay until the plane took off, but I assured him I would be fine. "Are you sure you don't want some *tsenene*?" he joked, pointing to the roasted termites in convenient aluminum packing for sale in the airport lobby.

My childhood dream had been to come to Africa. Ocham's childhood dream had been to go to America one day. I had been able to live mine, and I felt very guilty as I said good-bye to him knowing that he had not been able to fulfill his dream yet. We promised to stay in touch and continue the projects we had started together but with a tinge of the uncertain that comes with such idealism.

Then we stood there together very quietly for a moment. We just stared at each other. I don't know what he was thinking, but I was thinking that I might actually never see one of my best friends ever again.

He carried my bags to security, gave me a final hug, turned away and soon was riding on the back of a motorcycle calling out, "See ya, buddy!" and waving to me until he disappeared into the lush trees of Kanazi Road.

Inside the airport (which was really a bungalow opening up to the landing field), I was stunned to find Sister Clara, one of the nuns from the college, and Janet waiting for me. They helped me through security and sat with me on the little patio overlooking the tarmac until it was time to board the plane.

Janet would be leaving soon too, returning to her grown daughter in England. She told me that she finally agreed with me about the beauty of our encounter with the lions. She still believed they wanted to eat us, but at least we finally shared a sense of beauty and wonder about those moments when we were inches away from lions in the Serengeti Desert.

I crossed the unpaved tarmac with six other passengers

while little birds flitted about in front of us. We boarded the fifteen-seat plane to Mwanza. From there I would take another plane to Dar es Salaam. Since there were only seven of us on the plane, we could choose our seats. I sat right behind the pilot next to a window. With an incredible gentleness, we ascended quickly into the air. I had a bird's eye view of the airport, including the little café where family members and loved ones waved to planes ascending or descending. For a second, I thought I saw Father Joseph standing there, too.

The plane flew graciously over the cathedral and marketplace, then over the port where HMV Victoria docked, then along the rock cliffs and the Waalkgard Hotel. I could see the pool, the forests and even the rooftops of DESIRE. I recognized every road and landmark. As we floated higher and further, I once again felt simultaneously very close to and very far away from home until there was nothing left to see except for the clear sky above and the shadow of the plane gliding across the rippling canvas of the water below.

THE RETURN

I spent two days in Dar es Salaam with Rebecca before flying back to California. It was a good thing too because although I hadn't cried hysterically (like I usually do) when I left Bukoba, I was emotionally exhausted. I was already showing signs of reverse culture shock.

As I was taking the taxi from the airport to Rebecca's home, my eyes grew wide, and I felt like a country bumpkin in the big city for the first time.

"Golly, jeepers! Look at all them fancy buildings and bright lights—they sure look purdy!" I thought passing along the paved and busy roads.

Rebecca's dog, Addie, was the first one out the door to greet me. I had to leave my boots out on the porch because they were covered in dried red mud and dust.

No sooner had Rebecca shown me to my room than I took the first of many showers there. The reliable flow of gloriously warm water, once a normal expectation of daily life, now felt like an absolute luxury. I slept atop cloud-like padding and underneath soft blankets worthy of a princess in Zanzibar.

I also spent a lot of time in front of the ice dispenser.

Sitting at the dining room table the first night while feasting on a series of delicious homemade dishes, I noticed that the bird nest that had been in the dining room when I first came here was gone. I asked Rebecca about it.

"They can't live here *forever*" she explained, describing the proliferation of birds that had started from a single mother multiplying into an entire adult, "slacker" brood. The avian family had relocated just outside under the eaves near the back door thanks to her tough love.

After two days of excessive water consumption and sleeping, it was time for me to leave, and I returned Rebecca's books.

"What'd I tell ya about that these books, eh?" she remarked as she put them back on her perfectly stocked shelves.

I tried to thank her adequately for the experience, but there was little to say that she didn't already know.

I took a taxi to the airport. It made no sense to have Rebecca or Chris drive me. Although the drive was only about 15 miles from their home, with traffic the drive could take up to two hours each way. Although I left at the crack of dawn, Rebecca and Chris were both awake to see me off, waving good-bye as they stood there together on their front porch, their arms wrapped around one another with Addie at their feet.

"See you later, Lee Lee," Rebecca called out, unknowingly using my family nickname. And somehow, I knew that indeed she would.

I had arrived in Tanzania with a lot more literal and figurative baggage than I had upon leaving. In addition to leaving some of my clothes with Doreen back in Bukoba, I had also given her one of my massive suitcases, so check-in was easy.

As I went through border patrol, the officer asked me why

I had so many different Tanzanian visas in my passport. When I explained, he laughed. Apparently, the original visa I had obtained before even arriving here had been valid all along.

"This is still good for two more weeks," he said pointing to the very first Tanzanian stamp in my passport. He apologized profusely as I explained all of the immigration rigmarole I had gone through.

"*Hamna shida,*" I laughed. No problem.

This was my first indication of how I had changed during this year because it really was no problem: If I hadn't thought I needed another visa, I wouldn't have had that great day with Cesi.

As I walked across the tarmac toward the plane, I took one last look around. Climbing the steps, I paused just before entering, wanting one last second of that Tanzanian warmth. Before I stepped into the plane, a sudden blast of hot hair blew my hair everywhere, wild tresses of flame flickering in the early morning light. Once seated, I put on my headphones and pressed play on George Harrison's "All Things Must Pass." Looking out the window, I admired the trees, then watched them, at first very slowly and then very quickly, rush past as we gained momentum on the runway. Then they were a blur. Then they were gone. Once we were airborne, I looked out over the harbor, then over Oyster Bay. Gradually there was nothing left to look at except the expanse of the Indian Ocean, a universe of liquid jade which slowly shrank away into the pale violet void of space as the plane, that giant *ndege,* followed the sun.

VENUS IN TRANSIT

En route home to California, I visited my daughters in Washington D.C. We ate a lot of foods with pumpkin spice in them and engaged in some aggressive snuggling. I slept in Victoria's bed for over seventeen hours at one point while she brought me cups of tea and kisses on the forehead. Although my daughters would be coming to California soon for winter break, I wanted to see them as soon as possible.

The Man I Love was waiting for me at the airport in Los Angeles, and it felt as if he had actually been with me the entire time that I was gone. We talked non-stop in the car ride home, and it felt as if we had never left each other's sides. Our future was uncertain, and I realized that this is the only kind of future there is.

The reverse culture shock upon returning back home to California was overwhelming. Wherever I went, people seemed impatient, impolite, anxious and constantly complaining. Drivers yelled at each other and flipped each other off. No one seemed to notice all the good, let alone praise it.

Even those dearest to me became easily irritated by minutiae like unacceptable parking spaces or lines at

Starbucks while ignoring the riches of our health, financial security and everyday conveniences. I felt slightly scandalized by the culture and wondered if I had, in fact, turned into a nun after all. I was so happy to be reunited with my family, but I struggled to reintegrate.

"Welcome back to civilization," many said to me. How can I ever explain that I did not feel like that at all? Instead, I felt that I had departed a wonderfully civilized world and been thrown back into a jungle of anxiety, ego and vulgarity.

When people asked me about my time in Tanzania, they often used words like "primitive" or "hardship" or even "brutal." I explained that no words could be further from what I experienced in Tanzania, but few really listened or believed my stories.

For the first few weeks after my return, I e-mailed my friends and family from Bukoba regularly. I contacted Francis on several occasions to see how Simba's transition was going. At first, I was concerned because he reported that he hadn't yet been able to coordinate the pick up of the dog with the fathers. First, they told him it would be better to wait for a weekend so that Francis wouldn't be away at work, leaving the dog alone. Then there were other excuses until we realized what was happening. The fathers had decided to keep Simba after all.

As the weeks passed, daily contact gave way to occasional phone calls, e-mails, Facebook, and Skype.

Only when Ocham came to California did I begin to feel like myself again. True to her word, Rebecca made sure that this was indeed a reciprocal cultural and educational exchange. Just as I had received a grant to work with him in Tanzania, Ocham received a grant to work with me in California. Just as I had been able to experience my dream, he got to experience his.

Six months after we had said good-bye at the tiny Bukoba

airport, we said hello again at the tiny Long Beach airport. Once I saw his smiling face emerge from the plane, I finally felt reassured that everything I had experienced in Tanzania had really been more than just a dream.

In between conferences, poetry readings and visits to my college campus, Ocham and I tried to fit in a lifetime of memories, and I made sure he never went anywhere alone, just as he had with me when I first came to Bukoba.

I showed him around Hollywood and Universal Studios, pointing out a studio that no one used because it was believed to be haunted. We went on the back-lot tour where he could see the movie backdrop of a fictitious and non-existent American city as well as the fake towns and neighborhoods.

We went to the Getty Museum and laughed hysterically when we saw that the main exhibition was called "The Age of Queen Victoria."

"That woman seems intent on following us everywhere," Ocham cracked.

After I apologized for an unusually busy day of activities he said, "We *must* do it all. We were supposed to have grown up together, so we still have a lot of catching up to do!"

As we drove down the 405 freeway one afternoon, he remarked that there were sure a lot of Coca-Cola ads here.

Like a tourist on safari, Ocham observed the unusual adornment practices and behaviors of some Southern California natives: septum piercings, tattoos, massive breast implants, cursing, untamed and conspicuous consumption. He was incredulous when he saw a blonde woman begging for money.

"You have a real African family," he remarked on his last day as we got in the car to go to the airport, giving my tribe just about the greatest compliment one could have. As I drove home from dropping him off at the airport, I felt like my culture shock had departed with him. I realized that what I felt was no longer a temporary condition. Although it seemed that the world where I had grown up had been transformed, I was the one who had changed.

During the year I was gone, California experienced one of the worst droughts in its history. Mountain lions, coyotes and bobcats descended the highlands looking for food and water; humans fled to the seashores to splash in the shallows. And that was the one place that still seemed the same to me.

Although I returned to California in the winter, the ocean was still warm enough to swim in. In early December I found sanctuary by running right into the water, swimming past the wave breaks and letting myself be carried up and down by the tides. Two dolphins floated between water and air. Surfers and pelicans skimmed the smooth surface of the water near the pier, their reflections glimmering in the light. The sun melted into the ocean, a swirl of purple, orange and pink.

I looked out over the ocean, knowing that the grey whales had begun their southern migration. Like those other magnificent aquatic mammals, my own daughters would soon make their annual winter migration home, and I felt happy.

I also felt better when I went to visit my dad who lives up in the Sierra Nevada Mountains of Northern California. The peaceful forests, the sound of birds, the dogs, the forest cat, the unpredictable electricity and the fresh air were all peacefully reassuring.

While I was in Tanzania, I had purchased a DNA kit so that my dad could participate in the National Geographic Genographic Project. He had wanted to wait until I returned to share the results with me.

"You're not gonna believe it, kid."

But actually, I wasn't as surprised as he expected. As anticipated, his genes (and consequently mine) could be traced back to Ireland within the last few thousand years, then through the Middle East over ten thousand years ago. The great surprise for him was the tracing of his "deep ancestry" to a spot on the map that was precisely where I had just spent the last year of my life—on the Western shores of the largest lake on the continent of Africa.

After cleaning up after dinner one night, my dad went out onto the back porch to set up the telescope so that we could enjoy one of his favorite pastimes while I checked my e-mails. There was a flood of messages from Bukoba. I opened one from a former student, and my heart stopped.

"I'm sorry to tell you this, but Mrs. Ocham is dead, Mom."

This was the message so many were trying to send me.

While out in the field doing teacher observations, Pauline had died in her sleep.

I tried to call Ocham but couldn't reach him. I texted him with my deepest sympathies and the promise to be there for him and the children in the weeks, months and years to come.

I thought about Pauline and her now-prescient words about wanting to ensure her children would be able to emotionally survive if anything ever happened to her. Had she known that she might die young? Had she been sick and never told me directly? Or was the possibility of dying young just, as she once told me, the reality of the "life of an African woman?"

I remembered our last moment together in my office holding hands when I promised I would never forget her family. Had she known then that she was sick?

I remembered all of the dreams and hopes she had for her children, how everything she did was to secure a future for them. I thought about that New Year's Day with her, Ocham and the kids, of how she shared her dreams for her children's education. I remembered how we were all pressed together in the taxi singing and laughing. This is how I will always remember her, happily surrounded by her children and husband.

I frantically began to message everyone in Bukoba that I

could in order to find out what had happened and what I could do. I tried to read through my tears the entire chain of responses and explanations of how Pauline had fallen ill with a fever and had "fallen asleep and never woken up."

I tried again to reach Ocham.

"He is in no condition to talk now, Mum," one of our students said. "We will look after him."

I tried to find out exactly what had happened.

"Maybe it was malaria, or maybe it was her heart," one of our colleagues offered.

I asked question after question about the various types of possible causes of her early death.

"What does it matter *how* she died, Mom? She is gone. There is nothing we can do for her now."

But there *was* something to do. In the future, many of us in both California and Bukoba would come together to take care of her legacy. But at that very moment, there was only one thing for me to actually do, what Pauline had told me to do when I first met her, so I joined my father and finally started to count my seemingly infinite constellations of precious, lucky stars.

ACKNOWLEDGEMENTS

The stories in this book are true as I remember them, and I have tried to respectfully and accurately document the events, locations, translations and conversations as I experienced them. To protect privacy, in some instances I may have changed names or other identifying characteristics.

My deepest gratitude go first and foremost to all of the people I met in Tanzania who contributed to the experiences in this book. This includes the students, faculty and staff of St. Augustine University and the visiting scholars from the University of Vechta; the archdiocese of Bukoba; the United States Embassy in Dar es Salaam and the Peace Corps. I cannot adequately express my respect and appreciation for you. My year in Tanzania was possible thanks to the English Language Fellow Program and Georgetown University. Thank you for providing me with unparalleled support, resources, training and opportunities. I am particularly indebted to Rebecca Smoak, Ocham Olanda Collins, Father Charles Gervas, Father Pius Mgeni and Father Joesph Meli Kamugisha.

To the friends, family and colleagues who contributed to encouragement, editing, and feedback during the process of writing this book, please know that I am so grateful for the time and attention you have given these stories.

Thank you to the team of talented editors and designers at Atmosphere Press who brought this book to publication. Thank you for helping to make my vision a reality.

To my brother Neal McIlroy, who gave me excellent editing feedback and encouragement, thank you so much for the time and love you offered during this process.

I am indebted forever to Monica Nash. I would never have had this experience without her. Her detailed and thorough editing of several drafts were a true act of love. I will always be grateful for not only getting me through one of the hardest times of my life, but for insisting that I document and share my experiences. You are the true definition of a friend.

Paul Kareem Tayyar relentlessly insisted that I finish this book, and provided indispensable editing and revision suggestions. I am so thankful for your constant support and encouragement throughout this project.

Finally, to my daughters who gave me permission to share details of our life together, thank you for your unwavering love, support, and inspiration. I hope you feel what one of the editors called your "heartbeat in every chapter."

REFERENCES

Chami, Felix A. *Zanzibar and The Swahili Coast from 30,000 Years Ago*. E & D Vision Publishing (2009)

Dineson, Isak, 1885-1962. *Out of Africa*. New York: Modern Library (1952)

Fitzpatrick, Mary and Tim Beyer. *Tanzania*. Lonely Planet (2012)

Gabriel, Peter "Here Comes The Flood," and "Solsbury Hill." *Peter Gabriel*. Charisma (1977)

Geldof, Bob and Midge Ure. "Do They Know It's Christmas?" Columbia Records (1984)

Harrison, George. *All Things Must Pass*. Apple Records (1970)

Harrison, George. *Living In The Material World*. Apple Records (1973)

Markham, Beryl. *West with the Night*. III. [gift] ed. San Francisco: North Point Press (1987)

Mohammed, Amir. *Zanzibar Ghost Stories*. Good Luck Publishers (2000)

Morgan, Elaine. *The Descent of Woman: The Classic Study of Evolution*. Stein and Day (1972)

Murakami, Haruki. *1Q84*. Vintage International (2013)

Myachina, E.N. *The Swahili Language: A Descriptive Grammar*. Routledge and Kegan Paul (1981)

Reader, John. *A Biography of a Continent: Africa*. First Vintage Books (1999)

Stevenson, Terry and John Fanshawe. *Birds of East Africa: Kenya, Tanzania, Uganda, Rwanda, Burundi*. Bloomsbury. (2004)

Wayman, Erin. " A New Aquatic Ape Theory." Smithsonianmag.com (April 16, 2012)

Ruete, Emily, Sayyida, Princess of Zanzibar. *Memoirs of an Arabian Princess from Zanzibar*. (1886)

World Book Encyclopedia "A." Field Enterprises Educational Corporation. (1971)

ABOUT ATMOSPHERE PRESS

Atmosphere Press is an independent, full-service publisher for excellent books in all genres and for all audiences. Learn more about what we do at atmospherepress.com.

We encourage you to check out some of Atmosphere's latest releases, which are available at Amazon.com and via order from your local bookstore:

Sit-Ins, Drive-Ins, and Uncle Sam, by Bill Slawter

Black Water and Tulips, by Sara Mansfield Taber

Ghosted: Dating & Other Paramoural Experiences, by Jana Eisenstein

FLAWED HOUSES of FOUR SEASONS, by James Morris

Words for New Weddings, by David Glusker and Thom Blackstone

It's Really All About Collaboration and Creativity! A Textbook and Self-Study Guide for the Instrumental Music Ensemble Conductor, by John F. Colson

A Life of Obstructions, by Rob Penfield

My Northeast Passage – Hopes, Hassles and Danes, by Frances Terry Fischer

Love and Asperger's: Jim and Mary's Excellent Adventure, by Mary A. Johnson, PH.D

Down, Looking Up, by Connie Rubsamen

God? WTF?!, by Charmain Loverin

ABOUT THE AUTHOR

photo by Victoria Langdon

Lee Anne McIlroy was the Senior English Language Fellow in Tanzania for the U.S. Department of State as administered by Georgetown University. She has also worked as an English Language Specialist in Tanzania and the Comoros Islands through the embassies of Tanzania and Madagascar. Born and raised in Southern California, she earned degrees in Linguistics from UCLA and California State University Long Beach. Currently, she is a tenured faculty member of English as a Second Language at Cerritos College in Los Angeles County where in 2021 she was named the Bhagavan Kunthunath Endowed Scholar of Jain Thought Leadership.

For more information, please visit
www.sleepingwithlions.com.

Printed in the USA
CPSIA information can be obtained
at www.ICGtesting.com
LVHW040057150823
755211LV00010B/784